QUEST FOR A CHRISTIAN AMERICA, 1800–1865

RELIGION AND AMERICAN CULTURE

Series Editors
David Edwin Harrell Jr.
Wayne Flynt
Edith L. Blumhofer

Quest for a Christian America, 1800–1865

A Social History of the Disciples Christ, Volume 1

David Edwin Harrell Jr.

THE UNIVERSITY OF ALABAMA PRESS

Tuscaloosa

To Dr. and Mrs. David Edwin Harrell, Senior

Reprinted by The University of Alabama Press
Tuscaloosa, Alabama 35487-0380
Manufactured in the United States of America

Preface to the 2003 Edition
Copyright © 2003 The University of Alabama Press

∞

The paper on which this book is printed meets the minimum requirements of
American National Standard for Information Science–Permanence of Paper for
Printed Library Materials, ANSI Z39.48-1984.

Library of Congress Cataloging-in-Publication Data

Harrell, David Edwin.
A social history of the Disciples of Christ / David Edwin Harrell.
v. cm. — (Religion and American culture)
Originally published: Nashville, Tenn. : Disciples of Christ Historical
Society, 1966–1973. With new pref.
Includes bibliographical references and index.
Contents: v. 1. Quest for a Christian America, 1800–1865 — v. 2.
Sources of division in the Disciples of Christ, 1865–1900.
ISBN 0-8173-5074-8 (v. 1 : pbk. : alk. paper) —
ISBN 0-8173-5075-6 (v. 2 : pbk. : alk. paper)
1. Disciples of Christ—History. I. Title. II. Religion and American
culture (Tuscaloosa, Ala.)
BX7316 .H27 2003
286.6'09—dc21   2003012350

CONTENTS

PREFACE TO 2003 EDITION

I AM PLEASED that The University of Alabama Press decided to reprint *Quest for a Christian America* (Nashville: Disciples of Christ Historical Society, 1966) and *The Social Sources of Division in the Disciples of Christ* (Athens, Ga.: Publishing Systems, 1973). These two books were published as volumes 1 and 2 of *A Social History of the Disciples of Christ*. Although these studies were written over a period of several years, most of the research was done while I was a graduate student in the history department at Vanderbilt University between 1957 and 1960. At the time that I began doing research, first to write an M.A. thesis and later a Ph.D. dissertation, the Disciples of Christ Historical Society was housed in the basement of the Joint University Library on the Vanderbilt campus. I struck up a lasting friendship with Claude E. Spencer, the curator and father of that remarkable collection, and we spent countless hours sharing our ideas and discussing the literature of the movement.

By the time I began writing my dissertation it was quite clear that I had done far too much research to include in one volume. I decided to end my dissertation at 1865, and in the years that followed I continued to write about the remainder of the nineteenth century. The end of the Civil War was a major watershed in American history and a natural place to break the study; I also had become convinced that it was a critical juncture in the life of the Disciples of Christ. Although most of the literature about the movement in the early 1960s assumed that the bitter national debate over slavery

This preface also appears in the companion volume, *Sources of Division in the Disciples of Christ, 1865–1900: A Social History of Christ, Volume 2.*

and the Civil War had little effect on the Disciples movement, the facts indicated otherwise.

It is impossible to write neat narratives about the history of the Disciples of Christ because throughout most of the movement's history it was a loose and amorphous collection of churches with little central organization and no creed to define orthodoxy. The movement changed a great deal in the nineteenth century, however, and in the years before and after the Civil War a loose denominational organization appeared and three separated circles of fellowship became more and more identifiable. The death of Alexander Campbell in 1865 signaled symbolically the end of the first generation leadership and the beginning of what I labeled in volume 2 the "Middle Period." These were critical years of debate and division.

It is hardly remarkable that a young history doctoral student would wonder how church leaders viewed the factious and tragic history of the nation in the middle of the nineteenth century and the rapid industrial development that made the United States a world power in the last quarter of the century. In *Religion Follows the Frontier* (New York: Harper & Brothers, 1931), distinguished University of Chicago historian Winfred E. Garrison, using the interpretations of historians Frederick Jackson Turner and William Warren Sweet, linked the origins of the Disciples to the nation's frontier heritage, but most of the movement's history had been written in a social vacuum. My reading of the contemporary literature led me to different conclusions. Extending from the liberal fringe of the movement to its most conservative niches, Disciples editors and writers had much to say about the society in which they lived. Thousands of articles offered conflicting moral and political advice on topics ranging from prohibition and blue laws to economic injustice and labor unions. It became increasingly clear to me that diverging social profiles were as critical in understanding the divisions within the movement as were theological arguments.

In *Quest for a Christian America, 1800–1865,* I emphasized the sectional tensions engendered by slavery and the Civil War. After all, every intersectional Protestant church in the United States divided by 1861. The looseness of the Disciples movement and its lack of a central denominational apparatus dictated that there would be no official division, but I became convinced that the gradual separation of the Churches of Christ from the mainstream of the movement in the late nineteenth century owed much

to the sectional tensions generated by slavery, the Civil War, and reconstruction (a theme developed in volume 2). Both before and after the publication of *Quest for a Christian America,* I wrote a number of articles ex-
panding on this interpretation: "The Sectional Pattern: The Divisive Impact
of Slavery on the Disciples of Christ," *Discipliana* (Mar. 1961): 26–28;
"Brother Go to War," *World Call* (Oct. 1961): 6–15; "Disciples of Christ
Pacifism in Nineteenth Century Tennessee," *Tennessee Historical Quarterly*
(Sept. 1962): 263–74; "The Sectional Origins of the Churches of Christ,"
Journal of Southern History (Aug. 1964): 261–77; "Pardee Butler: Kansas
Crusader," *Kansas Historical Quarterly* (winter 1968): 386–408; and "James
Shannon," *Missouri Historical Review* (Jan. 1969): 135–70. The truth of
this interpretation still seems absolutely clear to me. Of course, sectional
lines in the United States were never precisely drawn. There were Copperheads in the North and Unionists in the South, and in the Border States
(where the Disciples were strong) loyalties were sometimes impossible to
predict. But one can hardly explain the starkly sectional nature of the Christian Church–Churches of Christ division without acknowledging that it took
place amid the cultural diversity of the United States of America.

Volume 2 is appropriately titled *Sources of Division in the Disciples of
Christ 1865–1900.* By 1900 the outlines of the three-way division of the
movement into the Christian Church (Disciples of Christ), Independent
Christian Churches, and the Churches of Christ were clearly visible, and
the doctrinal fault lines had been pretty well marked out. Volume 2 documents the sociological basis of these schisms. Church leaders elaborated
three general responses to the critical issues raised by rapid urbanization
and economic change in the last quarter of the nineteenth century. Their
social and economic ideas, like their theological pronouncements, would in
the twentieth century define them as mainstream liberal Protestants, conservative evangelicals, and sectarian separatists. The sectional nature of the
divisions within the movement was probably more linked to urban-rural
and diverging economic profiles than to the lasting influence of the Civil
War. I subsequently wrote a series of articles that developed this interpretation: "The Disciples of Christ and the Single Tax Movement," *Encounter*
(winter 1964): 261–77; "Sin and Sectionalism: A Case Study of Morality in
the Nineteenth Century South," *Mississippi Quarterly* (fall 1966): 157–70;
"The Disciples of Christ and Social Force in Tennessee, 1865–1900," East

Tennessee Historical Society's *Publications* 38 (1966): 30–47; and "The Agrarian Myth and the Disciples of Christ in the Nineteenth Century," *Agricultural History* (Apr. 1967): 181–92.

These two volumes, then, explore the social issues that contributed to the divisions within the Disciples of Christ movement. I am not now an economic determinist, nor was I when these books were written. I do believe, however, that groups tend to behave in rather predictable ways—whether nations, businesses, or churches. The vast literature on the sociology of religion offers useful models for understanding the history of the Disciples of Christ. How groups evolve is clearly related to the economic and social status of their members. The children and grandchildren of the mostly rural leaders of the early Disciples of Christ movement were better educated and more affluent than their ancestors, and it is not surprising that they came up with different ideas about how to build a church and a nation.

While institutional changes often seem predictable, the choices made by individuals about what they believe and where they will worship is far from predictable. Individual choices are rooted in psychological profiles and theological convictions; there are no models for predicting individual behavior. So, these are not "anti-theological" or anti-intellectual books. Chapter 2 of *Quest for a Christian America* is titled "The Mind of a Movement"; it explores the diverging intellectual context of the movement that provided a template for the social divisions that took place.

Much fine work has been done on Restoration history since these two books were published. My assessment of the twentieth-century developments in the Churches of Christ was published by The University of Alabama Press in 2000, *The Churches of Christ in the Twentieth Century: Homer Hailey's Personal Journey of Faith*. That book offers some analysis of the recent literature on the Churches of Christ, though it does not undertake a general assessment of the growing literature on the movement.

I confess that it is a little painful to reread one's own dissertation after nearly fifty years have passed. I would probably suggest a good deal of rewriting, if this material were submitted to me by a student today, but I never considered trying to edit these volumes. They have an integrity of their own, and they deserve to be read as the author originally intended them. And, as far as interpretations go, there is little that I would change; I must say that I was wiser in those student days than present memory recalls. Or perhaps I have just not learned much with the passing of nearly five decades.

Finally, I want to thank The University of Alabama Press for reprinting these volumes. A generation has come along since these books went out of print, and copies have been increasingly difficult to find.

David Edwin Harrell Jr.
Daniel F. Breeden Eminent Scholar in the Humanities
Auburn University
April 9, 2003

PREFACE

ACCORDING TO THE 1964 *Yearbook of American Churches* over 4,000,000 Americans now trace their religious heritage to the Disciples reformers of the nineteenth century. These twentieth-century Disciples span from virtually one end of the spectrum of American Protestantism to the other— from ecumenical denominationalism to legalistic sectarianism. The proclivity of the "restoration movement" to proliferate has not weakened since the separation of the Disciples of Christ and the Churches of Christ around the turn of the century. Two distinct religious bodies have grown out of the Disciples of Christ by midtwentieth century—one ecumenical in outlook and theologically sophisticated; the other largely sectarian. In the Churches of Christ the same pattern has been followed. The more cultured element of the group is well on its way to denominationalism (or at least to a position much nearer the mainstream of American Protestantism), while a smaller segment of the church remains committed to the most legalistic implications of the restoration plea.

As varied as these recent manifestations of the restoration emphasis may be, this account of the beginnings of the movement belongs to all of them. It is not the history of any one of the modern groups—it is the history of each of them. This is the story of the first travails of the "common mind of the movement," the varied reactions of Disciples to these trials, and the divisive influence of social pressures on the mind of the Disciples.

The thought of any intellectual current is as diverse as the personal convictions of every individual in the stream. Too often historians are inclined to assume that the beliefs of the gifted few are invariably the convictions of the less articulate masses. The premise that such is not the case is fundamental in this study. Within the Disciples of Christ—

where change, growth, retrenchment, strife, and division are a part of the very texture of the movement—it is seriously misleading to ignore the views of minorities, nonconformists, and even the fanatics on the fringes.

And yet every historian compromises somewhere short of telling what all of the people thought and did. The vast majority of people in all times have been inarticulate in their own day and remain a silent statistic to the most diligent historian. In truth, their story could hardly be told were it known—time and patience wear thin with much less elaborate plots. While a primary objective of this study has been to broaden the base of the history of the Disciples of Christ to include the significant and almost endless diversity within the church, it is certainly not the story of all Disciples. Not all of the characters discussed were preachers or editors but these leaders are the main players.

There is some justification for assuming that one can write a history of the Disciples of Christ by studying the church's leaders. It is not unreasonable to presume that the church members who paid preachers' salaries and the readers who financed editors' efforts generally agreed with the views expressed by these religious spokesmen. In short, if this is not a history of the Disciples of Christ, it is about as close to it as patience and labor can get.

More specifically, this is a study of what Disciples thought and did on social subjects. While most religion (in the Christian tradition at any rate) first centers around the efforts of man to come to terms with the unknowable, another important area which has generally been considered a proper sphere for the pronouncements of religious leaders includes the moral and ethical problems involved in man's relation to man. Most American religious historians (and Disciples are no exception) have concerned themselves primarily with the first of these questions—the theological and ecclesiastical history of religious groups. This study is basically concerned with the second. Of course, there are many and obvious interrelations between the theological and the social in the thought of the Disciples of Christ; in fact, the impact of each of these forces on the other is one of the major themes of this work. The primary story to be told, however, is what the Disciples thought and did with regard to social problems, and theological and ecclesiastical developments are discussed only when they are related to this basic theme.

Two significant limitations on the scope of this study were imposed after it was well on the way to completion. The work originally was to include chronologically the period from the beginnings of the movement, around the turn of the nineteenth century, to 1900. It has long since become apparent, however, that to investigate such a time span thoroughly would require much too massive a volume. Consequently, the study ends 1866. A second volume, now underway, will take the story to 1900.

A second self-imposed limitation is the exclusion of the subject of education. To examine the thought of the Disciples on this broad subject and to trace the development of educational institutions within the movement would have extended too far the already burdensome labor involved in the project. In addition, while no definitive study has yet been written on the Disciples and education, this area of the social history of the group has been much more thoroughly explored than other phases of the church's history. Where Disciples leaders have combined their thought on such social issues as economic morality, nativism, and slavery with theories of education, the subject has been included; otherwise it has been ignored.

Whatever contribution this investigation may make to American social history is derived from the depth of research into one religious stream. This is a vertical study in American religion. Most recent studies of American Protestant thought have been interdenominational in scope—they have been horizontal studies. As a result, the views of a limited number of significant spokesmen from each denomination have been presented as the social creed of American Protestantism. The weakness of such projects is that they fail to reach that huge base of less important farmer-preachers, part-time evangelists, and seldom-paid pastors who were above all the religious prophets of the common people. The omission of this class has encouraged the unrealistic conclusion that illiterate and poverty-stricken Protestant pastors preached social reaction to their hardhanded parishioners. This simply is not the case in the tradition of Disciples. The truth of the matter is that the sectarian Christian expression has several different emphases, but whatever the emphasis and wherever the location, the sect has been an active and creative force in American society. Further studies in depth of the social thought of other lower-class sectarian emphases might well produce similar findings.

Finally, something should be said for the benefit of the diverse variety of modern Disciples who will read this book. Although just as subject to human frailties as other mortals, the historian tries to tell his story simply as it happened—less interested in who was right than in what happened and why it happened. It so happens that I am a supporter of the conservative emphasis within the restoration rationale, but this study is not intended as theological propaganda. Whatever the merits and shortcomings of the book may be, it is an effort to set the facts straight.

Acknowledgments

OF COURSE, the author is indebted to many for their aid in this sizable undertaking: first, and foremost, to my wife, Deedie, for her patience and encouragement; then to my father and mother for their assistance, financial and otherwise, throughout the somewhat extended process of "aging" the author.

Two men have had especially important influences on the production of this manuscript. Professor Henry Lee Swint, a warm man and a skilled master teacher, spent many hours laboring over this text. Much of what is commendable in it is the result of his acumen; the errors that remain are a result of the limitations of the student. Dr. Claude E. Spencer, now curator emeritus of the Disciples of Christ Historical Society, has been my friend, confederate, booster, and supplier of information. No one knows so much about the source materials of Disciples and no one could have been more anxious to share his information and his ideas.

The Disciples of Christ Historical Society, of course, has been the key to the production of this book. The magnificent facilities of the society are equaled only by the friendliness and competence of the staff. The vast body of material which has been collected under Dr. Spencer's guidance has made it possible to base this book on a broad research foundation which was simply not available to Disciples historians a few years ago. I also owe a lasting debt of gratitude to the society and its president, Dr. Willis R. Jones, for their interest in the publication of my book in particular and for their enthusiastic encouragement of scholarship in general.

Other libraries and librarians were helpful. Roscoe Pearson of the Lexington Theological Seminary library in Lexington, Kentucky, and Dr. Henry Shaw of the Christian Theological Seminary library in Indianapolis, Indiana, were both very generous. I am indebted to B. C. Goodpasture of Nashville, Tennessee, for the use of his large private collection of material. Indeed, it was the fascination of the dusty and aging books that he magicianlike pulled from the debris of his library that first convinced me that I should know what was in them.

I am grateful to President Burgin E. Dossett, Dean Mack P. Davis, and Dean George N. Dove of East Tennessee State University for recommending that my teaching load be reduced during the time that I was revising my manuscript. I am indebted to a number of my colleagues here, Professors Robert G. Crawford, Morton Brown, and Frank B. Williams, for their critical readings of sections of my writing. Professor Herbert Weaver of Vanderbilt University read the entire manuscript and made many valuable suggestions.

A number of people aided in the preparation of the manuscript. Mrs. Lillian Swingley typed the entire text twice. Others who have worked with me are Mrs. Peggy Moore Biddy, Mrs. Myra Deal, Mrs. Majorie Swift, and Miss Rita Adams. Much of the work involved in assembling the index was done by my graduate assistant, Miss Leah O'Dell.

This book is a revision of a doctoral dissertation written at Vanderbilt University in 1962. Both the text and documentation have been considerably reduced.

Table of Periodical Abbreviations

A.A.—*Apostolic Advocate*
A.C.Q.R.—*American Christian Quarterly Review*
A.C.R.—*American Christian Review*
B.A.—*Bible Advocate*
C.B.—*Christian Baptist*
C.E.—*Christian Evangelist*
C.Ev.—*Christian Evidences*
C.Ex.—*Christian Examiner*
C.I.—*Christian Intelligencer*
C.J.—*Christian Journal*
C.L.—*Christian Luminary*
C.Mag.—*Christian Magazine*
C.M.—*Christian Messenger*
C.Mon.—*Christian Monitor*
C.P.—*Christian Pioneer*
C.Pr.—*Christian Preacher*
C.Pub.—*Christian Publisher*
C.R.—*Christian Record*
C.Rev.—*Christian Review*
C.T.—*Christian Teacher*
C.U.—*Christian Union*
E.R.—*Ecclesiastic Reformer*
G.A.—*Gospel Advocate*
G.P.—*Gospel Proclamation*
H.D.—*Heretic Detector*
L.Q.—*Lard's Quarterly*
M. and A.—*Messenger and Advocate*

M.H.—*Millennial Harbinger*
N.W.C.M.—*North-Western Christian Magazine*
N.W.C.P.—*North-Western Christian Proclamation*
O.P.—*Orthodox Preacher*
P. and R.—*Proclamation and Reformer*
P.U.—*Protestant Unionist*
P.U. and C.A.—*Protestant Unionist and Christian Age*
W.C.R.—*Weekly Christian Record*
W.G.E.—*Weekly Gospel Echo*
W.E.—*Western Evangelist*
W.R.—*Western Reformer*

QUEST FOR A CHRISTIAN AMERICA, 1800–1865

CHAPTER I

THE SETTING

RELIGION AND AMERICAN SOCIETY, 1800-1865

FROM THE BANKING HOUSES of New York to the steel mills of Pittsburgh, the cotton fields of Alabama, the one-horse farms of Indiana, the gold fields of California—nineteenth-century America was a titan in adolescence. In the sixty-five years from 1800 to 1865 the United States increased in area by three times and increased in population by eight times, the frontier was rolled back well beyond the Mississippi River, a significant exodus into urban centers began, the national struggle for political democracy was consummated, and the groundwork for an economic revolution was laid. Such a metamorphosis was not accomplished without growing pains. Sectional frictions and the struggle of the common man against class interests generated persistent and perplexing internal problems. Gaudy growth and bitter and bloody discord—such is the antebellum American saga.[1]

The story of American religion during these years is of the same cloth as the story of the American nation.[2] Organized religion in the United States shared the growth of the nation, was embued with its youthful

---

[1]The three volumes of the *History of American Life Series* which cover the years 1790-1865 provide a good survey of general developments during this period. John Allen Krout and Dixon Ryan Fox, *The Completion of Independence 1790-1830* (New York: The Macmillan Company, 1944); Carl Russell Fish, *The Rise of the Common Man 1830-1850* (11th ed.; New York: The Macmillan Company, 1950); Arthur Charles Cole, *The Irrepressible Conflict 1850-1865* (New York: The Macmillan Company, 1934).

[2]For general treatments of American religion from 1800 to 1865, see Clifton E. Olmstead, *History of Religion in the United States* (Englewood Cliffs, N. J.: Prentice-Hall, Inc., 1960), pp. 238-398; William Warren Sweet, *The Story of Religion in America* (rev. ed.; New York: Harper & Brothers Publishers, 1950), pp. 189-326.

I

vitality, and was jolted by the same internal quakes which divided and redivided the country over sectional and economic issues.

The religious history of the United States has been marked by recurrent cycles of decline and revival. The early religious interest which played such a major part in the founding of several of the colonies declined in the late seventeenth and early eighteenth centuries. After 1740 this decline was followed by a second period of enthusiasm, the Great Awakening, which worked its way through all the colonies by the 1770's. Although the vitality of American religion never quite died in the years before and after the Revolutionary War, there was a marked decline and "there was probably never a time when there was as large a percentage not only of religious indifference, but of active hostility to religion, as during the last two decades of the eighteenth century."[3] Around the turn of the century a second awakening stirred the American religious scene. A significant revival had erupted in the East as early as the 1740's in the universities, but more spectacular was the religious outbreak all along the American frontier known as the Great Revival in the West. This new evangelical surge caused a significant revamping of several religious bodies and the establishment of several new sects. It culminated in an unprecedented growth of those sects most suited to meet the religious needs of the ebullient and individualistic society of the frontier; the Baptists, the Methodists, the Disciples of Christ, and the Cumberland Presbyterians.[4] The frontier was also "a natural breeding ground for bizarre cults and utopian societies" and the first half of the nineteenth century witnessed the rise of the Mormons, the Shakers, the Rappites, the Adventists, and other similar groups.[5]

While the development of the evangelistic sects of the West is one of the dominant themes in ante-bellum American religious history, the urban churches continued to play a significant part in the molding of the religious thought of the nation. The intellectual leadership of American

---

[3]Winfred Ernest Garrison, *Religion Follows the Frontier* (New York: Harper & Brothers Publishers, 1931), p. 53. See, also, Will Herberg, *Protestant—Catholic—Jew* (rev. ed.; Garden City, N. Y.: Doubleday & Company, 1960), p. 103. Mary Alice Baldwin presents a different point of view in *The New England Clergy and the American Revolution* (Durham: Duke University Press, 1928).

[4]William Warren Sweet, "The Protestant Churches," in *Organized Religion in the United States*, ed., Ray Abrams, *Annals of the American Academy*, CCLVI (March, 1948), 47.

[5]Olmstead, *Religion in the United States*, p. 335.

religion remained unalterably connected with the names of the great Eastern preachers such as Theodore Parker and William Ellery Channing, who pushed toward a more liberal understanding of the Christian tradition. Nor was evangelical religion confined to the West. In the East, especially in the cities, a long list of revivalists, beginning with Charles G. Finney, and including clergymen from most major American churches, adopted the fervor and techniques of the frontier camp meetings and roused the growing masses of city population with their Christian message.

In short, the history of American religion in the nineteenth century was a story of challenge and response. The challenge of bringing religious order out of the chaos of the frontier and the challenge of rampant immorality and irreligion in the restless young cities were met by new bursts of vital religion. Sometimes the older churches remodeled to meet the new demands; sometimes new ones emerged; but whatever the institutional form might be, in the first half of the nineteenth century organized religion made large gains toward reasserting its dominance of American life.

The eruption of fervent and revivalistic religion in the West and the urban centers of the East produced an extraordinary shuffling of the American religious census. In 1800 the largest American denomination was the Congregationalist, the Presbyterians were second, and Baptists, Episcopalians, Lutherans, Reformed, Quakers, German Sectaries, and Methodists followed in that order. By 1850, the Methodists were first with 1,324,000 members; Baptists second with 315,000; Presbyterians third with 487,000; Congregationalists fourth with 197,000; Lutherans fifth with 163,000; the Disciples of Christ, after only about twenty years of independent existence, sixth with 118,000 members; and the Episcopalians seventh with only about 90,000 members. William Warren Sweet emphasizes the tremendous impact these developments had on the continuing pattern of American religion: "The proportional numerical strength of the American Protestant churches today may largely be explained by the relative effectiveness with which they followed the population westward in the years after independence had been achieved."[6]

American religion again responded to the pressures in American society by the multiplication of organized churches during the great slavery crisis. Almost unanimously churches became deeply enmeshed in the North-

---

[6]Sweet, "Protestant Churches," *Annals*, CCLVI, 45. See, also, Olmstead, *History of Religion*, p. 242.

South frictions which plagued the nation in the decades before 1861. When the nation divided in 1861, American religion also divided—in some cases the churches preceded the nation in the action, the Baptists and Methodists by as much as fifteen years, and in other cases religion followed, but every major intersectional Protestant church divided.

The evangelical religion of the country before 1865 was active, optimistic, and free. The variety of manifestations it took was shocking to European observers, but in it all there was a common Christian tradition in the nation as there was a common mind shared by all Americans. If American organized religion repeatedly crumbled under pressure from American society, there was an enduring unity in its fervor, evangelicalism, and moral seriousness. As Richard Niebuhr puts it, the common objective which permeated all of the evangelical tradition was the Christian dream of the establishment of "the Kingdom of Christ" in America.[7]

THE DISCIPLES OF CHRIST, 1800-1865

During the period of religious enthusiasm and ferment around the turn of the nineteenth century, numerous protest and reform movements broke out in the restless young American nation. The central theme of several was an embattled plea for the restoration of New Testament Christianity as a basis of Christian union. In such diverse places as New Hampshire, North Carolina, Kentucky, and Pennsylvania new prophets of the ancient order began seeking the elusive dream of many Christian reformers— the rebirth of the primitive church. They generally conceived that this would be possible if all would wear the name "Christian" or "Disciples of Christ" and return to the pattern of the first-century church in doctrine, worship, and practice. The two largest of these reforming streams united in 1832—one led by Barton Warren Stone and the other by Alexander Campbell.[8] The American religious movement which had its source

---

[7]H. Richard Niebuhr, *The Kingdom of God in America* (Torchbook ed.; New York: Harper & Brothers, 1959).

[8]The most useful general accounts of Disciples history are: Winfred Ernest Garrison and Alfred T. DeGroot, *The Disciples of Christ* (St. Louis: Christian Board of Publication, 1948); Winfred Ernest Garrison, *Religion Follows the Frontier* (New York: Harper & Brothers Publishers, 1931); Earl Irvin West, *The Search for the Ancient Order* (2 vols.; Nashville: Gospel Advocate Company, 1953); James DeForest Murch, *Christians Only* (Cincinnati: Standard Publishing, 1962). The first two of these works are by liberal Disciples historians; the third is by a Church of Christ minister; while the last is by an independent Disciple.

in these two streams has never had an exclusive name; Alexander Campbell preferred "Disciples of Christ," Barton Stone's followers preserved
the popularity of the name "Christian Church," while in many localities
the name "Church of Christ" was most widely used.[9]

Barton Warren Stone was born in Maryland in 1772 and soon moved
with his family to the frontier in western Virginia where he received a
back-country academy education about as good as the frontier had to offer.
While still a young man, he had a moving conversion experience and
became an ordained Presbyterian clergyman. In 1796 the young preacher
migrated westward, finally settling in southern Kentucky, where, around
the turn of the century, he was one of the leaders in the revival which
swept that area. Stone had always had reservations about the traditional
Calvinistic doctrines of total depravity and unconditional election and
during his revivalistic campaigns he became convinced of the error of
these doctrines. He began to preach that the love of God opened salvation to all men who would accept Him. This action led to the expulsion
of Stone and his followers, along with several other preachers, by the
Synod of Kentucky in 1803. After uniting in an outlaw presbytery of
their own creation—the Springfield Presbytery—for about a year, the
group in 1804 announced the dissolution of the presbytery in one of the
basic documents of Disciples history, "The Last Will and Testament of
the Springfield Presbytery." In this document the bolters announced their
intention to call themselves simply "Christians," renounced the rite of

---

[9]Throughout most of the nineteenth century all of the divergent elements within
the church accepted all three of the names as permissible. As the conservative-
liberal rift became clear in the decades following the Civil War, however, the
conservatives more and more adopted the name "Church of Christ" while "Disciples of Christ" and "Christian Church" were generally associated with the liberal
wing. In the course of time these distinctive names have become quasi-official for
each group, although they are still not exclusive. The title "Disciples of Christ" is
used in this work to describe the movement as a whole as it is probably the most
widely accepted all-inclusive name at the present time. A good discussion of the
early differences between Campbell and Stone on this question may be found in
William Garrett West, *Barton Warren Stone* (Nashville: The Disciples of Christ
Historical Society, 1954), pp. 153-157. See, also, Garrison and DeGroot, *The
Disciples of Christ*, pp. 14-16. Several other early nineteenth-century religious reform movements used the name "Christian." Two of these groups, one initiated
by Abner Jones and Elias Smith in New England and the other started by James
O'Kelly in North Carolina, formed the "Christian Connection" church shortly after
the turn of the century.

ordination, and agreed that the Bible was the only source of authority in religion. Soon afterward they began to practice baptism by immersion. The young Christian church's growth was rapid in Kentucky, Ohio, and Tennessee and by 1830 it numbered about 15,000 members.[10]

Thomas Campbell, until he moved to America in 1807, was a Presbyterian minister in northern Ireland. Campbell was thoroughly familiar with the distressingly divided state of his own church in Ireland and had been an active leader of church-union sentiment before his decision to come to America. His contact with the radical reform movement led by Robert and James Alexander Haldane in Scotland had also introduced him to the idea of "restoration" before he came to the United States. Immediately upon his arrival Campbell was given a charge in western Pennsylvania by the Synod of North America of the Seceder Presbyterian Church, one of the many minority wings of the Scottish church. His desire for unity led him to admit nonmembers of the church to communion services and this brought him into immediate conflict with the church authorities. In 1808 he was suspended by the synod and the next year he and his followers formed "The Christian Association of Washington" (Pennsylvania) which was a religious society composed of members of all denominations. They did not consider themselves a "church" until four years later. Campbell summarized their views at the formation of the society in a phrase which became the battle cry of the movement: "Where the Scriptures speak, we speak; where the Scriptures are silent, we are silent." In 1809 Thomas Campbell wrote a document of fifty-six pages for the Association which was called the *Declaration and Address.* The *Declaration and Address* enumerated the shortcomings of contemporary religion and outlined the steps necessary for the restoration of primitive Christianity.

In 1809, just as the *Declaration and Address* was completed, Thomas Campbell was joined by his son, Alexander, who, with the remainder of the Campbell family, had delayed his coming to America until called by his father. The younger Campbell had spent his last months before his departure for America in Scotland where he was considerably influenced by the Haldane movement and another small religious group known as the Sandemanians, which, founded by John Glas and under the leader-

---

[10]Garrison and DeGroot, *The Disciples of Christ*, p. 115.

ship of Robert Sandeman, had reached startlingly similar conclusions to those emerging among the various "Christian" groups in the United States.

Alexander Campbell was concerned that his newly formed religious convictions might be offensive to his father. When his father greeted him with the *Declaration and Address,* he was overjoyed. He immediately threw the vigor of his youthful zeal (he was twenty-one years old upon his arrival in America) and profound and expanding intellectual powers behind the new movement and soon assumed its leadership. In 1812 infant baptism was renounced by Campbell and his followers and immersion began to be practiced as the only correct form of baptism. Largely because of their adoption of immersion, in 1815 the Campbells found fellowship in the Baptist Church but the partnership proved to be an uneasy and unsatisfactory working agreement and ended in the early 1830's.

During his years as a Baptist, Campbell founded his first paper, the *Christian Baptist,* which he used from 1823 to 1830 with devastating proficiency in gaining followers among the Baptists of western Pennsylvania, western Virginia, Ohio, and Kentucky. The fundamentals of the restoration plea, as well as the basis of separation from the Baptist church, appeared in the pages of the *Christian Baptist.* Campbell mercilessly attacked the clergy, creeds, and authoritative councils and pled for a "restoration of the ancient order of things." By 1830 the Campbell movement was rapidly crystallizing and thousands of converts were being gained yearly.

The acquaintance of Stone and Alexander Campbell began in 1824. Their differences were slight and as the two streams converged upon each other in Kentucky in the late 1820's, the two leaders, after some negotiations, agreed in 1832 to unite. The actual process of union took place in an amazingly successful merging of local congregations at the grassroots level, or by simply agreeing to fellowship one another, that is, to accept one another as true "Churches of Christ." Although the union was imperfect (many of the Stone "Christians" refused to accept the "Campbellite" union and rather remained with the James O'Kelly "Christian" group in North Carolina which was called the Christian Connection Church), it was tremendously significant in increasing the membership and the range of the newly formed church.

The years following the Stone-Campbell union were marked by a solidification of doctrine and organization along with an impressive growth.
Alexander Campbell's influence until his death in 1866 was enormous.
A series of debates, including one with the renowned atheist Robert Owen
in Cincinnati in 1829, spread his reputation and accelerated the progress
of the movement.

A growing troop of rough-and-ready pioneer preachers scattered the
vital message of the Disciples of Christ from Ohio to Texas and from the
Carolinas to Missouri. But these fiery backwoods exhorters were only a
part of the Disciples story. Although it is true that the movement made
great gains among the common folk of the West during the ante-bellum
period, it is also true that the Disciples made considerable progress among
the people of culture, wealth, and social position as the crudest stages of
frontier life moved farther west. Many of the early preachers in the
church were men of real social standing and distinction—and often of
wealth. They often addressed and converted the most stable elements in
the rapidly developing society of the West. The Disciples sold their gospel in all segments of society, in all sections of middle-America. Their
leaders were as diverse as the society they worked in—some were rich
and some were poor; some were illiterate and some were university gradu-
ates; most were farmers, but a few lived in the mushrooming Western
cities such as Cincinnati, Pittsburgh, and Louisville; some were known
throughout the church and others never preached outside their native
county—they were united only in their determination to "restore the
ancient order."

One early historian of the Disciples of Christ has suggested that one of
the two most important events in the history of the church was "the organization of the American Christian Missionary Society."[11] The significance of the founding of the society in 1849 is difficult to overestimate for
it not only marked the weak beginnings of national organization within
the group but it also initiated rumblings of discontent which were the
first signs of an internal difference in interpretation of the restoration
plea. Half a century later, when the movement finally accomplished a

---

[11]Frederick D. Power, *Life of William Kimbrough Pendleton* (St. Louis: Christian Publishing Company, 1902), p. 128.

practical division, the missionary society was to be one of the "issues."[12]
The society was the herald of greater union and of ultimate division.

The establishment of the American Christian Missionary Society was
the result of growing agitation by many for more co-operation; a result

---

[12]The first official major division among the Disciples of Christ came in 1906
when the United States census for the first time made separate entries for the Church
of Christ and the Disciples of Christ. Actually the twentieth-century date is un-
important since the two factions had been vocally and institutionally represented
in the church since the 1850's and had clearly understood that a division was in
progress for several decades before 1900. There was simply no "official" organization within the movement with the power to authoritatively announce a separation.
The motives for the division were complex: they were a combination of theological,
economic, social, and psychological forces; they reached far back into the basic conceptions of the restoration plea and the sociological complexion of the church's membership; they involved fundamental differences in personality and attitudes. Divisive
forces worked within the movement from its inception and the early manifestations
of these forces are discussed in this work. The ingredients necessary for actual
division at the local level were the development of some basic "issues" which were
clear enough and important enough for congregations and individuals to break
"fellowship"—to cease to recognize one another as "true churches of Christ"—and
the development of institutions to act as brotherhood-wide propagators of the
divergent views and to serve as tangible power concentrations for the factions to
unite around. In short, what constituted division among the Disciples of Christ
was simply the rupturing of the tenuous union which existed—a union which
consisted of "fellowship" and common institutional loyalties. In the Disciples-
Church of Christ division the support of or opposition to the use of instrumental
music in worship and organized missionary societies supplied the major "issues."
In the absence of extra-congregational organization, the factions developed a nebulous sort of group consciousness by identifying with the outstanding institutions
supporting their position. The "antis" were *"Advocate* men" while the "progres-
sives" were "society men" or *"Standard* men." The process of division took place
at the local level where congregations, parts of congregations, and individuals
eventually drifted into the orbit of one of the power concentrations. Actually the
schism of the nineteenth century was not a clear-cut halving. There remained for
several decades a strong "middle-of-the-road" group which refused to "disfellow-
ship" either of the two factions. Although these moderates eventually accepted the
liberal position on the "issues," they remained a conservative complex within the
Disciples which in the twentieth century generated a new division with new "issues" and new power concentrations. Within the Churches of Christ today the
same complex theological and sociological partitioning is slowly becoming clear.
"Antis," "liberals," and "middle-of-the-roaders" are slowly dividing the local congregations into three distinct factions which are definable only in terms of "issues"
and institutional loyalties. For a discussion of the sociological origins of the Dis-
ciples-Churches of Christ schism, see David E. Harrell, Jr., "The Sectional Origins
of the Churches of Christ," *Journal of Southern History,* XXX (August, 1964),
261-277.

which was foreshadowed in the thirties and forties by increasing numbers of local and state organizations which were themselves the succes-
sors of the old "conferences" and "co-operative meetings" of the early
years of both the Stone and Campbell movements. Although the annual
conventions of the society had no authoritative powers in the church, and
generally avoided discussion of any controversial theme, they acted
throughout the years as a unifying force as well as a means of furthering
missionary activity. The society had the hopeful beginning of receiving
widespread support from the most influential leaders in the group. Especially important was the blessing received from the aging Alexander
Campbell, who in his earlier years had been quite disrespectful of such
organizations. But there was by no means solid approval of the new venture even at this early date. During the decade of the fifties important
figures like the Kentucky evangelist, Jacob Creath, Jr., and the Nashville educator and preacher, Tolbert Fanning, began to give vocal leadership to the anti-society faction within the church.

As the controversy over the missionary society and other "issues" progressed in the years following the Civil War, it became more and more
obvious that a basic dilemma which faces all ideological movements was
involved in the strife. The basic theological issue which ultimately caused
a division of the Disciples was the question of a "liberal" or "conservative"—"loose" or "strict"—interpretation of the restoration plea of
Thomas Campbell: "Where the Scriptures speak, we speak; where the
Scriptures are silent, we are silent." The question of whether the silence
of the Scriptures was "binding" or "loosing" was a fundamental one
which was to disturb the Disciples for fifty years. The absence of scriptural precedent for the missionary society and, later, other "innovations,"
brought this question slowly into focus.

The division which began to spread through the ranks of the church
in these early years also found expression in the point of emphasis of the
two-fold ideal of the original reformers. Their desire was for "Christian
union" through the "restoration of the ancient order of things." While the
two goals seemed perfectly compatible, indeed, inseparable, in the minds
of the early reformers, in later years the dividing parties began to feel
a closer kinship to one or the other of the two—the liberals, "Christian
union" and the conservatives, "the restoration of the ancient order of
things."

Underneath this theological facade deep and turbulent undercurrents had long troubled the waters of peace within the sect. The sectional, economic, cultural, and psychological diversities within the movement from its beginning were blurred in the early years by fervor and lack of organization. National organization and increased brotherhood communication in the decade of the 1850's, along with a long series of national crises, slowly brought the antagonistic elements into focus. A significant part of this study deals with the formative impact of these sociological forces on the course of Disciples history.

By 1865 the Disciples of Christ had over 200,000 members.[13] The church apparently had passed through the bloody national ordeal without a division and in 1866 Moses E. Lard, widely known Kentucky editor and preacher, confidently boasted, *"we can never divide."*[14] The new and vigorous leaders who directed the movement in the years following the Civil War (by 1866 such names as Thomas and Alexander Campbell, Barton Stone, Walter Scott, and John T. Johnson were no longer on the church rolls) found out that Lard was wrong in his church division prophecy. The church could divide and did divide. In fact, it was already dividing when Lard made his prophecy. One of the foremost intellectual preoccupations of the post-Civil War Disciples' leaders was to explain theologically how the church could divide; one of the primary aims of this study is to examine the sociological process by which it did divide.

RELIGION AND SOCIETY

The recurrent outbursts of active, vital religion in American history have left deep imprints on the nation's thought. In his introduction to a study of American religion made by the American Academy of Political and Social Science, Ray Abrams comments that "religion is quite obviously one of the most powerful and persistent of all the social forces."[15] The social historian Ralph Gabriel also emphasizes the impact of American religion on the nation's social thought: "The twentieth-century student is often astonished at the extent to which supernaturalism permeated

---

[13]Garrison and DeGroot, *The Disciples of Christ,* pp. 328-329.

[14]"Can We Divide?" *Lard's Quarterly,* III (April, 1866), 336.

[15]Ray Abrams, Introduction, in *Organized Religion in the United States,* ed., Ray Abrams, *Annals* of the American Academy, CCLVI (March, 1948), vii.

American thought of the nineteenth century."[16] But the relationship between religion and society in America has by no means been one-sided. One of the most persistent patterns in American religious history has been the "Americanization" of religious expression in this country. Abrams also notes this influence: "On the other hand, in the pattern of the inter-relationship of our social institutions, organized religion has been greatly influenced by the political, economic, and educational system. . . . Social change has deeply affected church life."[17]

Since the pioneering studies of Max Weber, Ernst Troeltsch, and Richard Tawney early in the twentieth century, religious historians and sociologists have done a good deal to clarify the complex relationship between religious and social thought.[18] The historic expressions of Christianity have been sorted into categories, each of which represents a describable mixture of the Christian "ethos" and a particular socio-economic tradition. While nomenclature often differs, the broad divisions generally used are: 1. The church, *ecclesia,* or ecclesiastical body, which includes such European national churches as the Lutherans and Anglicans—groups growing out of the right wing of the Protestant Reformation. 2. The independent body or denomination, including most of the American religious groups which have the established sociological characteristics of European ecclesiastical bodies without their unique relationship to the state. 3. The sect, which includes the left wing of the Christian movement both in Europe and America.[19]

---

[16]Ralph Henry Gabriel, *The Course of American Democratic Thought* (2d ed.; New York: Ronald Press Co., 1956), p. 14. Also see pp. 26-38; and Timothy L. Smith, *Revivalism and Social Reform in Mid-Nineteenth-Century America* (New York: Abingdon Press, 1957), pp. 34-44; William Warren Sweet, *Revivalism in America* (New York: Charles Scribner's Sons, 1945), pp. 140-161; Olmstead, *Religion in the United States,* pp. 347-361.

[17]Abrams, "Introduction," *Annals,* CCLVI, vii.

[18]Max Weber, *The Protestant Ethic and the Spirit of Capitalism,* trans., Talcott Parsons (New York: Charles Scribner's Sons, 1958); Ernst Troeltsch, *The Social Teachings of the Christian Churches,* trans., Olive Wyon (2 vols.; New York: Harper & Brothers, 1960); R. H. Tawney, *Religion and the Rise of Capitalism* (10th ed.; a Mentor book; New York: published by the New American Library, 1960).

[19]Often other subdivisions are made but these three remain the basic types. See J. Milton Yinger, *Religion, Society and the Individual* (New York: The Macmillan Company, 1957), pp. 142-155.

The three-fold sociological division which includes the ecclesiastical body is less meaningful in a study of American Christianity than in the European scene where the established church type is prominent. Recent students of American religion have emphasized that denominationalism is the natural state of religion in America; the denominational expression of the Christian tradition is final in this country and does not represent, as it often does in Europe, a transitional stage between sect and ecclesiastical body. Pluralism in religion is considered normal and even desirable by most Americans, and denominationalism is the natural and final expression of this philosophy.[20]

Sects and denominations are defined in terms of both theological and sociological common denominators. A denomination, while it considers itself the "true religious community," is "less exclusive, owing to a less institutional and more spiritual notion of Christian fellowship."[21] Such a group is not only inclined to be more tolerant of other religious bodies it is also more tolerant of the society in which it exists. The denomination is a "culture-centered religion" and, in effect, becomes the religious expression of the leading element in the social order.[22]

On the other hand, sects are "characterized by a rigid exclusiveness" which distinguishes them from denominations.[23] The sect is also "indifferent towards the authority of the State and the ruling classes" and quite critical of the cultural norms of the society in which it exists.[24] It is an expression of the Christian message in terms of protest against society and is "connected with the lower classes, or at least with those elements in

---

[20]Herberg, *Protestant,* pp. 85-86; Herbert Wallace Schneider, *Religion in 20th Century America* (Cambridge, Mass.: Harvard University Press, 1952), pp. 22-23.

[21]Joachim Wach, *Types of Religious Experience Christian and Non-Christian* (Chicago: University of Chicago Press, 1951), p. 194.

[22]A very useful description of differences between sects and denominations may be found in Liston Pope, *Millhands and Preachers* (New Haven: Yale University Press, 1942), pp. 122-124. See, also, Troeltsch, *Social Teaching,* I, 331; Wach, *Religious Experience,* p. 201; H. Richard Niebuhr, *The Social Sources of Denominationalism* (5th ed.; New York: Meridian Books, Inc., 1960), pp. 30-32.

[23]Wach, *Religious Experience,* p. 195.

[24]Troeltsch, *Social Teaching,* I, 336. See, also, Pope, *Millhands and Preachers,* pp. 122-124. There are, of course, many different types of sects. A good discussion of this problem may be found in Elmer T. Clark, *The Small Sects in America* (rev. ed.; Nashville: Abingdon Press, 1949), pp. 20-24.

Society which are opposed to the State and to Society."[25] In sum, sect and denomination are different expressions of the Christian message designed to meet the needs of the socially contented and the disinherited.

While these sociological divisions are useful in tracing the development of, and relating religious groups, they do not give a clear-cut picture of the status of all religious bodies. As a matter of fact, many churches do not fit snugly into any one of the divisions; some churches have the characteristics of more than one of them; and there is a persistent tendency among sectarian groups to evolve into denominations. The sects, originating among the lower classes, are communities formed on "a genuine religious basis" and from them "all great religious movements based on Divine revelation which have created large communities have always issued." But the very vitality and creativity of the sect holds within itself the seeds of denominationalism because "inevitably, as the movement develops, the early naïve vital religious content always fuses with all the higher religious forces of the intellectual culture of the day; apart from this fusion faith would be broken by the impact of the cultural environment."[26]

Although many sects evolve into denominations, others have shown a remarkable ability to preserve their sectarian characteristics for generations. Other radical groups develop in such a distinctive way that some recent students have seen the need for a new classification—the "established sect" or the "institutionalized sect."[27] The evolution of the sect is often determined by the character of its peculiar protest. Sometimes the protest of the group is too radical, too incompatible with the social milieu, to be accommodated within the broad mainstream of socially established religion. Such a sect may develop organizationally and institutionally in the same manner as other groups which evolve into denominations but its unique plea keeps it out of the mainstream of the denominational movement. It remains a halfway stopping place between anarchic sectarianism and acculturated denominationalism.

[25]Troeltsch, *Social Teaching*, I, 331.

[26]Troeltsch, *Social Teaching*, I, 44-45.

[27]Yinger, *Religion, Society*, pp. 150-152; Harold W. Pfautz, "The Sociology of Secularization: Religious Groups," *American Journal of Sociology*, LXI (September, 1955), 121-128.

In studying the social thought of a religious body many of the most intriguing problems are questions of why the Christian message was expressed in the way that it was and why the particular form in which it was molded attracted the group of people it did. What was the tenuous complex of motivations which prompted some to formulate and others to accept the unique social philosophy of a particular sect? What were the sociological motivations which prompted an evolution from sect to denomination or which preserved the sectarian emphasis? The answers to these questions are neither simple nor subject to comprehensive generalization. The motivation for the social philosophy (as well as the theology) of each religious group is an intricate mixture of sociological and spiritual forces.

One sociological factor which has influenced the social thought of many religious groups is the ethnic composition of the body. Many churches within the Christian system have evolved primarily as the religious expression of an ethnic group. H. Richard Niebuhr has emphasized the importance of the immigrant church in the explosive development of denominationalism in America.[28] Often, as the second and third generations of immigrant children began to lose their peculiar national status in the American melting pot, they continued to use the ethnic church as the preeminent connection with their immigrant heritage.[29]

Generally an isolated ethnic group also forms a congruous economic unit in society and the immigrant church in America is sometimes better understood as an economic expression than an ethnic one. It has long been apparent that the vital and emotional religious expression of sectarianism met the needs of the lower classes. Through the sect the dispossessed found an avenue for their simple and ebullient spiritual expressions. The sect also supplied the vehicle for the propagation of their economic and social philosophies within the Christian tradition.

H. Richard Niebuhr, in *The Social Sources of Denominationalism*, relates the history of American religion as the story of churches being formed and torn apart, stagnating and growing, in cadence with the violent sectional economic struggles which racked the American nation

---

[28]*Social Sources*, pp. 106-134; 200-235.

[29]Herberg, *Protestant*, pp. 7-45. See, also, Oscar Handlin, *The Uprooted* (Boston: Little, Brown and Company, 1951), pp. 117-143.

in the nineteenth century. Dividing the nation into economic and cultural
units of East and West and North and South, Niebuhr pictures the rise
of new sects and the development of new denominations as basically responses to sectional religious needs. He writes:

> The part which the sectional conflict between North and South has played in the
> history of church schism in America is well-known. Less obviously but not less
> effectively the constantly recurring strife between East and West has left its mark
> on religious life in the United States and has been responsible for the divergent
> development of a number of denominations.[30]

While the American pattern of sect creation and development has basically
followed in the European tradition, the history of "churches of the disinherited" in this country has been influenced by the peculiar sectional
flavor of American economic struggles. American religion in the nineteenth
century rent first into religious groups which satisfied the needs of the
East and the West and later divided again into groups which represented
the economic and cultural interests of the North and the South.

As the economic and cultural climate of the American sections changed
with the development of the nation in the nineteenth century, the religious
groups which had been generated by the sectional needs also changed.
As the American frontier passed, the sectarian groups which had flourished
in its atmosphere became "rural churches" in which the sectarian emphases
were "modified by the influence of social habit."[31] The "rural church"
was a transitional stage for the great evangelical churches of the West in
which they were less fervent and vigorous than in their radically sectarian
stage but in which they were only slightly less suspicious of the virtues
of urban communities and urban churches. It was not until the late nineteenth century that these frontier groups developed a close interrelationship with the new industrialized and urbanized America and concurrently
passed into the status of religious denominations. William Warren Sweet
notes that as this evolution took place within the great Western evangelical
groups, there were recurrent resurgences of sectarianism. He accounts for
the widespread generation of new sects in the 1880's by the "cultural
metamorphosis" which had "taken place in these great evangelical bodies,

---

[30]*Social Sources*, p. 136.
[31]*Ibid.*, p. 182.

transforming them into upper middle-class churches."[32]

It would be a mistake, however, to think that the development of religious bodies and the motivation of their social thought can be understood simply in terms of the relation of a church to an economic group. If Christian thought has been shaped historically to fit the economic presuppositions of certain sociological groups, it is no less true that the economic and cultural philosophy of Western man has been cast in the mold of the Christian tradition. It would be ridiculous to say that the force of the religious stream in American history has never flooded over the embankments of class dictates. In his 1937 study, *The Kingdom of God in America*, Niebuhr stated that he was dissatisfied with the unbalanced picture he had presented in *The Social Sources of Denominationalism:*

> Though the sociological approach helped to explain why the religious stream flowed in these particular channels it did not account for the force of the stream itself; . . . while it could deal with the religion which was dependent on culture, it left unexplained the faith which is independent, which is aggressive, rather than passive, and which molds culture instead of being molded by it.[33]

Nor have social historians been oblivious to this truism. Ralph Gabriel writes:

> But social beliefs are affected by other forces than economic change. If a man on earth must eat, so also must he adjust his life and thought to the mysteries surrounding him. . . . For this reason the reigning cosmic philosophy is as fundamental to a particular climate of opinion as are its economic foundations to a selected social scene.[34]

The persistent force of the vital, creative Christian message has unquestionably been a powerful influence in the development of American social thought.

Finally, religion is born of and molded by deep-seated psychological needs. The "individual psychology" of the members of any religious group must be considered in order to understand the peculiar characteristics of

---

[32]Sweet, "Protestant Churches," *Annals,* CCLVI, 47. See, also, William Warren Sweet, *American Culture and Religion* (Dallas: Southern Methodist University Press, 1951), pp. 89-92; Clark, *Small Sects,* pp. 18-20.

[33]H. Richard Niebuhr, *The Kingdom of God in America* (Torchbook ed.; New York: Harper & Brothers, 1959), pp. ix-x.

[34]Gabriel, *Democratic Thought,* p. 26.

that group. Joachim Wach asks the intriguing question: "Are there, generally speaking, types of personality roughly corresponding to the sociological types of fellowship which have been outlined?"[35] Elmer T. Clark has also suggested that the sectarian impulse in America has psychological undertones: "That so many persons attach moral meaning to what most people regard as trivial details is a psychological problem in itself."[36] Dilemmas in the thought of a religious group which defy explanation simply in terms of economic, ethnic, and religious factors often may be resolved in terms of the common mind which drew the group together. The psychological character of the leader, especially in sectarian bodies, acts as a magnet which draws around him people of like mind and leaves a permanent imprint on the thought of the church.

All of these complex and tenuous factors are involved in understanding the social thought of a religious movement. Perhaps more than in any other ideological area, the convictions of men in the name of religion are rooted in the innermost subsoil of his mystical, spiritual, practical, socio-conditioned, and sometimes twisted experience.

DISCIPLES SOCIAL THOUGHT, 1800-1865

Very little work of any significance has been done in the history of social thought of the Disciples of Christ in the nineteenth century;[37] in fact, Winfred Garrison, the outstanding historian of the church, prefaced his three-page summary of this area of the movement's history with an explanation of why the Disciples had been almost totally unconcerned with social problems:

---

[35]Wach, *Religious Experience*, p. 204.

[36]Clark, *Small Sects*, p. 16.

[37]Harold Lunger's excellent book, *The Political Ethics of Alexander Campbell* (St. Louis: The Bethany Press, 1954), is the outstanding exception to this statement. A number of useful works have been written in specialized areas but for the most part the few studies which have appeared in the field of social thought have been woefully lacking in a sound research foundation and totally ignorant of the larger implications of the social views of Disciples leaders. Oliver Read Whitley's recent book, *Trumpet Call of Reformation* (St. Louis: The Bethany Press, 1959), is an important attempt to trace the sociological development of the movement. However useful Whitley's book might be, it is seriously marred by the author's failure to delve deeply into the primary sources and by his uncritical acceptance of several stereotyped interpretations of Disciples history.

It was in the early years of the twentieth century that the Disciples began to have a new sense of the ethical and social responsibility of the churches. . . . Disciples in the earlier period had special reasons for aloofness from social problems, and even for hesitating to make positive pronouncements on disputable questions of personal conduct. The primary reason for this was their concentration on restoring the unity and the apostolic order of the church and on the conversion of individuals according to the spiritual "plan of salvation."[38]

The history of the Disciples of Christ, as that of most other religious groups, has been written largely in terms of theological and organizational development.

It is true that Disciples were first concerned with establishing the kingdom of Christ on earth, but this spiritual preoccupation had tremendous social implications. They thought and wrote a great deal about what society ought to be like. While divided on the question of whether they ought to become involved in political attempts to regenerate American society, as were most American Protestant leaders, they were consistently vocal in expressing their views on social questions, even while insisting that the only way to accomplish the needed reform was through spiritual revolution. Disciples vocalized their social ideologies, they intricately connected them with their theological concepts and, perhaps even more significant, there was often a striking and significant diversity of viewpoints—but they were not "aloof."

Aside from the lack of interest in social history, two other erroneous basic assumptions have plagued Disciples historiography. They are both vividly illustrated in Oliver Read Whitley's *Trumpet Call of Reformation*. Although Whitley repeatedly states that he has based his conclusions on "an extensive research in the most important source material of Disciples [*sic*],"[39] his documentation, as far as primary materials are concerned, is taken almost completely from the periodicals edited by Alexander Campbell and from twentieth-century publications. Whitley supports that portion of his study dealing with the period to 1870 solely with citations to the *Christian Baptist* and the *Millennial Harbinger* (with the exception of one reference to *Lard's Quarterly*) and then skips to the publications

---

[38]Garrison and DeGroot, *The Disciples of Christ*, p. 421. Historians of American religion have generally accepted this interpretation of the Disciples. Clifton Olmstead writes: "The Disciples of Christ eschewed social reform in favor of personal evangelization." *Religion in the United States*, p. 383.

[39]Whitley, *Trumpet Call*, pp. 9, 68, 159.

of the twentieth century—for the most part articles written after 1930.[40]
Whitley's book is not a unique example in Disciples historiography. Assumptions that the early history of the Disciples is synonymous with the story of Alexander Campbell and that the period from 1865 to 1900 was an era when the church was without competent leaders and in which very little was achieved have often distorted the history of the movement.[41]

Unquestionably the influence of Alexander Campbell on the early history of the Disciples of Christ was enormous. But to attempt to understand the broad scope of the movement simply on the basis of the material in the *Christian Baptist* and the *Millennial Harbinger* is absurd. There was tremendous diversity in the body from the beginning, and a meaningful explanation of the tensions which developed in the church in the latter half of the nineteenth century without an understanding of these diversities is impossible. If Alexander Campbell was the uncrowned monarch of the church before 1860, he reigned over a turbulent and unruly kingdom. Other important ante-bellum leaders left deep and permanent imprints on Disciples thought. Noel L. Keith's work, *The Story of D. S. Burnet: Undeserved Obscurity*[42] is typical of what needs to be done with other early leaders.

Within the framework of this understanding of Disciples history this study develops as a three-part story. The first is a narrative of what the Disciples thought and did on social issues. Not only has the variety of thought on social questions often gone unnoticed and many unique and significant individuals been ignored by the students of the church, but the actual course of the social thought of the movement has often been misjudged, or, more frequently, misguessed. Interpretation without the aid

---

[40]*Ibid.*, see footnotes, pp. 239-250.

[41]Only the first of these assumptions is significant for the period included in this volume. It is perhaps less glaring, however, than the second. A cursory examination of the space-allotment in the major general studies of the movement is a simple illustration of the disproportionate significance assigned to the early and recent periods of the movement's history by most of its students. Winfred E. Garrison has called the post-Civil War period "the Dark Ages of the Disciples," *Religion Follows the Frontier*, p. 223. See, also, W. E. Garrison, "1896-1946," *The Scroll*, XLIII (September, 1945), 1-3. William E. Tucker's recent book, *J. H. Garrison and Disciples of Christ* (St. Louis: The Bethany Press, 1964) is a splendid and important addition to the literature on the "middle period of Disciples."

[42](St. Louis: The Bethany Press, 1954).

of information has too often been the case and it is to the correction of
this problem that a considerable portion of this work is directed.

But the most intriguing facet of this study involves interpretations of
impact and motivation. The hard facts which tell the story of what men
did and thought on a specific social issue are coherent and meaningful in
terms of Disciples history and American history only if they are put into
the context of people being molded by a vital, creative Christian message
and in turn being shaped by the turbulent society of nineteenth-century
America. In short, the problem of interpretation is two-fold: a study of
the contribution of Disciples to the social consciousness of the nation and
an analysis of the sociological impact on the church's social thought.

The first of these questions has important implications in American
social and religious history. If the social crusades of the early nineteenth
century had their most famous leaders among the religious dignitaries of
the established churches of the East, revivalistic and evangelical religion
in both East and West supplied religious fervor and the mass of the
storm troopers. Ralph Gabriel comments: "Evangelical Protestantism
dominated the social thought of Trans-Appalachia and ultimately captured
the Atlantic States of the cotton kingdom. . . . Religion was the most
powerful drive behind the humanitarian movements of the age."[43]

Timothy L. Smith, in his recent book, *Revivalism and Social Reform
in Mid-Nineteenth-Century America,* forcefully demonstrated the fact that
revivalistic religion continued to flourish in the period from 1840 to 1870
and that it had a tremendous impact on American social thought. Smith
also shows, as Richard Niebuhr had earlier, that the evangelical sects during these years not only nurtured the practical reform movements which
led to the alleviation of many of the major social injustices in the nation,
but that they also displayed an "ethical seriousness" and social concern
for sinful men which later proved a solid foundation for the social gospel
movement in the last decades of the nineteenth century. While no serious
student of social and religious history would contend that the social gospel movement was an inevitable development of the evangelical tradition,

---

[43]Gabriel, *Democratic Thought,* p. 161. See, also, Herberg, *Protestant,* pp.
106-107; Charles C. Cole, Jr., *The Social Ideas of the Northern Evangelists
1826-1860* (New York: Columbia University Press, 1954), pp. 96-131; and
Whitney R. Cross's study of enthusiastic religion in western New York, *The
Burned-Over District* (Ithaca, New York: Cornell University Press, 1950).

neither is it any longer tenable to stereotype the vital religious emphasis of midnineteenth-century American Protestantism as the seed ground of social reaction. It remains true that the social gospelers of the 1890's were the peculiar children of their peculiar environment but they inherited a humanitarian and socially concerned birthright from the evangelical tradition in which they had deep roots.

Smith's book is essentially an effort to rescue the "holiness" movement of the Northeast from an undeserved reputation as social reactionaries. This study demonstrates that another of the vital sectarian streams in American religious life shared this concern over the social ills of the nation. The truth of the matter is that the sectarian Christian expression, the churches of the dispossessed, had several different emphases (of which the "holiness" craving for Christian perfection was one and the legalistic "search for the ancient order" of the Disciples was another), but whatever the emphasis and wherever the location, the sect has been an active and creative force in American society. All through the nation midnineteenth-century evangelical religion throbbed with the socially significant anticipation of the coming of the "kingdom of Christ."[44]

This study, then, is designed to trace the strivings of one group of religious people to deal with the complexities of their social environment within the framework of Christian principles. The Disciples of Christ were Biblical literalists with a gigantic faith and again and again they gave their views of the social mold in which Christian America should be cast. The Disciples furnish vivid evidence that the humanitarian impulse in American Christianity was generated neither in Eastern or Western, nor urban or rural, religion but in the sectarian Christian expression of the dispossessed—whatever the peculiar emphasis of the movement might be. Vital religion, as Arthur M. Schlesinger, Jr. has suggested of vital politics, was not the possession of any section; it was the fervent birthright of the common man.

The antitypic question to that of the importance of the Disciples of Christ in the forming of the social thought of the nation is the problem of how much the thought of the church was molded by sociological forces. It is absurd to try to departmentalize the complex reactions of men to the challenges of their environment into neat packages of ideologi-

---

[44]Niebuhr, *The Kingdom of God*, pp. 150-163.

cal, economic, and psychological responses. And yet, even if the historian cannot account for every individual's conduct, he can suggest any number of motivating forces which were at work and which influenced the thought of a religious group to flow in the channels which it did. In addition to the theological presuppositions and the sectarian vitality which unquestionably influenced the course of Disciples social thought, there were powerful economic, ethnic, and psychological motivations which directed the flow of the movement.

Thirty years ago Winfred Ernest Garrison, in what remains the most meaningful study of the church, *Religion Follows the Frontier*, brilliantly interpreted the Disciples as the Christian expression of American frontier society.[45] Since that time the Disciples have consistently been interpreted within this context by social and religious historians.[46] No serious student of the movement can ignore its frontier heritage.

And yet the interpretation of the Disciples as an American frontier religion is inadequate. The group has never fit snugly into such a simple package without some untidy remnants hanging over the sides. With the passing of the frontier the Disciples were increasingly faced with the problem of adjusting and readjusting to a changing socio-economic environment. Garrison, in his re-evaluation of the history of the movement in 1945, significantly changed the title of his work to *An American Religious Movement*.[47] The evolution of the church's social thought can be understood only in the context of the changing economic and social structure of middle-America.

The reactions of Disciples to the economic and social pressures of changing America were as varied as the almost incredible diversity of the nation. Richard Niebuhr's description of the socio-economic process through which most of the frontier evangelical sects passed from sect to

---

[45]For an even earlier sociological interpretation see, Rodney L. McQuary, "The Social Background of the Disciples of Christ," *The College of the Bible Quarterly*, XIII (March, 1924), 3-16.

[46]See Niebuhr, *Social Sources*, p. 178; Herberg, *Protestant*, pp. 104-105.

[47](St. Louis: Christian Board of Publication, 1945), pp. 5-6. See, also, Royal Humbert, "Convention Resolutions: A Case History," *The Scroll*, XLIII (October, 1950), 54-59. Actually Garrison showed real insight into the evolving character of the sociological pressures on the Disciples in his earlier work. See *Religion Follows the Frontier*, pp. 224-227.

rural church to denomination is clearly applicable to Disciples history.[48] But this is not the whole story of Disciples thought. The Disciples are preeminently typical of the phenomenon which Herbert Schneider calls a "religious movement." They were not a "body" in the early years of the nineteenth century but simply a vital religious movement united around sometimes vague poles of emphasis.[49] A denomination does emerge out of the movement in the last half of the nineteenth century but the sectarian emphasis flowed on in the same old channels still united around the same loose but fertile ideas. In the process of the nineteenth century this movement demonstrated the fertility common to all sectarian emphases— there were in it the seeds of sectarianism, of institutionalized sectarianism, and of denominationalism. The whole spectrum of the possibilities of sociological expressions of Christianity slowly comes into focus in nineteenth-century Disciples history. The variety of expressions which emerged out of the church's objectivistic and legalistic emphasis under the economic and cultural pressures of American society are not in general any different from those which developed within other sectarian expressions, although there are specific peculiarities due to the uniqueness of their plea. In short, all of the divisive elements in the complex American economic and cultural life of the nineteenth century were at work molding the Disciples emphasis—East and West, North and South, rural and urban, dispossessed and middle-class, all of these sociological forces forged their own Christian message out of the Disciples plea.

The sociological approach to an understanding of Disciples social thought also raises other significant questions of interpretation. Ethnic presuppositions unquestionably influenced their social thought. It is apparent to the casual observer of nineteenth-century Disciples history that the church was the ethnic religious expression of Anglo-Saxon middle America. In some areas of Disciples social thought the group's version of the Christian message was profoundly influenced by this fact.

Finally, when all is said and done, this is the story of the Disciples of Christ. While Disciples shared the economic and cultural heritage of most of middle America and the ethnic heritage of much of it, they had their

---

[48]*Social Sources*, pp. 181-187. See, also, Herberg, *Protestant*, pp. 108-110. This, of course, is the theme of Oliver Read Whitley's *Trumpet Call of Reformation*.

[49]Herberg, *Protestant*, pp. 107-108; Schneider, *Religion in 20th Century America*, pp. 22-23.

own sectarian emphasis and their own religious psychology, similar to that of others but never quite the same. They had their own powerful personalities who left deep marks on the movement; they had their own eccentrics and their own prophets. The story of what they thought is as broad as the American nation and as narrow as the small clique of devotees bound to a unique leader; it is a story in which exciting interrelationships are everywhere apparent and in which sweeping generalizations are never quite true.

CHAPTER II

THE MIND OF A MOVEMENT
HALF LAW—HALF LOVE

"And this commandment have we from him, That he who loveth God love his brother also." I John 4:21.

ALTHOUGH MOST Protestants recognize the Bible as the ultimate authority in religious matters, they are by no means all Biblical literalists. One of the persistent threads in the American religious tradition, however, has been the sectarian emphasis on literal Biblical interpretation. In his study of American sectarianism, Elmer T. Clark describes this theme:

An intense devotion to the very word of Holy Writ characterizes the little groups classed as legalistic. "The Bible not only *contains* the word of God, it *is* the word of God," is a well-known attitude. From this position the bodies in question draw the principles which mark them as legalistic.[1]

The Christian faith expressed in these terms becomes a very concrete and tangible system of thought and, within the bounds of revelation, an intensely rationalistic one. Starting outside of reason by accepting the Bible as the "word of God" which contains all truth, the legalist then proceeds to decipher this body of revealed truth rationally.

This particular sectarian emphasis has been recurrent in the history of Christianity and was especially prominent in nineteenth-century evangelical religion in America. Although there were some beginnings of liberal theology in this country before 1865, for the most part church and Biblical authoritarianism remained unchallenged until after the Civil War.[2] Baptists, Methodists, Presbyterians, and most of the splinter evangelical movements of the early nineteenth century would all ultimately resort to logical exegesis of Biblical texts to defend their peculiar doctrines. While

---

[1]Clark, *Small Sects*, p. 159.

[2]For a general discussion of American religious thought during this period see, Olmstead, *Religion in the United States*, pp. 295-320.

there were vast differences in doctrine and emphasis, the revivalist leaders of the early nineteenth century were as much the children of the Enlightenment as deists and freethinkers; they based their investigations on a different set of presuppositions, but they all shared the methodology of eighteenth-century philosophy.

The Disciples of Christ in the first half of the nineteenth century is perhaps the purest and most striking American example of the legalistic and objectivistic sectarian expression.[3] One of the basic articles of faith which cut deeply through the whole movement during the period 1800 to 1865 was that the Bible was authoritative and final and that intelligent investigation of this source would result in the discovery of truth. From the "Last Will and Testament of the Springfield Presbytery" which pleaded with all men to take "the Bible as the only sure guide to heaven"[4] and the statement in the *Declaration and Address* that the Christian Association of Washington "holds itself engaged . . . in promoting a pure evangelical reformation, by the simple preaching of the everlasting Gospel, and the administration of its ordinances in an exact conformity to the Divine Standard,"[5] the thought of the group was rooted in the central conviction that there was a divine pattern of apostolic Christianity and that the answer to the problems of contemporary Protestantism was to return to these Biblical standards.

In short, the Disciples were Biblical rationalists. As Winfred E. Garrison has noted, there was a "definiteness and positiveness" about the message of Christianity in their thought which "easily ran into legalism."[6] They conceived of their mission in terms of restoring the gospel to its original first-century purity and of reordering the church according to the "ancient order of things." The natural result of this spiritual revolution

---

[3]Among Disciples the rationalistic emphasis was more unmixed than in most evangelical sects. Disciples almost completely rejected emotion and "experience," although they inherited some of this emphasis through Stone.

[4]Charles Alexander Young, *Historical Documents Advocating Christian Union* (Chicago: The Christian Century Company, 1904), p. 2.

[5]*Ibid.,* p. 78.

[6]Garrison, *Religion Follows the Frontier,* p. 193. For a broad discussion of this emphasis see Garrison, *The Sources of Alexander Campbell's Theology* (St. Louis: Christian Publishing Company, 1900), pp. 185-210; and Homer Hailey, *Attitudes and Consequences in the Restoration Movement* (2d. ed.; Rosemead, California: The Old Paths Book Club, 1952), pp. 113-136.

would be the union of divided Christendom. The foundation upon which both ideas rested was Biblical literalism.

The whole of the intellectual, religious, and social environment in which the sect was born fertilized its rationalistic legalism. If the Methodists and frontier Presbyterians were more emotional than the Disciples, they had no less respect for the "word of God" and they were no less prepared to smother an opponent with proof texts. In the countless and colorful debates between Disciples and Presbyterians, Methodists, Baptists, Mormons, and almost every other religious species, both sides used the Bible and both sides dissected it with the cold logic of an eighteenth-century rationalist.

Many early leaders among the Disciples were deeply influenced by the writings of John Locke, Francis Bacon, and the Scottish "common sense" philosophers.[7] Sterling W. Brown suggests that it was "their philosophical background inherited from John Locke" which was the most important formative influence on the thought of the Disciples of Christ.[8] The Disciples simply adopted the philosophical methodology of the day and used it within the framework of their own Christian emphasis. While they "reacted against the results" which came from the philosophy of the eighteenth century, they "accepted in the main the principles upon which it was based."[9]

The rationalistic and optimistic philosophy of the Enlightenment was simply a sophisticated expression of the spirit that prevailed in the American West. If many of the first-generation leaders of the Disciples of Christ were influenced by the writings of Locke, Reid, and Bacon, the practical rationalism of the frontier reached into the pulpits and pews of every country church. The self-confident American frontiersman lacked respect for all authority, especially ecclesiastical and clerical, and his individualism

---

[7] A basic study which remains valuable after many years is Garrison's *Alexander Campbell's Theology*. See, also, Robert Frederick West, *Alexander Campbell and Natural Religion* (New Haven: Yale University Press, 1948); Sterling W. Brown, "The Disciples and the New Frontier," *The Scroll*, XXXII (May, 1936), 153-165. Bacon's name is recurrent in Disciples history. For an excellent example of the Baconian impact on Biblical interpretation see J. S. Lamar, *The Organon of Scripture* (Cincinnati: H. S. Bosworth, Publisher, 1860).

[8] Brown, "Disciples and the New Frontier," XXXII, 158.

[9] Garrison, *Alexander Campbell's Theology*, p. 108.

led him to believe that every man had the innate ability to discover religious truth simply by a rational investigation of the Scriptures. The Disciples "formulated a simple, practical, straight-from-the-shoulder statement of their faith," says Sterling W. Brown, "which found a ready response in the minds and hearts of the frontiersman in the Middle West."[10]

To a large degree the Disciples were not simply Biblical primitivists, they were New Testament primitivists. Early in the history of the Disciples Campbell gave the church significant direction in his famous "Sermon on the Law" in which he stressed differences between the Old and New Testaments.[11] As this covenant theory developed in the thought of the Disciples, the Old Testament was increasingly discarded as authoritative in the "Christian age" and the New Testament emerged as the only guide to Christian action. Perhaps even more significant was the emphasis placed on the Book of Acts and the Epistles. Their interest in the restoration principle made the post-Pentecost portions of the Scriptures particularly important to Disciples, and the bulk of the scriptural precedent for their actions was based on the "approved examples" in the Book of Acts and the "precepts" recorded in the Epistles.[12]

The preoccupation of Disciples with scriptural authority was one of the fundamental factors which directed the church's social thought. When a Disciple looked for answers in the pre-Civil War period, he looked in the Bible—more specifically he looked in the New Testament. No important leader in the church during these years would have seriously attempted to defend a position on any issue without Biblical proof texts. Occasionally the "higher law" concept was appealed to during the slavery controversy but invariably even the abolitionists would attempt to substantiate their

---

[10]Brown, "Disciples and the New Frontier," XXXII, 158. See, also, W. C. Bower, "The Frontier Mind," *The Scroll*, XL (June, 1943), 300-309.

[11]Garrison, *Alexander Campbell's Theology*, pp. 161-182.

[12]Although, of course, this varied a great deal with the individual. For instance, William Garrett West, in his book on Barton Stone, points out that Stone leaned heavily on the Gospels and the Sermon on the Mount. *Barton Warren Stone: Early American Advocate of Christian Unity* (Nashville: The Disciples of Christ Historical Society, 1954), pp. 209, 222-223. This is certainly true of many other leaders in the church. And yet, the Acts-Epistles emphasis is inherent in the "restoration plea" and more often than not these were the portions of Scripture where most early Disciples looked for authority. See Lunger, *Political Ethics of Alexander Campbell*, p. 33.

claims with Biblical proof—the Scriptures remained the "highest law."[13]

Another important implication of the literalistic New Testament orientation of Disciples was that this emphasis opened a wide area where diversity of opinion was tolerated. "For Campbell and the movement generally," notes Harold Lunger, "only those things that were set forth 'in express terms or by approved precedent' were considered matters of 'faith' and therefore binding upon all members of the church. Other inferences and deductions from scriptural premises fell into the category of 'opinion' and could not be made terms of communion."[14] While the early leaders of the group thought there were a number of specific elements in the original gospel and in the order of the first-century church which were clearly and indisputably established by New Testament authority, they also believed there were many areas where scriptural teaching was not so positive or clear and in these areas Christians were free to follow their own private judgments. This distinction was theologically important to Disciples—the union of Disciples and Stoneites, who were suspected of Unitarianism, could hardly have been accomplished without it—but probably even more important were its implications in the area of social ethics. The proper application of the sweeping principles of Christian morality almost always were regarded as matters of "opinion." If one was loyal to the basic doctrinal statements of the New Testament, he was allowed the widest sort of liberty in the area of Christian social thought. A second important implication of this faith-opinion distinction was that while every individual had the right to make any application of the principles of Christian ethics which he thought proper, the church could make no formal commitment in these disputed areas. Legalism freed the individual Christian and restricted the activities of the church.

The evangelical Christianity of the early nineteenth century, even of the most legalistic variety, was not without an important humanitarian

---

[13]There were, of course, differences in degree in the New Testament legalism of Disciples leaders from the beginning but there were hardly any real "liberals" in the church prior to 1865. Preachers such as Lewis L. Pinkerton, Burke Hinsdale, James Garfield, George Longan, and Alexander Proctor, who were the first Biblical liberals in the group, did not openly advocate such views until the years following the Civil War. For a discussion of the general doctrinal emphasis of the movement during these years see Whitley, *Trumpet Call*, pp. 47-91.

[14]*Political Ethics of Alexander Campbell*, p. 27. See, also, Whitley, *Trumpet Call*, pp. 92-96.

emphasis. The evangelical sects were the "heirs of the religion of the poor" and, according to H. Richard Niebuhr, they were "more interested in the ethics than the theology of the faith."[15] American Protestantism during the years 1800 to 1865 was a religion of action and it imbibed deeply of the humanitarian spirit which was a fundamental part of American social thought. "Practical Christianity" was the heart of the message of the nineteenth-century evangelist in his crusade for the establishment of the kingdom of God in America. The compassionate message of a first-century vagabond Jew was readily comprehended by the itinerant, underpaid prophets to the poor in every section of the nation.[16]

This emphasis on practical religion was firmly rooted in the early thought of the Disciples of Christ. Although they were objectivistic legalists and often seemed totally preoccupied with doctrinal disputes, they were never unconcerned about the more practical applications of Christian principles. Humanitarian concern was always directed toward helping the individual and was often motivated by a legalistic conscience— the phrase "law of love" was not uncommon—but it was real and activistic.[17]

Although the chief concern of the early reformers among the Disciples was the "restoration of the ancient order," they never failed to stress the importance of Christian living. "Were all the common . . . virtues of justice, truth, fidelity, honesty, practised by all Christians," wrote Alexander Campbell in 1833, "how many mouths would be stopped, and how

---

[15]*Social Sources*, pp. 191-192. See, also, Niebuhr, *Kingdom of God*, pp. 112-126; Cole, *Northern Evangelists*, pp. 96-131; Olmstead, *Religion in the United States*, pp. 347-361.

[16]This is the emphasis of the whole latter half of Timothy Smith's *Revivalism and Social Reform*, pp. 148-237. The fact that the leaders of American evangelical religion were concerned about men's lives as well as their souls in the years before and after the Civil War has certainly been well established. Whitney R. Cross, in his study of enthusiastic religion in western New York during the period 1800-1850, has carefully and convincingly demonstrated the complex interrelationship between revivalism and social humanitarianism. *The Burned-Over District* (Ithaca: Cornell University Press, 1950).

[17]Charles C. Cole, Jr., says that Lewis Tappan was "keynoting the spirit of the times" when he expressed concern for other people in these dogmatic terms: "If I think you are losing your soul it is my duty to attempt to save you." *Northern Evangelists*, p. 130.

many new arguments in favor of Jesus Christ could all parties find!"[18] Barton Stone early warned Disciples of the "danger of dwelling too long upon doctrinal disquisitions, to the neglect of practical piety" and challenged them to "labor to have our own hearts and lives reformed."[19] In short, from the sect's beginnings to 1865 the emphasis on practical religion was an important part of the common mind of the Disciples of Christ.

William Garrett West, in his biography of Barton Stone, has suggested an interesting comparison between Alexander Campbell and Stone as representatives of the opposing extremes of "legalism" and "love" in Disciples thought. Speaking of Stone, West says, "Love reigned in his life."[20] On the other hand, he believes that the "legalistic element in Alexander Campbell's thought" left a deep and permanent mark on the restoration movement.[21] There is probably truth in West's comparison (Stone's teachings may have centered less around the Epistles and Acts and more around the Gospels, as he points out), yet it can easily be distorted. The truth of the matter is that it was never an "either-or" proposition in the mind of either man but a "both-and." They both could be, and were, legalists and they both could, and did, preach practical Christianity. Humanitarianism and legalism were part of the equipment of every first-generation Disciple and it is a tedious and unsure process to determine which of the two was the dominant theme in the thought of most of the early leaders.[22]

---

[18]"The Regeneration of the Church," *Millennial Harbinger*, Extra, VI (August, 1833), 366. In all quotations from nineteenth-century sources the original spelling and punctuation has been retained.

[19]"Editor's Address," *Christian Messenger*, VII (January, 1833), 3.

[20]*Barton Stone*, p. 223.

[21]*Ibid.*, p. 224.

[22]There is certainly a broad and challenging area here which would make an interesting study. The assumption that the humanitarian emphasis within the movement has its roots in Stone and the legalistic emphasis in Campbell has certainly never been proved. The exceptions to such a generalization are overwhelming at first appearances. Such early leaders of the "liberal" spirit, in social matters at any rate, as David S. Burnet, John T. Johnson, and Isaac Errett were from the Campbell stream. On the other hand, John Rogers says that "a large proportion of the friends of Stone received the teachings of Brother Campbell almost from the very beginning of his writings in the *Christian Baptist*." Elder John Rogers, *The Biography of Eld. Barton Warren Stone. . . .* (Cincinnati: J. A. & U. P. Jones, 1847), p. 115. A thorough study of this thesis remains to be done.

By 1865, however, it was evident that there were significant and expanding differences in emphasis within the church. If every important Disciples leader prior to 1865 remained nominally loyal to the legalistic restoration principle, and if every important Disciples leader had always insisted that a man could not be a Christian unless he was a "practical Christian," the intricate mixture of these two emphases showed signs of being jolted out of balance.

In March, 1857, Robert Richardson, long-time personal friend of Alexander Campbell, professor at Bethany College, and associate editor of the *Millennial Harbinger*, began a series of articles entitled "Faith *versus* Philosophy," which ran in the *Harbinger* throughout most of that year.[23] Richardson was soon locked in debate with Tolbert Fanning, the President of Franklin College in Nashville, editor of the *Gospel Advocate*, and probably the most influential church leader in Tennessee. Although the Richardson-Fanning debate centered specifically around the function of the Holy Spirit in conversion, the real crux of the difference between the two men was in their attitude on the question of literalistic and practical religion. Richardson believed that the restoration movement had not yet reached a successful culmination and that all that really had been effected was "an exchange of opinions, rather than a change of condition."[24] Such an idea was heretical to Fanning; he insisted that the legalistic "search for the ancient order" was the heart of the church's uniqueness and denounced Richardson as a "spiritualist." The Richardson-Fanning controversy flared throughout most of the year until finally, much to Richardson's embarrassment, Alexander Campbell, who apparently favored Fanning's position, at least through the early phases of the debate, closed the columns of the *Harbinger* to further discussion.

The discussion evoked widespread interest throughout the brotherhood and similar debates erupted over such issues as open communion, the meaning of baptism, and the propriety of special education for preachers. Beneath this turbulent surface lurked deep-seated internal tensions. While the intricate balance of "legalism" and "practical religion" had not tipped

---

[23]See the *Millennial Harbinger*, beginning March, 1857. For a good general discussion of the Richardson-Fanning debate see Cloyd Goodnight and Dwight E. Stevenson, *Home to Bethphage* (St. Louis: Christian Board of Publication, 1949), pp. 168-187; West, *Ancient Order*, I, 125-126.

[24]Stevenson and Goodnight, *Home to Bethphage*, p. 169.

over by 1865, it had become extremely delicate. The common mind of the
Disciples of Christ still contained both emphases in 1865 but in the minds
of many it was no longer a mixture of "both-and" but a process of first
one and then the other.

HALF PROPHET—HALF PEACEMAKER

"But he said, I am not mad, most noble Festus; but speak forth the words of
truth and soberness." Acts 26:25.

While Elmer T. Clark's statement that it is "a peculiar type of mind
which is convinced that God is interested in whether his worshipers sing
with or without instrumental accompaniment" is itself the product of a
"peculiar type of mind," it is none the less both true and meaningful.[25]
It is a "type of mind" which is essentially out of step with midtwentieth-
century American thought and yet it is one that is recurrent in Christian
history. It is the mind of a legalistic fanatic. The fanatic, legalistic or
otherwise, was not out of place in the midnineteenth-century Disciples
of Christ.

Religion is essentially an answer to the problems of death, suffering,
frustration, and tension—the basic psychological problems of man. An
individual's reactions to these problems are conditioned by both personal
and social factors. J. Milton Yinger, in his study of the sociology of religion, points out that there are "wide individual variations of frustration, tolerance for frustration, and sense of injustice, but there are also
wide variations in the degree to which social systems produce these personality tendencies."[26] While all individuals in all societies must deal with
these problems at some level, "those who feel it most acutely may struggle
with it in religious terms" and "for a few—the mystics, the ascetics, the
prophets—they become the dominant preoccupation of life."[27] The psychological needs of an individual may mold his religious personality into
that of a fanatic, into a state of relative complacency, or into any of the
infinite number of stopping places in between these two extremes.

There is much of the mind of the religious fanatic in the pre-Civil War
thought of the Disciples. For the most part it was a rationalistic and

---

[25]*Small Sects*, p. 16.

[26]*Religion, Society, and the Individual* (New York: The Macmillan Company,
1957), p. 79.

[27]*Ibid.*

THE MIND OF A MOVEMENT

legalistic fanaticism, but the enthusiast is not circumscribed within any doctrinal system and there were zealots on both extremes of Disciples thought.[28] The Christian movement was born amidst the emotionally loaded revival fervor in the first decade of the nineteenth century. Barton Stone recalled that during the early years of the sect "some of us were verging on fanaticism."[29] The Campbell group also began in an atmosphere of excitement and tension. Campbell himself led the way: "His hand was against everything; and every man's hand was soon against him. His spirit of iconoclasm led him to demolish very many useful and indispensable customs of organized Christianity."[30] Pioneer prophets scoured the fermenting American West with the "restored gospel," heralding the rejuvenation of the New Testament church, and, as Jacob Creath put it, delivering "a blow at the root" of every false religious system. By the 1830's enthusiasm reached a peak intensity within the church and culminated in widespread anticipation of the imminent approach of the millennium. To call a Disciple a fanatic has always been considered the grossest insult; but the movement was never without its prophets—and every Disciple had a little of the zealot in him.[31]

In commenting on the impact of social conditions on the individual's religious psychology J. Milton Yinger says, "social systems may reduce somewhat the individual religious needs by lowering the level of frustration and reducing the sense of injustice."[32] The Disciples were born in a society which nurtured an intense religious psychology—a society in which tensions and frustrations were unquestionably large. While the pragmatic philosophy and practical experience of the frontiersman made him receptive to rationalistic and legalistic religion, his insecurity and

---

[28]Jacob Creath, Jr. and Lewis L. Pinkerton were on the opposing extremes of Disciples thought and yet it would not be inaccurate to say that each of them had a fanatical temperament. It is the nature of a man and not the doctrinal message he preaches that marks him as a zealot.

[29]Rogers, *Biography of Stone*, p. 64.

[30]Errett Gates, *The Early Relation and Separation of Baptists and Disciples* (Chicago: The Christian Century Company, 1904), p. 40.

[31]For more than any other reason, early Disciples probably objected to being called fanatics because of the emotional connotations of the word. They considered the emotional excesses of the frontier camp meetings most objectionable. But it is apparent that they were just as extreme in their own rationalistic way.

[32]Yinger, *Religion Society*, p. 79.

the instability of the society in which he lived made him equally receptive to fervent and enthusiastic religious expressions. The Disciples of Christ shared the same heritage in the violent social and religious climate of early nineteenth-century America that almost every other evangelical sect had; if they were less emotional than most of them, they were hardly less enthusiastic.

From the beginning of the movement, however, the radical element in the Disciples mind was mellowed and tempered by a recurrent emphasis on moderation. Eva Jean Wrather, probably the outstanding student of Alexander Campbell, describes him as a moderate:

> In a world of extremes . . . only the uncommon man of sound sense and fine sensibility is able to pursue a sane and moderate course. . . . Alexander Campbell proved himself such a man. . . . For he was naturally of a rational and tolerant temperament, and he was reared in the common-sense school of Scottish philosophy.[33]

Amos S. Hayden reported that from the beginning Campbell, William Hayden, and other important leaders among the Disciples in Ohio opposed all radical religious and social expressions. They checked rampant antiorganizational prejudice, tried to calm premillennial excitement, and completely quashed the introduction of radical economic schemes.[34] By 1831 the most fanatical fringe of the movement in the Western Reserve had been drained off by the defection of the erratic Sydney Rigdon, along with several other preachers and a number of churches, to the Mormons.[35]

The same spirit of moderation was evident in the early Christian stream in Kentucky. Barton Stone became an early and unrelenting opponent of the most radical religious and social expression to emerge from the Kentucky revivals—the Shakers. In 1805 three missionaries from New Lebanon, New York—Benjamin Seth Youngs, Isaachar Bates, and John Meacham—introduced Shakerism into the West. By the end of April, at least five of the leading preachers of the Christian movement had accepted the prophetic doctrine of the Shaker missionaries. Stone, however, quickly

---

[33]Eva Jean Wrather, "Alexander Campbell and Social Righteousness," *Christian Standard*, LXXIII (September 17, 1938), 907. See, also, Whitley, *Trumpet Call*, pp. 60-61.

[34]Amos S. Hayden, *A History of the Disciples on the Western Reserve* (Cincinnati: Chase & Hall, Publishers, 1875), pp. 295-300, 183-190.

[35]*Ibid.*, pp. 209-222.

became the "center of an anti-Shaker movement" in the West.[36] In his autobiography Stone wrote: "Never did I exert myself more than at this time, to save the people from this vortex of ruin. I yielded to no discouragement, but labored night and day, far and near, among the churches where the Shakers went. By this means their influence was happily checked in many places."[37]

The inroads of the Shakers into the nascent Christian movement were significant. They not only took a considerable number of the members but also drained off a good portion of the ablest leaders of the young movement.[38] Stone recognized that the Shaker missionaries had come at a propitious time:

> Some of us were verging on fanaticism; some were so disgusted at the spirit of the opposition against us, and the evils of division, that they were almost led to doubt the truth of religion *in toto*. . . . The Shakers well knew how to accommodate each of these classes, and decoy them into the trap set for them.[39]

In the final analysis, the Shaker defection among the Christians and the Mormon defection among the early Disciples had similar effects; they drained off the most radical fringes in both of the movements.[40] David Purviance, who with Stone resisted the Shaker intrusions, believed that the purging had a lasting good effect on the movement:

> I have thought there might be something providential in the coming of the Shakers, although some honest and precious souls were seduced and ruined by their means; yet a growing fanaticism was drawn out of the church, which threatened the most deleterious effects.[41]

The moderate mood deepened in Disciples thought in the decades following 1830. In 1840 Campbell wrote: "I will only farther premise, that

---

[36]Edward Deming Andrews, *The People Called Shakers* (New York: Oxford University Press, 1953), p. 73. See, also, Marguerite Melcher, *The Shaker Adventure* (Princeton: Princeton University Press, 1941), pp. 75-76.

[37]Rogers, *Biography of Stone*, p. 63.

[38]Melcher, *Shaker Adventure*, pp. 69-77.

[39]Rogers, *Biography of Stone*, p. 64.

[40]H. Richard Niebuhr describes these two groups as "the radical wing of the frontier movement." *Social Sources*, p. 160.

[41]Levi Purviance, *The Biography of Elder David Purviance* (Dayton: B. F. & G. W. Ells, 1848), p. 148. Another of the early Christian leaders, Nicholas Summerbell, came to a similar conclusion: "Those who went to the Shakers were too much inclined to fanaticism; and had they remained they would have caused trouble." Quoted in J. P. MacLean, "The Kentucky Revival in the Miami Valley," Ohio Archaeological and Historical *Publications*, XII (1903), 271.

as extremes always beget extremes, I fear the logic and the declamation of all enthusiasts on all questions, political, moral, religious."[42] Most of the rising young leaders in the church in the decades preceding the Civil War were firmly dedicated to the policy of moderation. In 1847 Benjamin Franklin, an influential young editor in Indiana, warned that "abusive fanatics are the most unsafe guides both in politics and religion in all the world."[43] Although every Disciple had some of the religious enthusiast in him and some were real prophets, there was inherent in the sect from the beginning an aversion to religious and social radicalism of the most wild-eyed variety—even when expressed in legalistic terms.

Not only did the rationalistic and "common-sense" heritage of the Disciples create a practical aversion to "extremes" of every sort but there was also much in their environment to encourage a moderate mood. For the most part the Disciples arrived late on the frontier. During the period 1830-1865, when the group made such large gains in the Middle West, the most riotous and unrestrained features of frontier society were giving way to a more settled and sedate pattern of Western life. Although the frontier was unquestionably important in the development of Disciples thought, perhaps, as H. Richard Niebuhr points out, they were even more "representative of a West which had passed the storm and stress period of social adolescence and was recovering from its youthful extremities of hope and fear."[44] From the group's beginning the Disciples included many leaders and members from the most stable segment of Western society—from that element least likely to be influenced by religious and social fanaticism. Many of the church's leaders had something of the "aristocratic temperament" and shared an appreciation for stability, order, and moderation.[45]

---

[42]"Morality of Christians—No. XVIII," *M.H.*, N.S., IV (March, 1840), 99. See, also, A. C., "Church Organization—No. 1," *M.H.*, 3d S., III (February, 1849), 92. The series numbers of such periodicals as the *Millennial Harbinger* are hereafter cited as N. S. (New Series), 3d S., 4th S., etc.

[43]"Remarks," *Western Reformer*, VI (December, 1847), 114.

[44]*Social Sources*, p. 181.

[45]Lunger, *Political Ethics of Alexander Campbell*, p. 145. Although Campbell was a spokesman for liberal Western views in the Virginia Constitutional Convention in 1829-30, he was never a political radical. See, also, the biographies of such men as John T. Johnson, William K. Pendleton, Philip Fall, Thomas M. Allen, David S. Burnet, and Isaac Errett.

To sum up, the religious personality of the Disciples of Christ had decided schizophrenic tendencies. They were fanatics with a compulsive sense of mission; and yet they were nineteenth-century rationalists with an almost psychotic aversion to fanaticism. Most Disciples were a perplexing mixture of these two elements. They could be tolerant or intolerant; they could be dogmatic or broad-minded; they could be sectarian or denominational—and it was never quite obvious which course they would follow. The schizoid middle-of-the-road psychology always comprised the broad and slow-moving mainstream of the movement but it became more and more apparent in the years before the Civil War that it was the fanatical fringes of Disciples thought which were determining the direction of the flow.

THE MILLENNIAL ORDER

"Blessed and holy is he that hath part in the first resurrection: on such the second death hath no power, but they shall be priests of God and of Christ, and shall reign with him a thousand years." Revelation 20:6.

The Disciples of Christ during the pre-Civil War period were more rationalistic and legalistic than many of their contemporary American sects but they were hardly less interested in the prophetic and eschatological portions of the Bible. Not one first-generation leader of the church ignored the apocalytical portions of the Scriptures and some of them were almost totally preoccupied with discussing prophetic passages.[46]

Disciples interest in prophecy centered, as it did in other groups, around anticipation of the millennium. Millennialism, says Elmer T. Clark, has always been "the leading principle of the so-called Fundamentalist movement" and has historically been "found in nearly all of the denominations and in many small sects."[47] There are two distinct schools of millennialists, divided basically over their understanding of the time of the coming of the Christ in relation to the thousand-year period referred to in Revelation 20:1-6. One group, the postmillennialists, believes that the

---

[46]John Thomas' *Apostolic Advocate,* which began publication in 1835, and Arthur Crihfield's *Heretic Detector* (1837-41) and *Orthodox Preacher* (1843-46) are perhaps the outstanding examples of this. But almost all of the editors of the movement demonstrated intense prophetic interest at times. Walter Scott's *Evangelist* and Barton Stone's *Christian Messenger* were frequently crowded with interpretations of prophecy.

[47]*Small Sects,* p. 23.

second coming of Christ will be delayed until after the completion of the millennium. The millennium will be a period when the world is governed according to Christian principles rather than an era when Christ will literally reign on earth and it will be introduced by the gradual triumph of the church over the wickedness of the world rather than by a cataclysmic reappearance of the Lord. The social implications of post-millennialism are both obvious and profound. Optimism, a belief in progress, and a desire for reform are inherent in such a religious interpretation of history.

Although there are broad differences among premillennialists about just what will happen during the apocalyptical period, they are generally agreed that the world has been hopelessly evil and degraded since the fall of Adam. According to the premillennialist, the world must become more and more turbulent and confused until the crucial hour when Christ will return and banish the wicked from the earth, "chain the Old Serpent," and personally reign with the "true church" in a kingdom of glory. After the thousand-year millennium, the battle of Armageddon and the final judgment will take place. The pessimistic implications of premillennialism are at least equal to the optimistic ones of postmillennialism. Clark points out: "One finds little or no social consciousness among them. It is no part of the church's duty to reform and redeem the social order. Its function is to prepare a 'true church,' a comparatively small body of saints, for membership in the coming kingdom."[48]

Social and moral laxity in the church, combined with political, social, and economic maladjustments, have caused recurrent outbursts of millennialist enthusiasm throughout the history of the Jewish-Christian tradition. A vibrant millennialist fervor was an important element in the turbulent and unstable American religious scene in the 1830's and 1840's. Ante-bellum American premillennialism centered around the personality and work of William Miller, a devout Baptist licentiate from Low Hampton, New York, whose studies on the Book of Revelation and the Old Testament prophecies led him to the conclusion that the millennium was imminent and probably would begin between March 21, 1843, and March 21, 1844. He began to preach his message of the "soon coming of the Lord" in 1831 and his views were favorably received by leaders of many

---

[48]*Ibid*, p. 26.

of the American churches. Although the movement reached its culmination in 1844, the year of the prediction, and there was widespread disillusionment when the Lord failed to appear, there remained many premillennialists within the evangelical sects and in 1845 an independent
adventist body was formed.[49]

Probably more important in early nineteenth-century American thought
was the widespread acceptance of postmillennialist views. "The most significant millennarian doctrines of the mid-nineteenth century," writes
Timothy Smith, "were not those of William Miller, but those which grew
out of evangelical Protestantism's crusade to Christianize the land."[50] All
of the great evangelical preachers of this period believed that the new
order was "at hand" and that it was their duty to blot both sin and injustice from the world. While the revivalists were as determined as ever
to save men's souls, they also preached the "hope of a radical transformation of life upon earth."[51]

Postmillennial presuppositions were deeply entrenched in Disciples
thought prior to the national eruption of premillennialist enthusiasm in
the 1830's.[52] Prior to 1830 both Alexander Campbell and Barton Stone
linked their religious reform efforts with the eventual spiritual and social
regeneration of the world. In 1829 Stone wrote that the greatest obstacle
in introducing the millennium, when "Christ will reign in spirit on earth
a thousand years," was the religious degeneration of his day.[53] The following year Campbell summarized his early millennialist view in the pro-

<hr>

[49]For general information on Miller and pre-Civil War premillennialism see
Olmstead, *Religion in the United States*, pp. 343-345; Cross, *Burned-Over District*, pp. 287-321; Alice Felt Tyler, *Freedom's Ferment* (Minneapolis: University
of Minnesota Press, 1944), pp. 68-78.

[50]Smith, *Revivalism and Social Reform*, p. 236. See Timothy Smith's fine chapter, "The Gospel of the Kingdom," for an analysis of the widespread impact of
postmillennialism, pp. 225-237. See, also, Niebuhr, *Kingdom of God*, pp. 127-163.

[51]*Kingdom of God*, p. 151.

[52]Although the impact of millennialism on the thought of the movement has
largely been ignored, there have been two very able studies of Alexander Campbell's millennial views in recent years. See West, *Alexander Campbell and Natural
Religion*, pp. 163-222; Samuel M. Whitson, Jr., "Campbell's Concept of the Millennium" (unpublished Master's thesis, Division of Graduate Instruction, Butler
University, 1951).

[53]"Remarks on Liberty of Conscience," *C.M.*, III (February, 1829), 91.

spectus of his new and significantly named journal, the *Millennial Harbinger:*

> This work shall be devoted to the destruction of Sectarianism, Infidelity, and Antichristian doctrine and practice. It shall have for its object the development, and introduction of that political and religious order of society called THE MILLENNIUM, which will be the consummation of that ultimate amelioration of society proposed in the Christian Scriptures.[54]

By the early 1830's a number of significant church leaders had become ardent premillennialists. Both Walter Scott and Barton Stone lent the support of their periodicals to speculation about the imminent advent and millennial reign of the Lord.[55] Scott wrote:

> The Christian of the 19th century has been permitted to witness the accomplishment of wonderful events; Providence has stationed him on a sublime eminence, from which he can behold the fulfillment of illustrious prophecies, and look backwards upon nearly the whole train of events leading to the *Millennium*.[56]

Stone, when queried about the meaning of the "fiery stars" and other "phenomenon" [*sic*] which one of his readers had observed, replied: "I have no doubt that awful things are just ahead. May the Lord prepare us to meet them unappalled."[57]

But by 1834 Campbell began to lead a counterattack against the premillennial enthusiasm. The question was handled delicately by the editor but Campbell's postmillennialist position was meticulously outlined in a long series of articles signed, "A Reformed Clergyman."[58] Campbell

---

[54]"Prospectus," *M.H.,* I (January, 1830), 1. In *Religion Follows the Frontier* Winfred Garrison says that the name of the new paper did not "indicate any special interest in the second coming of Christ in a spectacular way or any marked devotion to either premillennial or postmillennial view," p. 147. This is quite incorrect. Garrison gives some recognition to the importance of Campbell's millennial views in his later work: Garrison and DeGroot, *Disciples of Christ,* pp. 206-207. But by and large historians of the movement have seriously neglected this area of thought of the Disciples.

[55]See the *Evangelist* and the *Christian Messenger* for the years 1832-34.

[56]"Extract of a Circular Letter, for the Mahoning Association of 1830," *Evangelist,* I (February, 1832), 40.

[57]"Remarks," *C.M.,* VIII (January, 1834), 29.

[58]Hayden identifies Campbell as the author, *Western Reserve,* pp. 188-189. This series begins with the article, "The Millennium—No. I," *M.H.* V (September, 1834), 454-459.

urged his readers to "hear both sides" before they decided on the merits of pre- and postmillenniallism.[59] According to one early historian of the movement, the Bethany reformer's articles were decisive and "in the course of a few years the excitement subsided."[60]

That the death of premillennial excitement among the Disciples was either so sudden or so complete is by no means obvious. In 1846, when the young editor of *The Reformer*, Benjamin Franklin, was trying to account for the seeming lag in religious interest among Disciples, one of the things he blamed was the widespread "second advent excitement" in the church.[61] Actually, premillennial sentiment remained strong until the mid-1840's, retaining the support of such leading editors as Barton Stone, Walter Scott, Arthur Crihfield, and John R. Howard. Stone's *Christian Messenger* and Scott's *Evangelist* were crowded with premillennialist material during the early forties. Although neither of these men was willing to give unqualified backing to Miller's chronological calculations, they both thought them "worthy of all attention."[62]

The Millerite debacle of 1844 ended most of the serious premillennial agitation among the Disciples. In the November issue of the *Christain Messenger* the editors observed that "the subject of prophecies has too much engrossed the attention of our periodicals, and our brethren in general" and announced that they intended to avoid any further discussion "on that subject in the Messenger."[63] Walter Scott was crushed by the failure of Miller's prediction. While as late as 1846 he defended Miller as a "good pious Baptist, having the hope of the gospel,"[64] he slowly returned to his old postmillennialist views. In 1859, when he wrote *The Messiahship or Great Demonstration*, he was again a staunch postmillennialist: "The long-looked for age, popularly styled 'The Millennium' must belong to the history of human progress, and be of gradual

[59]"The Millennium—No. I," *M.H.*, V (September, 1834), 454.

[60]William Thomas Moore, *A Comprehensive History of the Disciples of Christ* (New York: Fleming H. Revell Co., 1909), p. 303. This is also Hayden's conclusion, *Western Reserve*, pp. 188-189.

[61]Quoted in West, *Ancient Order*, I, 131.

[62]B. W. S., "The Second Coming of Christ," *C. M.*, XII (May, 1842), 218; W. S., "New Government and New Society," *Evangelist*, IX (January, 1841), 5-7.

[63]"To Our Patrons," *C.M.*, XIV (November, 1844), 216.

[64]"The Adventist," *Protestant Unionist*, II (May 13, 1846), 90.

introduction."[65] By 1856 Alexander Campbell frankly called the "Millerites" "Bastard Millennarians"[66] and seldom did premillennialist articles go unchallenged after 1845.

The postmillennial emphasis remained strong in Disciples thought in the last decades before the Civil War but it was both less enthusiastic and more practical than during the early years of the church. It was apparent before 1840 that the preaching of the "ancient gospel" was not going immediately to dissipate all religious division and social sin. In the early years of the movement Alexander Campbell felt that the "new age was near at hand" but as it became more and more apparent that social and religious evils were not to be so easily solved he postponed "the arrival of the millennium . . . to around the year two thousand."[67] Perhaps even more significant was the rise of second-generation leaders who had not shared in the enthusiasm of the sect's youth and who were openly disinterested in millennialist speculation.[68] In short, millennialist interest was on the decline in the years immediately preceding the Civil War and that postmillennialism which remained was less urgent and more practical and constructive than it had been in the pre-1840 period.

THE AMERICAN MILLENNIUM

"Nevertheless we, according to his promise, look for a new heavens and a new earth, wherein dwelleth righteousness." II Peter 3:13.

The philosophy of history of nineteenth-century Disciples was inextricably interwoven with their millennialist presuppositions. Premillennialists were apt to view the idea of progress with a disinterested pessimism

---

[65](Cincinnati: H. S. Bosworth, 1859), p. 335.

[66]"Millennium," *M.H.*, 4th S., VI (December, 1856), 698. See, also, West, *Alexander Campbell and Natural Religion*, pp. 176-183.

[67]West, *Alexander Campbell and Natural Religion*, p. 214. See, also, Whitson, "Campbell's Concept of the Millennium," pp. 171-172.

[68]Both Isaac Errett and David Lipscomb were persistently unwilling to discuss the subject. Although the social ideas of second-generation leaders were not so different from those of the first, the millennial rationale is much less significant in their thought. See "The Second Coming of the Lord," *Christian Standard*, I (June 2, 1866), 68; "Queries," *Gospel Advocate*, XL (June 23, 1898), 397; "Queries," *G.A.*, XXXVII (July 11, 1895), 437. Charles C. Cole, Jr. emphasizes that this fading of interest in the millennium was a part of a general pattern of declining revival enthusiasm. *Northern Evangelists*, p. 224.

while the most outspoken postmillennialists were Enlightenment optimists. The destiny of the American nation and the necessity and possibility of social improvement were more often than not prophetically interpreted.

Outstanding premillennialists such as the prominent Ohio preacher and editor, Arthur Crihfield, believed that "the present amount of spiritual influence is not likely to produce a better state of society; that, it is probably that the coming of the Lord is nigh."[69] The editor concluded that "man is incapable of self-government" and that the proper course for Christians was to withdraw their "minds from all secular affairs as to give them only the necessary attention" and "learn the laws of the Lord."[70] Crihfield's pessimism is typical of the premillennialist leaders of the Disciples and yet his attacks on those who predicted a "millennium brought about by science and theology" clearly indicate that a more optimistic philosophy dominated the thought of the church.[71]

A belief in inevitable social progress before the millennium order could begin was almost everywhere a part of the Christian message of Disciples leaders. Alexander Campbell early connected religious and social reform and confidently predicted the "speedy overthrow of superstition, false religion, oppressive governments."[72] The European political revolutions of the 1830's and late 1840's were repeatedly linked with the rearranging of society necessary for the triumph of religious truth and the introduction of the millennium.[73] By and large, Campbell, and other leaders of the group, retained through the ante-bellum period a profound "faith in progress" and in the "fore-ordained destiny" of man.[74] In 1845 Robert Forrester wrote: "progressiveness seems to be an established and universal law in the economy of Divine procedures."[75]

---

[69]"Coming of the Lord—No. XVI," *O.P.*, I (November, 1843), 241.

[70]"Preface," *Heretic Detector*, V (1841), 3-12.

[71]"Coming of the Lord—No. III," *O.P.*, I (February, 1843), 31.

[72]"Conclusion of Volume II," *M.H.*, II (December, 1831), 568.

[73]See "Conclusion of Volume II," *M.H.*, II (December, 1831), 568; "Prefatory Remarks," *Christian Examiner*, II (January, 1831), 1-7; "Preface," *Gospel Proclamation*, II (1848), 3-6; "Europe," *P.U.*, IV (April 26, 1948), 82.

[74]"The Millennium," *M.H.*, 5th S., I (June, 1858), 336. See, also, James Egbert, *Alexander Campbell and Christian Liberty* (St. Louis: Christain Publishing Company, 1909), p. 47.

[75]"Progressive Development," *P.U.*, I (August 6, 1845), 138.

Another idea which was fundamental in the Disciples philosophy of history and which was inextricably connected with the group's views on the millennium and progress was a deep confidence in the providence of God. Repeatedly Christians were advised to "resign yourself entirely to the will of God" and reminded that "though all may not seem well in your feeble judgment, remember that it is God who directs it, and that it must be right."[76] Alexander Campbell concluded that it was "a thousand times more rational and blissful, to refer all things interesting to us . . . to the counsel . . . of the Lord, than to . . . 'our good fortune' or management."[77]

The American faith in progress, often rooted in millennial hopes and a God-centered philosophy of history, was expressed in the pre-Civil War period in a Christianized philosophy of the destiny of the American nation.[78] Faith in the future of the American nation was again and again identified with the Christian faith and in the minds of most Americans the "mission of American democracy to save the world from the oppression of autocrats was a secular version of the destiny of Christianity to save the world from the governance of Satan."[79] Protestantism and republicanism were the two great forces which God was using to reform the world and the American nation was leading the way to the millennium.

The millennialistic and providential world view of the Disciples of Christ was profoundly influenced by the patriotism of church leaders. Campbell, although there was some variation in the strength of his optimism, generally believed that the fate of the world rested on the American nation; that it was a land prepared by God for the restoration of the gospel and that from this country the message was to go into all the world. "To Protestant America and Protestant England," he wrote, "the world must look for its emancipation from the most heartless spiritual

---

[76]H.C., "Resignation to the Will of God," *Bible Advocate*, VII (December, 1849), 154.

[77]"Comments," *M.H.*, 4th S., I (November, 1851), 620.

[78]See Albert K. Weinberg, *Manifest Destiny* (Baltimore: The Johns Hopkins Press, 1935), pp. 1-223; Cole, *Northern Evangelists*, pp. 158-164, 232-233; Smith, *Revivalism and Social Reform*, pp. 225-237; Niebuhr, *Kingdom of God*, pp. 141-142; Tyler, *Freedom's Ferment*, p. 44.

[79]Gabriel, *Democratic Thought*, p. 37.

despotism that ever . . . degraded mankind. This is our special mission in the world as a nation and a people; and for this purpose the Ruler of nations has raised us up and made us the wonder and the admiration of the world."[80] When the "light which shines from our political institutions" had penetrated "the dungeons of European despots," the millennium would begin.[81]

Often Disciples leaders connected their duty of spreading Christianity with the mission of the nation. In his presidential address before the American Christian Publication Society in 1854, the prominent Cincinnati preacher, David S. Burnet, said: "The American church should do this work, because America is the divinely chosen theater of *new measures* as well as new men."[82] The American nation, declared the widely known educator, James Shannon, had been raised up by God to lead "the regeneration, political, social and moral, of a debased and down-trodden world."[83]

No pre-Civil War Disciple was more consistently nationalistic than Walter Scott and none had a more elaborate philosophy of American Christian destiny. Scott's intricate, nationalistic, postmillennial philosophy was published in its completed form in 1859 in his book, *The Messiahship or Great Demonstration.* He believed that the prophetic promises of a "new heavens and a new earth" should be interpreted to mean "a new government and a new people." "In this new political heavens and new political earth," wrote Scott, "Christianity was to have free course and to be glorified in the salvation of the nations." He believed that the millennium would begin when the "ancient gospel" had purified all the governments and all the societies of the world and that the United States, as the "first of the Messianic nations," had already passed through this transformation. He insisted that the "change in government and society"

---

[80]"Address on the Destiny of Our Country," *Popular Lectures and Addresses* (Philadelphia: James Challen & Son, 1863), p. 174.

[81]"An Oration in Honor of the Fourth of July," *M.H.,* I (July, 1830), 301-310.

[82]*Report of Proceedings of the Convention of Churches of Christ, at the Anniversaries of the American Christian Bible, Missionary and Publication Societies, Held in Cincinnati, October 17th, 18th, 19th, and 20th, 1854* (Cincinnati: American Christian Publication Society, 1854), p. 14.

[83]*Address to the People of the United States, Together with the Proceedings and Resolutions of the Proslavery Convention of Missouri, Held at Lexington, July, 1855* (St. Louis: Republican Office, 1855), p. v.

which had taken place in America would soon "obtain among all people" and that "revolution must succeed revolution in all lands, till the rights and liberties of humanity are understood and restored to all nations." The Protestant spirit and the American nation would lead to the "gradual introduction" of the millennium.[84] Walter Scott, the pioneer prophet of the "ancient gospel restored," was also one of the foremost prophets of the gospel of the American millennium.

THE ANGLO-SAXON MILLENNIUM

"These are the families of the sons of Noah, after their generations, in their nations: and by these were the nations divided in the earth after the flood." Genesis 10:32.

Such stately English names as Stone, Bentley, Pendleton, Fall, and Lamar, though hardly less common in the early history of the Disciples, are less conspicuous than the names Campbell, Scott, Richardson, Ferguson, Thompson, McCulloch, Mathes, Errett, Creath, and Shannon. Added to this English and Scotch-Irish base is a sprinkling of such names as Loos, Hoshour, Vawter, Hostetler, and Schmidt, an occasional Welshman named Longley, and an equally rare Huguenot named Reneau. Disciples of Christ of the first half of the nineteenth century were a cross section of Anglo-Saxon, Protestant middle America.

Aside from the internal migration of the more adventuresome and unsettled elements from the eastern sections of the colonies, the ethnic composure of the American backcountry in the last half of the eighteenth century was largely the result of two significant waves of European immigration. In the early part of the eighteenth century a series of religious, political, social, and economic disturbances led to a widespread influx of Germans into this country.[85] Although significant German settlement developed in New York during the colonial period, Pennsylvania became the center of German concentration. The immigrants moved first into the rich farming areas of southern and eastern Pennsylvania and then turned southward down the Valley of Virginia until "by 1750, an almost continuous zone of German settlements had been established along the fron-

---

[84]*Messiahship*, pp. 296-335. See, also, "Elements of Modern Society," *P.U.*, II (May 27, 1846), 98.

[85]For a general discussion of the German migration see Carl Wittke, *We Who Built America* (New York: Prentice-Hall, Inc., 1940), pp. 66-97.

tier from the head of the Mohawk, in New York, to Savannah, Georgia."[86]
After the American Revolution the Germans joined in the growing migration through the mountain gaps into Kentucky, Tennessee, and the
Trans-Appalachian West. For the most part this early German immigration was made up of Protestants who were "simple souls, devoted to the
accumulation of material goods, and conservative farmers" and they proved
to be a valuable and stable element in the development of the American
West.[87]

The second major stream of colonial immigration came from the Ulster
section of Ireland.[88] Most of these immigrants were the descendants of
the Scotch who had settled on the Ulster plantation in the seventeenth
century. The course of the Scotch-Irish migration was similar to that of
the Germans and, being unwelcome in New England and the tidewater
South, they came directly to Philadelphia and then rapidly sifted to the
frontier of Pennsylvania. Settling first along the river valleys of southern
Pennsylvania, they then followed the valleys between the Allegheny and
Blue Ridge Mountains into the Southwest. The Scotch-Irishman was in
the vanguard of the American frontier movement. Carl Wittke writes:
"He was bold, courageous, democratic to a point of lawlessness, highly
individualistic, querulous, a 'squatter,' an inveterate hater of Indians, and
a chronic opponent and critic of the established order."[89] Uncompromising
and militant Presbyterians, they were creative, tenacious, and often belligerent and unruly.

Among these peoples of the frontier (with the Scotch-Irish, perhaps,
as the dominant element) both of the early streams of the Disciples of
Christ had their beginnings.[90] The thought of the Disciples was influenced
in many obvious ways by these ethnic roots. The legalistic emphasis of the

---

[86]*Ibid.,* p. 71.

[87]*Ibid.,* p. 74.

[88]For a general discussion of the Scotch-Irish migration see Wittke, *We Who
Built America,* pp. 43-65.

[89]*Ibid.,* p. 54.

[90]A number of historians have linked the Disciples of Christ with the Scotch-
Irish ethnic tradition. See McQuary, "The Social Background of the Disciples of
Christ," *The College of the Bible Quarterly,* XIII, 3-16; Frederick Morgan Daven-
port, *Primitive Traits in Religious Revivals* (New York: The Macmillan Com-
pany, 1905) pp. 60-86; Wittke, *We Who Built America,* pp. 59-60; Niebuhr,
Social Sources, pp. 162-163.

movement was in the tradition of Scottish Presbyterianism and German sectarianism.[91] The intense individualism and iconoclasm of the early Disciples leaders, their fervent confidence in the destiny of the nation, and their practical "common-sense" approach to religion were all nurtured by their ethnic as well as their social heritage.[92]

Equally important in the thought of the Disciples was the idea of race itself. There is no simple and all-inclusive explanation for the racial presuppositions of a large segment of American society in the pre-Civil War period. As Oscar Handlin says, "Racism is a complex reaction, the strength of which inheres in its many-stranded nature."[93] Neither has the impact of racist ideas been simple. Although racist theories have most often influenced the Negro in American history, other groups have been important targets of race prejudice. American attitudes on Indian relations, immigration, and economic experimentation have been deeply influenced by racist convictions and the national faith in "manifest destiny" was often based on Anglo-Saxon superiority.[94]

A number of forces at work in American society in the early nineteenth century encouraged the development of racist theories. Unquestionably the most important factor in the formation of American racial views was the problem of the Negro. Only slightly less important, however, was the presence of the Indian, who formed a hostile, and often bitterly hated, barrier to westward expansion. After 1820 it became increasingly difficult to fit the Negroes and Indians into the picture of a multiracial United States. By the 1830's the idealistic hopes that by some method these two groups could be removed from American society had pretty largely been shattered. In the decades immediately preceding the Civil War many Americans simply ignored the problem posed by American racial inequalities but increasingly two extreme views were developing in the North and the South. In the North abolitionist agitators accepted

---

[91]See Clark, *Small Sects*, pp. 176-217; Sweet, *Religion in America*, pp. 102-126; Niebuhr, *Social Sources*, p. 158.

[92]See Wittke, *We Who Built America*, pp. 58-65; Niebuhr, *Social Sources*, pp. 130-134.

[93]Oscar Handlin, *Race and Nationality in American Life* (Boston: Little, Brown and Company, 1957), p. xii.

[94]See Weinberg's excellent chapter, "The Mission of Regeneration," for a description of the relationship between these two ideas, *Manifest Destiny*, pp. 160-189.

the inevitable conclusions of the doctrine of equality and announced that slavery was a sin and that it must be abolished. Economic and social necessity made the problem much less simple in the South and increasingly Southern radicals developed a philosophy which explained the obvious inequalities of their society on the basis of inherent biological differences in the races. Supported by biblical, anthropological, and scientific arguments, the most rabid racists in pre-Civil War America were the Southern proslavery radicals.[95]

Racist doctrines, however, were not confined to the proslavery agitators of the South; they did not have their origins there; they had important repercussions in several other areas of American social thought and action. Early in the eighteenth century a Swedish scientist, Carl Linnaeus, made the first basic attempt to classify the world of living organisms into species and genera. Linnaeus' work stimulated tremendous interest and soon the races of mankind became the subject of intensive studies by anthropologists, phrenologists, and philologists. Philosophers of the eighteenth century were not hesitant to point out the social implications of the intriguing findings of the new scientists of race. If the races of mankind had specific and hereditary physical characteristics, it was not unreasonable that they should also have certain hereditary mental and personality traits. More than any other man, Count Arthur de Gobineau of France popularized the racist conclusions of eighteenth-century science. Gobineau wrote a history of the human races which spanned from ancient times to modern and which glorified the white Aryan race as the creative and ruling people throughout the history of the world. The races of "inferior blood" were arranged in a descending scale below the Aryans. Although scientific racism had its greatest impact on American thought in the latter half of the nineteenth century, it had already made significant inroads before 1865.[96]

The Anglo-Saxon, middle-American Disciples of Christ were aware of and often influenced by the racist philosophies of the nineteenth century. William K. Pendleton, in an article in the *Millennial Harbinger* in

---

[95]For a discussion of this phase of American racism see Handlin, *Race and Nationality*, pp. 29-44; Gunnar Myrdal, *An American Dilemma* (5th ed.; New York: Harper & Brothers, Publishers, 1941), I, 50-67.

[96]See Handlin, *Race and Nationality*, pp. 71-92; Myrdal, *American Dilemma*, I, 84-101.

1846, demonstrated both a broad knowledge of the latest anthropological investigations and the typical Disciples disposition to link racist theory with biblical prophecy. Pendleton believed that the Caucasians had developed their "moral feelings and intellectual powers" to the "highest degree of perfection which human nature has ever exhibited." In the other races these admirable characteristics were present to an "inferior degree." The Asiatics had shown "limited intellectual powers" and had long "remained stationary"; the Negro race also had "remained stationary; but stopped at a point very much below that which the Asiatics have reached." Pendleton concluded his elaborate investigation by placing these racist conclusions within a biblical context:

Such are the results of physiological research; and we cannot fail to be struck with the remarkable agreement between their conclusions, based entirely upon the principles of comparative anatomy applied in a comprehensive and rigid induction, and those we rationally draw from the ninth chapter of Genesis. Shem, Ham, and Japeth are there represented as the heads of three races.[97]

Pendleton stated his racist convictions with more clarity and learning than most Disciples, and he was expressing a conviction which penetrated deeply into the movement. The idea that the races of men were the descendants of the three sons of Noah and that their destiny had been prophetically determined by God was a part of the intellectual equipment of a large majority of early nineteenth-century Disciples.[98] Only a few Disciples parlayed their racist convictions into radical proslavery arguments, and some even rejected the theories altogether, but that they were an important influence on the thought of the church is unquestionable.

Racist views were often combined with millennial faith in the destiny of the American nation. Alexander Campbell concisely pulled all these elements together:

[97]"The World," M.H., 3d S., III (April, 1846), 210-216.

[98]This whole subject is discussed in more detail in chapter IV. For a few examples see "Lectures on Genesis," Christian Magazine, I (May, 1848), 132-133; J.M.M., "Prophecy—II," C.R., V (August, 1847), 45-47; A.C., "Conversations at the Carlton House," M.H., N.S., IV (November, 1840), 493-501; James Shannon, The Philosophy of Slavery, as Identified with the Philosophy of Human Happiness (2d ed.; Frankfort, Kentucky: A. G. Hodges & Co., 1849). Robert Frederick West points out that when the conclusions of racist philosophers seemed antiscriptural, they were promptly rejected, Alexander Campbell and Natural Religion, pp. 123-126.

In our country's destiny is involved the destiny of Protestantism, and in its destiny the destiny of all the nations of the world. God has given, in awful charge, to Protestant England and Protestant America—the Anglo-Saxon race—the fortunes, not of Christendom only, but of all the world.[99]

The millennialistic triumph of freedom and pure religion was to be accomplished in God's providence by Protestantism, America, and the white man.

THE CHURCH AND THE WORLD

"Then saith he unto them, Render therefore unto Caesar the things which are Caesar's; and unto God the things that are God's." Matthew 22:21.

With the exception of the premillennial prophets of doom who remained rather consistently a minority element in the life of the Disciples prior to 1865, the leaders of the church generally believed that American society was progressing because of the influence of Christianity. Alexander Campbell wrote:

Society is not yet fully civilized. It is only beginning to be. Things are in process, in progress to another age—a golden—a millennial—a blissful period in human history. Selfishness, violence, inordinate ambition, revenge, duelling, even tyranny, oppression and cruelty, are yet exerting a pernicious influence in society.[100]

In 1830 Campbell surmised that all social progress had stemmed directly from the influence of Christianity:

It has enlightened men upon all subjects—in all arts and sciences. . . . It was the tongue and pen of controversy which developed the true solar system—laid the foundation for the American Revolution—abolished the slave trade.[101]

Thirty years later, on the eve of the Civil War, Aaron Chatterton wrote: "The Bible is the true basis of all that is worthy of the name of civilization."[102] But while the vast majority of Disciples believed that the Christian religion supplied the formula for a perfect society, they were by no means agreed about the Christian's function in bringing this society into being.

---

[99]"The Destiny of Our Country," *M.H.*, 4th S., II (August, 1852), 462.

[100]"Address on the Amelioration of the Social State," *Popular Lectures*, p. 69.

[101]"Religious Controversy," *M.H.*, I (January, 1830), 43.

[102]"Items," *Evangelist*, XI (May, 1860), 239.

As a matter of fact, American Protestant leaders were generally divided over the best way to initiate the American millennium. While some revivalists, such as Charles Finney, believed that politics was "an indispensable part of religion,"[103] Jonathan Edwards, John Wesley, Mark Hopkins, and many of the other great American evangelists had little confidence in "civil conflicts" but rather believed that the "Christian revolution" which would result from the conversion of individuals was the only real hope of the world.[104] In sum, American Protestant leaders were divided in the years preceding the Civil War on the best method of promoting social reform. Some were political activists, while others, whose hopes for a Christian America were equally strong, had little confidence in such methods.

Disciples of Christ occupied three basic positions on this question during the pre-Civil War period. The extremely conservative and sectarian element within the stream formulated a philosophy of absolute nonparticipation in civil government. They believed that Christians ought not to participate in political agitation in any way, either as candidates for office or as voting citizens. On the other hand, there were those in the church from the beginning who believed that the Christian had fundamental obligations to the government and that he ought actively to encourage the use of Christian principles to solve the problems of the nation. The third, and unquestionably the largest group during most of the pre-war period, represented something of a compromise between these two extremes. Most of the leaders of the group had a distinct aversion to "party politics" but they did believe that a Christian ought to be a good citizen and that he could use his rights as a citizen to try to improve the nation. They generally insisted that the church should not become involved in social agitation but agreed that individuals had the right to follow any course they thought would better society. While all Disciples had a social philosophy—they all had a set of standards which they believed society ought to comply with—they disagreed drastically about how society was to be converted.

The sectarian emphasis of nonparticipation in civil government cen-

---

[103]Cole, *Northern Evangelists*, p. 133. Cole notes that many of the revivalists were political activists, pp. 132-164.

[104]H. Richard Niebuhr stresses this view in *Kingdom of God*, pp. 149-150.

tered around the influence of Barton Stone in the early years of the church. Stirred by millennialist aspirations, Stone wrote in 1843: "Men by the light of truth are beginning to see that Christians have no right to make laws and governments for themselves. . . . We must cease to support any . . . government on earth by our counsels, co-operation, and choice."[105] In 1844 he wrote that he was "disgusted with the politicians" and prayed that the Lord would "deliver his people from their contagion."[106]

Other early preachers, such as Benjamin U. Watkins and James J. Trott, were equally fervent in insisting that God's people ought to have no association with the governments of the world. Watkins wrote: "But you may ask, is not Bro. W. a 'constituent' in this government. I answer, no, I am a pilgrim and a stranger as all my fathers were. . . . My citizenship is in Heaven! May the good Lord keep us all unspotted from the world!"[107] Probably the most important nucleus of this radical left-wing position among the Disciples during the ante-bellum period grew up in Tennessee in the years immediately preceding the war. Tolbert Fanning was the early leader of Tennessee radicalism, which in the years after the war was dominated by David Lipscomb. In 1861 Fanning, along with Robert B. Trimble, David Lipscomb, Elisha G. Sewell, and several other Southern preachers, petitioned the President of the Confederacy for exemption from the draft act. They wrote: "The measure and limit of the Christian's duty to, and connection with, the governments under which they live . . . is not an active participation in its affairs . . . but simply a quiet and cheerful submission to its enactments."[108]

---

[105]"Reflections of Old Age," C.M., XIII (August, 1843), 126. For a general discussion of Stone's left-wing concept of the church-state relationship see West, Barton Stone, pp. 135-136, 211-212.

[106]"Reply to T. P. Ware," C.M., XIV (October, 1844), 166-171.

[107]"Correspondence," G.P., I (January, 1848), 259. See, also, J. J. Trott, "Church and State," C.Mag., II (October, 1849), 379-382; A.C., "Notes on a Late Tour—No. II," M.H., N.S., VI (November, 1842), 506-507; "News," G.P., II (May, 1849), 549.

[108]Tolbert Fanning, "Church of Christ and World Powers, No. 11," G.A., VIII (July 3, 1866), 417. See, also, Earl Irvin West, The Life and Times of David Lipscomb (Henderson, Tennessee: Religious Book Service, 1954), pp. 87-111. For a concise statement of this philosophy of nonparticipation in civil government see D. Lipscomb, Civil Government (reprint; Nashville: Gospel Advocate Company, 1957), pp. 40-43.

There were also those in the church from the beginning who believed that the Christian had every right to participate in the political decisions of the nation. Walter Scott, avid nationalist with a prophetic confidence in the destiny of the American system, when asked in 1835 whether a Christian had the right to hold a public office, replied: "It is perfectly lawful . . . for any of the Disciples to fill the offices of the nations."[109] Samuel Ayers, editor of the Lexington, Kentucky, *Christian Journal* clearly stated the case of the interventionists in 1844:

Christians owe a duty to their country as well as to their God, and they cannot be released from the performance of the duty.—Again, if Christians who love religion and virtue, should leave politics and the polls entirely in the hands of the ungodly and the dissipated, we might well tremble for our country, and our liberties would soon be at an end.[110]

In practice, many early Disciples preachers and laymen were active in politics. The two most prominent Disciples laymen prior to 1870 were politicians, Judge Jeremiah Sullivan Black of Pennsylvania and James A. Garfield of Ohio. The persistent comments of disgruntled moderates at election time that "even the church of Christ is agitated by this fierce demon of discord" is good evidence of the political activity of Disciples at the local level.[111]

More than anything else, the critical debate over slavery and the outbreak of the Civil War forced more and more Disciples into an activist position. Henry Shaw, historian of Ohio Disciples, suggests that before 1849 the Ohio churches were "concerned only with what they called, 'Restoring the ancient order of things' " but during the decade of the fifties they became vitally concerned with social reform.[112] The abolitionist preacher, John Boggs, began the publication of his *North-Western Christian Magazine* in 1854 to discuss: "Primitive Christianity, General Edu-

---

[109]"Question," *Evangelist*, IV (June, 1835), 143.

[110]"The Christian and Politics," *C.J.*, III (October 5, 1844), 454. See, also, "What Should Christians Aim at as Citizens?" *C.Mag.*, I (September, 1848), 281; "Letter from M. Winans," *C.M.*, VII (October, 1833), 303-304; "Preface," *G.P.*, II (1848), 3-6.

[111]A.C., "Morality of Christians—No. XXI," *M.H.*, N.S., IV (September, 1840), 413.

[112]Henry K. Shaw, *Buckeye Disciples* (St. Louis: Christian Board of Publication, 1952), p. 129.

cation, The Temperance Reform, and Universal Liberty."[113] More and more in the decade of the fifties, and especially in the North, church leaders became convinced that Christians ought to be actively concerned about the failures of American society to conform to Christian principles. Increasingly, Northerners charged that the ban on "preaching politics" was a Southern stratagem designed to gag the Christian protest against slavery.[114]

Throughout most of the period before 1865, however, the dominant Disciples philosophy on the relation of the Christian to politics was characteristically moderate and ill-defined. Alexander Campbell was the early spokesman for this middle group. In answer to the question, "Ought Christians to take an active part in politics," Campbell bluntly replied: "I am decidedly of the opinion that they ought not."[115] Although he never advocated the "radical left-wing position that the Christian dare not hold public office or participate in political decisions in the use of the franchise,"[116] Campbell consistently warned Christians not to become involved in political controversies. He wrote on social questions and occasionally advised his readers to "vote like Christians"[117] but he was never a political agitator. Campbell believed that the way to reform a society was to reform the individuals who made up that society—he wanted a spiritual revolution rather than a political one.

Campbell's philosophy of avoiding "political strife" was shared by most of the important Disciples leaders prior to the Civil War. John T. Johnson, probably the most influential first-generation preacher of the movement in Kentucky, was strongly opposed to political involvement. Johnson was from a politically prominent Scott County, Kentucky, family (his brother Richard Mentor Johnson was Vice-President during the Martin Van Buren administration) and he himself served several terms in the

---

[113]See J.B., "Salutatory," *North-Western Christian Magazine*, I (July, 1854), 1-5.

[114]"Editor's Table," *N.W.C.M.*, IV (April, 1858), 320.

[115]"Morality of Christians—No. XXI," *M.H.*, N.S., IV (September, 1840), 414.

[116]Lunger, *Political Ethics of Alexander Campbell*, p. 63. See pp. 38-65; Dwight E. Stevenson, "Campbell's Attitude on Social Issues," *Christian Evangelist*, LXXVI (September 8, 1938), 977-979.

[117]See "Christian Politics," *M.H.*, 4th S., VII (March, 1857), 174; Lunger, *Political Ethics of Alexander Campbell*, p. 63.

United States House of Representatives from 1820 to 1830. After Johnson began preaching in 1830, he not only cut short his own promising political career but also persistently advised his brethren to beware of the dangers of political entanglement.[118]

In the decade of the 1850's this middle group was vigorously led by such moderates on the slavery question as the Cincinnati editor, Benjamin Franklin. The outspoken Franklin wrote: "Jesus and his apostles . . . never attempted to correct the political institutions of the country, no matter how corrupt they were." He insisted that while the Christian had the right to vote, he had no right to be an agitator: "When acting as a citizen of the civil government, be candid, quiet, peaceable, and kind, and do just what *you think right,* allowing every man the same privilege, as Christ has left us all free here, and leave the event with God."[119]

In sum, different attitudes on the relation of the Christian to politics existed from the beginnings of the restoration movement. The ill-defined and ambiguous moderate position dominated the thought of church leaders through most of the period before 1866. But increasingly after 1845 the stresses of the bitter slavery controversy and the Civil War threatened the Disciples tradition of unity in diversity. The crisis between political activists and pacifists which crested in the years 1861-1865 was an important milestone in the history of the movement.

THE MIND OF A MOVEMENT

"Now I beseech you, brethren . . . that ye be perfectly joined together in the same mind and in the same judgment." I Corinthians 1:10.

If peoples and civilizations and epochs have moods, then the Disciples of Christ had a common mind. It was a precariously balanced and often ill-defined mind—but it was common to the movement. Disciples were New Testament primitivists and Christian humanitarians; they were temperamentally fanatics and moderates; they were out-group iconoclasts

---

[118]See John Rogers, *The Biography of Elder J. T. Johnson* (Cincinnati: n.p., 1861), pp. 19-20; J. T. Johnson to Jacob Creath, November 22, 1844, Jacob Creath Collection, Disciples of Christ Historical Society, Nashville, Tennessee.

[119]"Where Is Safe Ground?" *American Christian Review,* I (July, 1856), 216-218.

and in-group constructive critics; they were noninterventionists in civil government and they were political activists; they were sectarian and they were denominational. The uniqueness of the mind of the movement rests not in the fact that there were Disciples who were each of these things but that most Disciples were all of them. The Disciple of the pre-Civil War period did not simply tolerate diversity—he was diversity.

Throughout the period 1800 to 1865 most Disciples remained a complex and unpredictable mixture of these diverse elements. But by 1865 it was obvious that the mixture was not in the same balance throughout the church. Harold Lunger has pointed to the decade of the thirties as a marked dividing line in Campbell's thought: "From about 1831 to the middle of the following decade Campbell's conception of the church underwent a gradual transformation from that of the radical sect form to that of the characteristic American church form—the denomination."[120] There is much to support the proposition that the mid-1830's was a significant turning point in Disciples history. By 1835 the *Millennial Harbinger* had become the more constructive replacement of the iconoclastic *Christian Baptist* as the leading periodical of the group; Disciples were no longer a dissatisfied and critical element within another communion but were now confronted with the demanding task of building a new religious body; both streams of the church had been purged of their most radical elements; the union of Disciples and Christians had had the effect of mellowing the most incompatible elements in the thought of both streams; phenomenal growth increasingly enhanced the social prestige of the church; and the accelerating retreat of the frontier rapidly increased the wealth and social status of the church's membership.

The transition that took place among the Disciples in the decades following 1830, however, was not so much a change as it was a dividing. There is truth in Alexander Campbell's contention in 1855 that he had not changed his views on "any Christian doctrine since I wrote the first volume of the *Christian Baptist*."[121] But Campbell's emphasis did change.

---

[120]Lunger, *Political Ethics of Alexander Campbell*, p. 115. See pp. 115-128. See, also, Garrison, *Religion Follows the Frontier*, p. 147.

[121]"Our Changes," *M.H.*, 4th S., V (June, 1855), 343. See, also, West, *Alexander Campbell and Natural Religion*, p. 164; West, *Ancient Order*, I, 181-195; Lunger, *Political Ethics of Alexander Campbell*, pp. 13-14, 264-274; Whitley, *Trumpet Call*, pp. 68-69, 92-103.

Within the movement, the schizoid common mind showed signs of fracturing by 1865. Two distinct emphases emerged. One group conceived of Christianity in the denominational framework of practical religion, social and political activism, and, often, a nationalistic postmillennialism. A second group emphasized the sectarian tradition of Biblical legalism, a fanatical disposition, and uncompromising separation from the world. Few Disciples fit snugly into one of these pigeonholes in 1865 but it also was becoming increasingly difficult to find a man who would fit in them both.

The fragmentation of the Disciples of Christ was inevitable. They were born of two seeds; they had two fathers; and no man could indefinitely serve two masters. That the Disciples divided in the way they did is, at least partially, a part of the story of the American nation. The United States divided in 1861; it was an economic and cultural fracturing as well as a sectional and political one. The national amputation of 1861 was not the clean and neat work of a skilled surgeon; there remained a large group of neutrals in the border states, there were Unionists in the South and Copperheads in the North—but Americans did divide into North and South. In the decades before 1865 the Disciples increasingly sifted into conservative and liberal camps and these alignments were perceptibly related to the sociological pressures in American society. Nor were the Disciples of Christ gathering neatly on each side of a geographic line; there were liberals in the South, conservatives in the North, and the ever-present block of moderates—but a socio-economic pattern was emerging in Disciples history. There was surely more perception than he knew in Alexander Campbell's statement in 1846: "In grand national concerns, I found it my duty to support principles and measures involving, as I conceive, the best interests of the community to which I belonged."[122] The social views of the Disciples of Christ vividly reflect how intricately cultural and economic presuppositions were linked with the theological in the composite mind of the movement.

The relationship of Disciples with the world around them was never one-sided, however. They were persistently concerned about the failures of their own society to fulfill the high standards of the Christian mes-

---

[122]"Impartiality of the Editor of the Harbinger," *M.H.*, 3d S., III (January, 1846), 4-5.

sage. Practical humanitarianism and prophetic vision combined in fervent
spirits to assault the sins of the nation. It is true that their aim was to
perfect society by perfecting men but they were never unconcerned. If
the legacy of individualistic love and millennial hope proved inadequate
in the years following the Civil War to meet the complex new problems
of industrial America, the post-war sons of pre-war Disciples prophets
were not without a heritage of Christian concern over social sin.

CHAPTER III

AN AMERICAN ECONOMIC GOSPEL

THE PRINCIPLES OF CHRISTIAN CAPITALISM

"Let him that stole steal no more: but rather let him labour, working with his hands the thing which is good, that he may have to give him that needeth." Ephesians 4:28.

THE FUNDAMENTAL TENETS of unrestricted capitalism were never seriously challenged in the first half of the nineteenth century in the United States.[1] And yet, if Americans were firmly committed to capitalistic economic principles, one of the primary aims of the common man during the pre-Civil War era was to "break the aristocracy."[2] The American common man was avidly antimonopolistic and antiaristocratic, if he was not anticapitalistic. The captain of industry was the American symbol of success but he was also the butt of lower class distrust and vituperation.

This basic dichotomy was persistently vocalized by the leaders of evangelical Protestantism in the years preceding the Civil War. While church leaders had a "profound distrust of money and material possession," they demonstrated an equally "strong impulse toward . . . the defense of the capitalistic system, and the appeasing of the monied classes."[3] The traditional virtues of the Calvinistic business ethic, such as thrift, frugality, and industriousness were interwoven with a Christian gospel which included warnings of the evils of riches and praise of Christian stewardship. American revivalists preached a Christian version of the optimistic, yet distrustful, American economic faith.

---

[1]For a general discussion of American economic thought, see Joseph Dorfman, *The Economic Mind in American Civilization* (5 vols.; New York: Viking Press, 1946).

[2]Fish, *Rise of the Common Man*, p. 325. See, also, Harvey Wish, *Society and Thought in Early America* (New York: Longmans, Green, 1950), pp. 394-414.

[3]Cole, *Northern Evangelists*, pp. 166-167. See pp. 165-191 for a general discussion of the economic views of the Northern evangelists during these years.

Most Disciples of Christ leaders during these years accepted and Christianized the economic principles of unrestricted capitalism. Their heritage in Enlightenment optimism, Biblical primitivism, and frontier experience convinced them that if a man was honest, diligent, and frugal he would prosper. The gospel of success, carefully documented with Biblical proof-texts, was intricately combined with their theological doctrines. Alexander Campbell, who, according to his biographer, Benjamin Lyon Smith, "died the richest man in West Virginia,"[4] recognized both in teaching and in practice that there "is nothing incompatible with diligence in business and fervor in spirit in serving the Lord."[5] Archibald W. Campbell, Alexander Campbell's brother, warned the Disciple "of humble station in society" not to "envy . . . his more prosperous brother, upon whom the Lord has bestowed more of this world's wealth."[6]

A growing respect for wealth was linked in the years after 1830 with the doctrine of Christian stewardship. "To labor for the purpose of having to distribute; to seek to be rich for the purpose of being rich in good works," was a variety of economic ambition which received persistent support.[7] The rising economic status of the church members during the years after 1830 made those "endowed with abundant means" prime targets for lessons on stewardship as well as more direct and specific pleas.[8] In 1851 the American Christian Bible Society passed a resolution that Christians, as "God's stewards," were "bound to dispense, in the succor of God's poor and the advancement of His kingdom, all that is not requisite to the actual supply of their wants."[9]

[4]*Alexander Campbell* (St. Louis: The Bethany Press, 1930), p. 147.

[5]"Short Sermons for Business Men," *M.H.*, 5th Series, III (July, 1860), 400. See, also, Lunger, *Political Ethics of Alexander Campbell*, pp. 179-181.

[6]"Christian Equality," *M.H.*, 4th Series, VI (January, 1856), 9.

[7]A. C., "Reformation—No. 8," *M.H.*, VI (August, 1835), 381.

[8]See C. L. L., "Munificent Donations to Colleges," *M.H.*, 5th S., VII (December, 1864), 560-562; A. C., "Liberal Donations to Bethany College," *M.H.*, 5th S., III (February, 1860), 107-108.

[9]*Report of the Proceedings of the American Christian Bible, Missionary and Publication Societies, for the Year 1851, Together with Other Documents* (Cincinnati: American Christian Publication Society, 1851), p. 21.

Although the basic tenets of capitalistic economics were almost every-where accepted by Disciples leaders, and increasingly after 1830 were combined with the doctrine of Christian stewardship, the antiaristocratic prejudices of the American common man were also deeply rooted in Disciples thought. The caustic Arthur Crihfield was perhaps the most outspoken critic of the economic injustices in American society: "Cor-ruption, fraud, intrigue, falsehood . . . and all the hateful passions of corrupt hearts, here embody, compound, commingle, coalesce."[10] Crih-field, a pessimistic premillennialist, combined real insight with Western prejudice in a provoking evaluation of American society:

Laws are made to favor the rich and oppress the poor. It will be soon that a poor man's voice will seldom be heard in the councils of his country; nay, it is generally so already. The rich blockhead, because he can command a quantity of *pork,* or rule a few hundred acres of *land* . . . may pretty easily be elected to the legisla-ture. . . . Do not the poor annually increase in all sections of the country? . . . Penury and want begin to bear heavily on the populace; and but for the vacant territories of the far west, they would soon be ground into the earth. It will soon become impossible for the poor to become rich, and we shall feel the oppression of England's *free slaves* without a government of sufficient strength long to sup-press the spirit of insurrection. The present peace of the world, political and re-ligious, is exceedingly deceitful.[11]

If most Disciples were less pessimistic about the solution to the prob-lems of economic injustice in American society, they shared Crihfield's bitterness toward "rich blockheads."

Most Disciples of Christ leaders prior to 1865 glorified the economic state of the common man.[12] Jeffersonian agrarianism was consistently preached in Christian terms. Alexander Campbell was convinced that the people of the cities were "neither so intelligent in the scriptures, nor

[10]"Preface," *Heretic Detector,* V (1841), viii.

[11]"Coming of the Lord—No. VIII," *Orthodox Preacher,* I (April, 1843), 76-77. Crihfield's reference to the frontier as a "safety valve" is quite typical of Disciples writers.

[12]One writer sweepingly condemned all "merchandizing." He wrote: "The an-cient Christian would not merchandize, because it opened such a door and tempta-tion to a man to *cheat, lie and defraud.* But the modern Christians will do all these things and live by trading, cutting and shaving notes, buying and selling stock to the South, trading in lands, loaning money upon usury, instead of following some honest and useful trade. Great evil is done to Christianity by such persons. Christ is wounded in the house of his friends." An Old Methodist, "The Charge of Wast-ing Our Master's Goods," *Christian Evangelist,* VI (June, 1855), 254-255.

so pious" as those in the country. "The American cities," wrote Campbell, "like all other cities, are not favorable to the prevalence of pure religious influences."[13] The site of Bethany College was chosen in a "rural location," according to Campbell, because such a setting was "more favorable to health, morals, and study than a village or city location."[14]

Nowhere did the Christianized Jeffersonian philosophy of the common man have deeper roots among Disciples, and nowhere did it have a more lasting impact on them, than in the South. Tolbert Fanning, the agrarian patriarch of the church in the South, indoctrinated the rising second-generation preachers of that section with the dignity and virtue of the laboring man. In an 1847 address to the graduating class at his manual labor school, Franklin College, Fanning first enumerated a number of "worthy objections" to professional and business careers and then clearly stated his preference:

For numerous reasons our prejudices are in favor of the laboring pursuits, although we own it is possible they are not in so high repute as others. . . . They are . . . favorable to the best morals and the acquisition of those qualities most essential to contentment and happiness.[15]

The lower-class emphasis in pre-Civil War Disciples thought was deeply rooted in their providential view of history. God's hand was in it all; if a man was poor, it was God's will. During the panic of 1858 Isaac Errett consoled his brethren by pointing out that the "trial" was probably a "great blessing" since nothing was "so hard for even Christians to bear as continuous prosperity." Errett reminded them: "Occasional chastenings from the hand of God call us back to a sense of dependence and accountability, and 'yield the peaceable fruits of righteousness in them that are exercised thereby.' "[16]

---

[13]"Notes of an Excursion to the Eastern Cities, No. II," *M.H.*, N.S., VII (February, 1843), 64.

[14]"Bethany College," *M.H.*, N.S., V (August, 1841), 378.

[15]Scobey, *Franklin College*, pp. 278-279.

[16]"Report of the Executive Board of the American Christian Missionary Society," *M.H.*, 5th S., I (December, 1858), 678. For similar statements by the leading evangelists of the North during these years, see Cole, *Northern Evangelists*, pp. 175-176.

The lower-class bias of the early church leaders was nowhere more apparent than in their insistence that the church be kept free of ostentation. In the *Christian Baptist*, Campbell mercilessly attacked the established denominations (especially the Presbyterians) as tools of the aristocracy: *"Money,* I think, may be considerèd not merely as the bond of union in popular establishments, but it is really the rock on which the popular churches are built."[17] He branded the Protestant clergy "hirelings," and charged that they were guided by the principle, *"no pay, no preach."*[18] Although Campbell consistently denied that he was opposed to paying evangelists, attacks on "clerical aristocrats" remained common in his papers.[19]

During the early years of the movement Disciples leaders insisted that the meetinghouses of the church should meet strict standards of simplicity—economic necessity would only rarely have allowed any other course. In 1834 Campbell gave a terse description of what he considered an adequate building: "A Christian meeting-house ought to be humble, commodious, and free from all the splendor of this vain and sinful world. . . . It should be a one story house, without steeples, galleries, or pulpit."[20] When asked about the propriety of "large meeting houses," Walter Scott gave a similar answer: "Whenever we see such meeting houses, we see pomp or show, and clerical power."[21]

---

[17]"The Clergy—No. V," *C.B.,* I (February, 1824), 127.

[18]*Ibid.,* 125. See, also, "A Review," *C.B.,* I December, 1823), 88-91; "The Clergy—No. III," *C.B.,* I (December, 1823), 85-88; "Tithes," *C.B.,* I (February, 1824), 144; "The Third Epistle of Peter," *C.B.,* II (July, 1825), 243-249. For a general discussion of the economic roots of Campbell's anti-clericalism see Whitley, *Trumpet Call,* pp. 54-58.

[19]See, for instance, A. C., "Is It the Duty of Christian Churches to Support Their Pastors," *M.H.,* 5th S., III (August, 1860), 462-466. As late as 1840 an Illinois Congregationalist minister complained of being harassed by a "Campbellite" who preached "against ministers who receive 'fat salaries.' " William Warren Sweet, *Religion on the American Frontier 1783-1850,* Vol. III: *The Congregationalists* (4 vols.; Chicago: University of Chicago Press, 1939), pp. 164-165. In 1846 an Arkansas Presbyterian evangelist reported to his missionary board that the "Campbellites" were opposed to "supporting the ministry." William Warren Sweet, *Religion on the American Frontier 1783-1850,* Vol. II: *The Presbyterians* (4 vols.; New York: Harper & Brothers Publishers, 1936), p. 697.

[20]"Meeting-Houses," *M.H.,* V (January, 1834), 8.

[21]"Questions and Answers," *Evangelist,* III (March, 1834), 62-64.

The frontier, lower-class orientation of Disciples of Christ, everywhere apparent before 1840, was markedly less conspicuous in the thought of many of the group's leaders by 1865. Although the church remained essentially in touch with the disinherited, it did not pass uninfluenced through the economic transformation of the nation. Prosperous, middle-class congregations were common in the small towns of Kentucky and the emerging midwestern cities by 1865. Winfred Garrison notes: "When they got better houses, they also wanted better churches."[22] While few really costly buildings were erected before 1865, "there was a noticeable tendency toward at least architectural respectability."[23] In 1865 Isaac Errett frankly admitted that "wealth is desirable for the erection of suitable houses of worship."[24]

Several writers showed concern over growing signs of the "aristocratic malady" within the church in the 1860's. Aaron Chatterton and Alexander Campbell objected to evangelistic reports sent in to their papers which emphasized the conversion of the "first citizens" and the "wealthy and influential" men of a community.[25] In 1864 William K. Pendleton denounced the "rage for building fine churches, gorgeous religious temples, cathedrals worthy of the glory of the Lord." He hopefully predicted that in the future the Disciples would avoid these "secular corruptions."[26]

The most ominous and prophetic symptom of diverging economic beliefs within the Disciples of Christ during the period before 1865 was the outbreak of scattered skirmishes over the propriety of the use of instruments of music in the worship. Although the music question did not assume major importance until after the Civil War, the pattern of reaction had become apparent before 1865. Significantly, it was in a Kentucky paper, where the church was more sophisticated and wealthier than

---

[22]Garrison, *Religion Follows the Frontier*, p. 226. For a description of this post-1840 transition see Whitley, *Trumpet Call*, pp. 104-119.

[23]Garrison, *Religion Follows the Frontier*, p. 226.

[24]"Spiritual Declension.—No. II," *M.H.*, XXXVI (December, 1865), 562.

[25]"Aristocracy," *Evangelist*, XIII (July, 1862), 312-315; "Aristocracy," *M.H.*, 5th S., VI (April, 1863), 168-170.

[26]"Pew-Renting and Organ Music," *M.H.*, 5th S., VII (March, 1864), 130.

in any other section, that the question was first seriously raised.[27] In 1851 the *Ecclesiastic Reformer* carried an extended series on the subject.[28] After several months of debate one of the bewildered pro-organ writers made a revealing condensation of his opponents' arguments:

> Just listen—"church music—unfashionable—important improvement—old hunkers —progress—reformers—dancing—accomplishment—gracefully—p a r l o r—right foot foremost—ball-room—awkwardness—clownishness—elegance—gesture—a t t i t u d e— money-saving machine—deep learning—ancient and modern lore—fine voice—gram-mar—rhetoric—logic—excellency—theological schools—chair of dancing," &c. Now can any one tell what all these mince pie articles have to do with the sub-ject of "instrumental music in all our churches."[29]

All of these diverse elements fit together quite logically in the mind of his assailant. Within the traditional framework of the lower-class heri-tage of the Disciples "instrumental music" became a symbol of all that was pretentious, aristocratic, and corrupt. When the subject again flared in the *American Christian Review* in 1860, the outspoken "old fogy," Benjamin Franklin, condemned the organ as an innovation of "fashion-able society."[30] Theological justifications for each of the contending parties were soon in abundance (an 1864-65 discussion in the *Millennial Harbinger* was almost totally Biblically oriented) but economic tensions increasingly influenced the diverging alignment of forces.

To sum up, through 1865 Disciples of Christ generally fit rather neatly into the dichotomic pattern of American economic thought. The basic presuppositions of capitalistic economics were seldom questioned; middle-class virtues were extolled; and Christian stewardship was persistently commended. On the other hand, the Disciples were deeply influenced by the antiaristocratic prejudices of the lower classes; established wealth was attacked; and the common man was lionized. In most early Disciples both emphases were present but by 1865 it was becoming apparent that in economics, as in theology, many church leaders were finding it in-

---

[27]For a general discussion of the early stages of the organ controversy among the Disciples see West, *Ancient Order*, I, 306-317.

[28]See *Ecclesiastic Reformer* beginning March 15, 1851.

[29]G., "Church Music," *Ecclesiastic Reformer*, IV (May 15, 1851), 272.

[30]"Instrumental Music in Churches," *American Christian Review*, III (January 31, 1860), 19.

creasingly difficult to remain loyal to both sectarian and denominational values.

THE TRIBUNAL OF BUSINESS ETHICS

"Dare any of you, having a matter against another, go to law before the unjust, and not before the saints?" I Corinthians 6:1.

Perhaps more than any other institution, the evangelical churches of the frontier were responsible for bringing some order out of the social chaos of the early West.[31] Church trials were commonplace and the jurisdiction of such courts extended into the area of business ethics as well as personal morality. The evangelical Protestant sects of the West were the theoretical and practical guardians of Christian ethics on the frontier.

Of the practical ethical problems discussed by Disciples leaders during this period, none received more attention than questions of business morality. While all of the leaders of the church agreed that honesty and charitableness ought to govern a Christian's business dealings, they were by no means agreed about the specific Biblical teachings on such subjects as usury and debt. The most radical sectarian element in the church insisted that it was sinful for a Christian to lend money for interest. Barton Stone, who lived close to financial disaster most of his life, asked: "He who said, 'From him that would borrow of thee, turn not thou away;' Did he mean, what his words signify?"[32] Some, such as Carroll Kendrick, expressed the more moderate view that while taking interest from fellow Christians was not lawful, it was permissible to demand interest of "strangers."[33] Alexander Campbell, unquestionably expressing the opinion of the majority of the brotherhood, insisted that the intent of the borrower determined the ethical propriety of interest. To extort money from a *"poor* brother" was wrong but if the borrower intended

---

[31]See William Warren Sweet, *Religion on the American Frontier 1783-1840,* Vol. IV: *The Methodists* (4 vols.; Chicago: The University of Chicago Press, 1946), pp. 640-679; William Warren Sweet, *Religion on the American Frontier 1783-1830,* Vol. I: *The Baptists* (4 vols., New York: Henry Holt and Company, 1931), pp. 203, 287, 316, 368-369; Sweet, *Presbyterians,* p. 564; Walter Brownlow Posey, *The Baptist Church in the Lower Mississippi Valley, 1776-1845* (Lexington: University of Kentucky Press, 1957), pp. 38-53; Walter Brownlow Posey, *The Presbyterian Church in the Old Southwest, 1778-1838* (Richmond: John Knox Press, 1952), pp. 93-101.

[32]"Usury," *C.M.,* XIII (June, 1843), 50.

[33]"Usury—A Test of Coveteousness," *C.J.,* IV (March 22, 1845), 14-15.

to use the loan for "trade, commerce, or speculation" then interest was "justifiable."[34]

The same difference in emphasis was apparent in the expressions of the church leaders on the subject of debt. Jacob Creath, Jr., writing in the *Christian Messenger,* summed up the radical sectarian case: "Many of our brethren have speculated in secular affairs; have fallen into debt, have brought dishonor upon the cause. . . . Beloved brethren, keep clear of *debt* and *speculation.* Owe no man anything. Be content to be poor and despised."[35] Although this sectarian emphasis remained prominent through 1865, repeated protests similar to Creath's are a good indication that many of the church members did not share such puritanical views. More important was the moderate emphasis on honesty and responsibility in business relationships. Alexander Campbell believed that debt should be avoided but when financial obligations were contracted (and there were conditions when a Christian lawfully could become indebted), then it was a "point of the highest honor" that the debt be paid.[36] Bankruptcy laws were condemned as immoral: "It is abhorrent to every principle of law, and justice, and honor, for any man to betake himself to the refuge of a bankrupt law to discharge a debt, which, by a rigid economy, industry and frugality, he may, at some time, be able to pay."[37] In short, the business ethic of the Disciples of Christ during the years 1800-1865 was essentially that of individualistic and optimistic American society. The major concern of most of the church leaders was to see that the capitalistic economy operated in accord with the Christian principles of honesty and benevolence.

Disciples leaders firmly believed that it was their duty to regulate the economic ethics of the church's members. There were frequent warnings against "defrauding one another," "extortion," "covenant breaking," and the exaction of "extravagant" profits.[38] Frontier churches often acted as

---

[34]"Usury," *M.H.,* N.S., VII (June, 1843), 254-259.

[35]"Speculations in Religion and Money," *C.M.,* XII (July, 1842), 264.

[36]"Sermon on Debt," *M.H.,* N.S., VI (July, 1842), 295-296.

[37]A.C., "Response to Jonathon Dymond, on Insolvency," *M.H.,* 4th S., III (October, 1853), 587.

[38]See, for examples, Iota Rho, "Difficulties in Churches, No. 4," *C.J.,* III (May 22, 1844), 145-146; B. W. S. "Selfishness," *C.M.,* XIV (May, 1844), 21-23; John Flick, "The Times—No. 2," *Gospel Proclamation,* I (August, 1847), 80-81.

tribunals to try those suspected of economic misconduct. Barton Stone wrote in 1831: "Not to pay a just debt when we have the means, is an open violation of the laws of our King, and suit against such a culprit should be made to the church of which he is a member, and judgment given by the church."[39] Numerous entries in the intriguing local church records of the period demonstrate that many of the churches scrupulously enforced their individualistic code of economic ethics. The church in Jacksonville, Illinois, where Stone long resided, excluded John Lennon for borrowing "money with no intentions of ever paying as the facts of the case clearly show."[40] In 1860 the South Elkhorn Church in Kentucky

cut off Richard Allen upon the ground of his reckless manner of doing business that is in purchasing property whenever he could get credit when he must have known he could not meet his promises which he failed to do by doing he had brought great reproach upon the Church of Christ.[41]

While such vigilance and thoroughness was probably not universal among the churches, these cases were by no means isolated incidents. In 1844 Alexander Campbell wrote: "Many of the controversies and cases of discipline which occur in churches, arise from this foredoomed and soul-withering passion for wealth."[42] As a matter of fact, the churches generally regarded it wrong to settle differences in any other manner than before the officers of the church.[43] In 1830 the Providence Christian Church in Jessamine county, Kentucky, reprimanded one of its members for "having instituted a suit at law instead of taking the Gospel steps with Brother Rutherford."[44]

In summary, the Disciples were never unconcerned about the practical problems of economic ethics in their society. Indeed, they considered it

---

[39]"Reply to Dr. Roach's Letter," *C.M.*, V (October, 1831), 227-228.

[40]Minute Book of the Christian Church of Jacksonville, Illinois, 1832-1889, Volume II, Disciples of Christ Historical Society, Nashville, Tennessee.

[41]Church Register and Record of the South Elkhorn Church, 1817-1897, Bosworth Memorial Library, College of the Bible, Lexington, Kentucky.

[42]"Morality of Christians—No. XX," *M.H.*, N.S., IV (June, 1840), 275.

[43]See "Lawsuits—No. I," *Christian Teacher*, IV (October, 1845), 264-265. William Warren Sweet points out that frontier Methodists also considered it sinful to "serve a brother." *Methodists*, p. 461. See, also, Posey, *Baptists*, p. 48.

[44]Church Record and Register of Providence Christian Church, 1817-1875, Bosworth Memorial Library, College of the Bible, Lexington, Kentucky.

one of the prime functions of the church to interpret and maintain the principles of Christian economics. If the economic morality supported by the church was individualistic and middle class, it was simply the ethic of the society in which they lived and the one they had inherited from the Protestant reformation. Insistence upon individual conformity to scriptural standards of honesty, integrity, and responsibility was not without its good effects in the unruly West of midnineteenth-century America.

HUMANITARIAN IMPULSES

"Pure religion and undefiled before God and the Father is this, to visit the fatherless and widows in their affliction, and to keep himself unspotted from the world." James 1:27.

It would indeed be strange if the poor had no sympathy for the poor. It was only natural that the humanitarian impulse was deep rooted in the evangelical sects of nineteenth-century America.[45] Much of the organized benevolent activity of the first half of the century stemmed directly from this humanitarianism in the churches of the dispossessed.

The Disciples were never apathetic about practical religion. In 1834 Alexander Campbell included among the five primary services demanded of Christians: "Direct contributions . . . for the poor saints, for widows, and other objects of sympathy."[46] Benevolence and charity were probably preached less often than repentance and baptism but they were certainly not ignored.

Systematic giving was a slow development in the church. The rank individualism and antiinstitutionalism of the early days of the movement, the early iconoclastic attacks on the "money foundation" of other groups, and the struggling local churches' own early economic inabilities all hindered the emergence of large benevolent projects. Generally, the churches simply attended to their most pressing financial needs by making "appor-

---

[45]For general discussions of this humanitarian impulse see Catharine C. Cleveland, *The Great Revival in the West* (Chicago: The University of Chicago Press, 1916), pp. 155-156; Smith, *Revivalism and Social Reform*, pp. 148-177; Olmstead, *Religion in the United States*, pp. 358-359; Cole, *Northern Evangelists*, p. 111.

[46]"Address to the Brethren of the Reformation, No. II," *M.H.*, V (April, 1834), 184.

tionments" or "subscriptions" among their members.[47] By the 1840's the general plan which had evolved demanded a weekly contribution in every congregation on the first day of the week with each individual contributing "as the Lord has prospered."[48] The "pledge system" developed slowly among the wealthier churches in Kentucky; John T. Johnson's Georgetown, Kentucky, congregation and Carroll Kendrick's Stanford, Kentucky, church had adopted such a system by the late 1840's.[49] In short, an emphasis on practical benevolence was a part of the birthright of the movement but not until the 1840's, and then only among the wealthier congregations, especially in Kentucky, was systematic giving very highly developed.

Until the 1840's the benevolent activities of the church were pretty largely limited to local congregations meeting immediate crises. Alexander Campbell, in one of his early articles on the "Restoration of the Ancient Order of Things," outlined the policy of dispensing charity at the congregational level:

Christian congregations, in primitive times, had need of money or earthly things, as well as we. . . . A deacon or deacons had the charge of this treasury, and were ex-officio treasurers. . . . They were not only to take care of the contributions, but to dispense or appropriate them according to the directions of the brethren.[50]

This plan of deacons and deaconesses attending to the needs of their fellow Disciples in a local church's own geographic proximity was universally accepted by the early Christian churches. Any effort to shift this responsibility to public or private charities was consistently opposed.[51]

It is evident that many of the churches of the movement were conscientious in relieving the severest needs of their poor members. In 1847

---

[47]See Church Register and Record of the South Elkhorn Church, 1817-1897; and Walter Scott Notebook, Bosworth Memorial Library, College of the Bible, Lexington, Kentucky.

[48]See "Reformation—No. 8," *M.H.*, VI (October, 1835), 472-475; Tychicus, "Tour, Incidents, Observations, &c.,—No. 5," *Gospel Advocate*, II (February, 1836), 23-25.

[49]See J. T. Johnson, "Scheme of Finance," *P.U.*, IV (December 15, 1847), 5; "The Weekly Contribution Again," *W.R.*, VI (August, 1848), 631-634; R. Milligan, "Systematic Benevolence," *M.H.*, 5th S., VII (February, 1864), 49-57.

[50]"A Restoration of the Ancient Order of Things. No. XIX. The Deacon's Office," *C.B.*, IV (May, 1827), 211.

[51]See W.S., "The Poor," *Evangelist*, VI (January, 1838), 7; J.F.R., "The Poor," *C.E.*, VII (February, 1856), 75-79.

Jessie B. Ferguson, minister of the strong Nashville, Tennessee, congregation reported that the church there had appointed

> brethren and sisters in each ward [of the city], whose duty it is to visit once every
> week, every member of the church in their several wards, and report their temporal
> and spiritual condition upon every Lord's day. We may thus have a full report every
> week, so that no one suffers in our midst.[52]

Some of the congregations expanded their benevolent activities into general community work. As early as 1840 Walter Scott reported that he had visited a church whose women met every week to "sew and make garments for the poor and needy" and he commended this "charitable custom to the sisters of the other churches."[53] By the 1850's such "sewing societies" were rather common.[54]

During the years before 1865 the most spectacular benevolent displays among the Disciples were two brotherhood-wide responses to disaster pleas. The extreme famines in the British Isles in 1847 and 1848 brought widespread appeals to America for help. Early in 1847 Walter Scott and William K. Pendleton began campaigns to raise funds for the famine sufferers through the columns of the *Protestant Unionist* and the *Millennial Harbinger*. By April 27 Scott announced that $320 had been raised by two churches in the Pittsburgh area, grain had been purchased, and was already "on its way to their relief."[55]

In April, 1847, a meeting was held by the Bethany church where it was resolved that it was the "duty" of every Christian to give to the suf-

---

[52]"Every City Church Ought to Have Its Sunday School," *M.H.*, 3d S., IV (April, 1847), 203. The church in Walnut Grove, Illinois, also had a remarkable benevolent program. An impressed visitor wrote: "These same brethren have reared up two poor houses within the bounds of the congregation, where the old and the maimed who love and obey the Lord, find comfortable homes with a good supply of the good things of this world.—This looks like old-fashioned Christianity, and very unlike that cold hearted . . . policy so prevalent with many churches." T. J. Matlock, "State Meeting in Illinois," *Western Evangelist*, II (October, 1851), 314-316.

[53]*Evangelist*, VIII (March, 1840), 72. See, also, A., "Our Reveries," *Ladies' Christian Annual*, III (February, 1855), 266-268.

[54]See J. T. Johnson, "Our Sewing Society," *E.R.*, III (February 2, 1850), 74-76; "Female Sewing Societies, etc.," *E.R.*, III (February 2, 1850), 35-36; S., "Sewing Societies," *E.R.*, III (March 30, 1850), 203-204; J.B., "Editorial Letters—No. 5," *North-Western Christian Magazine*, II (January, 1856), 209-211.

[55]"Contribution for Scotland," *P.U.*, III (April 28, 1847), 82.

ferers "each according to his ability." The church at Bethany decided to sponsor a special collection for the Disciples of the United Kingdom which would be "entrusted to the hands of Brother Campbell and distributed according to his judgment, during his tour through that country."[56] A total of $1,326.72 was finally collected in the Bethany fund and distributed by Alexander Campbell—mostly in the manufacturing centers of Scotland.[57]

This first brotherhood-wide benevolent campaign was typical of those that followed it in several ways. Contributions were made by both individuals and congregations and were channeled through such a diversity of clearing houses (some were sent direct, some through a local church, and some through a publishing office) that it is impossible to estimate accurately the amount given. A second feature common to nineteenth-century Disciples brotherhood benevolent campaigns was the persistent emphasis on helping the "brethren" in the distressed area—although broader humanitarian interest was not completely lacking.

In the fall of 1860 a general crop failure in Kansas set off another benevolent drive. Aaron Chatterton, Iowa editor, reported that there were "a goodly number of brethren in Kansas among the sufferers."[58] Most of the publishing offices in the church began immediately to collect funds which they distributed through individuals and churches in the disaster area. Within a few months the *Millennial Harbinger* reported receipt of $181.20;[59] the *Evangelist*, $160.90;[60] the *Christian Record*, $229.19;[61] and the *American Christian Review* over $900.00.[62] In addition, a Kansas Aid Society was organized by church members and it reported collections and disbursements of nearly $1,200.00.[63] Several local churches in Kansas and bordering states, including the congregations in Davenport, Iowa,

---

[56]"Relief for the Irish—Meeting at Bethany," *M.H.*, 3d S., IV (April, 1847), 229-231.

[57]"Distribution of Contributions," *M.H.*, 3d S., V (April, 1848), 213-217.

[58]"Destitution in Kansas," *Evangelist*, XI (December, 1860), 564.

[59]"Contributions for Kansas and Texas," *M.H.*, 5th S., IV (April, 1861), 233.

[60]"Kansas Fund," *Evangelist*, XII (March, 1861), 224.

[61]"Receipts for Kansas," *C.R.*, 3d S., V (May, 1861), 61.

[62]A. Crocker, "Relief for Kansas," *A.C.R.*, III (December 18, 1860), 203.

[63]See "Kansas Reports," *Evangelist*, XII (June, 1861), 322-323; "Kansas Aid Report," *Evangelist*, XII (August, 1861), 438-439.

and Leavenworth City and LeRoy, Kansas, served as clearinghouses for contributions which poured in from all over the country.[64] While it is impossible to estimate the amount raised in the Kansas relief drive, it is apparent that the response was both spontaneous and substantial.

Perhaps more important, but certainly more difficult to sustain, were the weak beginnings of organized benevolence among the Disciples prior to 1865. Church-supported institutional benevolence faced a number of obstacles. Before 1840 there was an almost chaotic lack of organization among the churches and this, combined with the precarious financial status of most of the young congregations, made any large-scale institutional enterprise impractical. Probably more important was the marked anti-institutional bias in early Disciples thought. A deep-seated distrust of both missionary and benevolent "societies" pervaded throughout the church before the decade of the forties. In the first issue of the *Christian Baptist* Alexander Campbell launched a frontal attack on all "societies:"

Their churches [early Christians] were not fractured into missionary societies, bible societies, education societies; nor did they dream of organizing such in the world. The head of a believing household was not in those days a president or manager or a board of foreign missions; his wife, the president of some female education society; his eldest son, the recording secretary of some domestic Bible society; his eldest daughter, the corresponding secretary of a mite society; his servant maid, the vice-president of a rag society. . . . They knew nothing of the hobbies of modern times. In their church capacity alone they moved.[65]

Barton Stone held similar views on "benevolent societies." He wrote:

These benevolent schemes are Bible societies, Tract societies, Rag societies, Cent societies, Theological Societies, Sunday School societies, Education societies, &c., &c. . . . I would simply ask, what have the divine writers of the New Testament said respecting these societies? They are all silent as the grave. . . . These benevolent societies, though good in their origin, we cannot but view as engines now used to build up sectarian establishments, and monopolise [*sic*] the wealth and power of the nation.[66]

[64]See "Kansas Reports," *Evangelist*, XII (June, 1861), 322-323; "Destitution in Kansas," *Evangelist*, XI (December, 1860), 563-564. It is virtually impossible to make any meaningful use of the figures given in the periodical accounts of the campaign. There is unquestionably some overlapping in their lists of receipts but this overestimation is probably far outweighed by the contributions which went directly to some agent or church in the stricken area.

[65]"The Christian Religion," *C.B.*, I (August, 1823), 6-7.

[66]"Dover Association," *C.M.*, VI (November, 1832), 344. See, also, "The Evangelizing System," *Christian Publisher*, N.S., I (November, 1839), 241-245.

In the decade of the 1840's, as the lower-class prejudices of the Disciples were becoming markedly less aggressive, the antisociety bias in their thought clearly weakened. This whole reorientation culminated in 1849 with the formation of the first national missionary organization in the denomination, the American Christian Missionary Society. Many factors were involved in this shift of emphasis: by this time the church had become "influential in point of numbers and resources;"[67] local preachers' meetings and co-operative gatherings had never completely ceased to function; the establishment of a number of colleges had illustrated the feasibility of co-operative financial efforts; and many of the larger churches were becoming well trained in the principles of systematic giving.

It seems apparent that such men as David S. Burnet, John T. Johnson, Lewis L. Pinkerton, and John W. Parish—the outstanding leaders of the church in the wealthy urban and northern Kentucky congregations—were the real fathers of systematic and organized benevolence among the Disciples.[68] Not only was the church better prepared financially to undertake institutional benevolence in these areas but also lower-class sectarian prejudices were less conspicuous. But while the Kentucky "liberals" led the movement for benevolent institutions, hardly less important was the support they received from Alexander Campbell who modified his old antiinstitutional views considerably in the decade of the forties. By 1849 Campbell had come to the conclusion that in "all things pertaining to public interest" the church was "unshackled by any apostolic authority" and could formulate any sort of organizational structure which was thought proper.[69]

Throughout the period before 1865, however, there remained an im-

---

[67] James Inglis, "A Baptist Preacher's View of Us," *M.H.*, 3d S., VII (April, 1850), 202.

[68] See, Keith, *Burnet*, pp. 191-199. For general discussions of Disciples organizational development, see Garrison and DeGroot, *Disciples of Christ*, pp. 234-241; Hailey, *Attitudes and Consequences*, pp. 147-152. For some typical examples of the benevolent emphasis among Kentucky preachers see J. T. Johnson, "Christian Knowledge and Practice," *C.M.*, VI (October, 1832), 316-318; C.K., "Systematic Benevolence," *E.R.*, III (July 20, 1850), 451-454.

[69] "Church Organization—No. III," *M.H.*, 3d S., VI (May, 1849), 270. Oliver Read Whitley suggests that Campbell's change was typical of "many of the thoughtful members of the Disciples Church." *Trumpet Call*, p. 125.

portant element in the church, led by Jacob Creath, Jr. and Tolbert Fanning, which refused to compromise their old anti-institutional prejudices. Significantly, their sectarian objections to organizational development had deep economic undertones. The American Christian Missionary Society early drew criticism because of its practice of selling life memberships.[70] Tolbert Fanning entertained grave doubts about the propriety of church-supported orphan homes as late as 1856:

Hence I state in conclusion, that I doubt the policy of establishing orphan schools to bring up unfortunate children without trades and professions, and still more on the ground, that these orphan schools, to my mind, are attempting to perform, in part, the labor which it is the imperious duty of each congregation to do.[71]

In 1846 an Arkansas Presbyterian preacher reported that the "Campbellites" opposed "sustaining any religious institutions with money."[72] In short, the anti-institutional bias which was so pronounced in the early movement did not die in the years after 1840. If the wealthier and more cultured churches of the bluegrass region were slowly diluting the most radical elements in the Disciples sectarian tradition, there remained a vocal group that was just as antiaristocratic and antiinstitutional as ever.

But by the mid-1840's, there was a large group of Disciples which was sufficiently prepared financially, organizationally, and intellectually to sponsor a successful project in institutional benevolence. In 1846 Lewis L. Pinkerton, outstanding Kentucky preacher and humanitarian, proposed the establishment of a girls' orphan school at Midway, Kentucky. The school was designed for "clothing, feeding, and educating orphan girls."[73] The institution filled a real need in Kentucky in the 1850's, where facilities for the education of young girls were scarce at best and virtually nonexistent for orphan girls.

Pinkerton received almost unanimous support for his plan from the leaders of the Disciples of Christ. Campbell commended the enterprise as "humane and Christian" and added that it "would seem to merit the

---

[70]West, *Ancient Order*, I, 200.

[71]"Institutions Originating in the Wisdom of Good Men—How Far Should They Be Encouraged," *G.A.*, II (October, 1856), 308-310.

[72]Sweet, *Presbyterians*, p. 697.

[73]Harry Giovannoli, *Kentucky Female Orphan School* (Midway, Kentucky: n.p., 1930), p. 29.

kind consideration of the philanthropic and wealthy portion of the Christian community."[74] William Baxter, minister of the historic Disciples congregation in Pittsburgh, Pennsylvania, praised the venture as a signal that the time of "mere theorizing and barren speculations has passed away" and that the brotherhood was ready to embark on a program of practical Christian action.[75]

In 1855 Walter Scott tried to promote the establishment of a similar male asylum in Covington, Kentucky. Scott called for a subscription of $50,000 to get the operation underway but, despite substantial early pledges from John T. Johnson and Alexander Campbell, the institution never materialized.[76] Disciples were simply not well enough trained in the habits of systematic giving by 1855 to sustain any broad expansion into the area of institutional benevolence; as a matter of fact, they were still groping in this area at the close of the nineteenth century.[77]

In summary, the Disciples of Christ was born as a religion of the disinherited and, above all, the group remained through the period to 1865 a church of the common man. Humanitarianism and sympathy for the poor were an inborn part of the movement's nature. Throughout most of the period before 1865 their benevolent activities were individualistic and even chaotic—but they made genuine efforts to relieve the sufferings of their fellow humans. When some of the church's leaders began to abandon their extreme sectarian theology in the decades following 1830, weak beginnings were made in systematic and institutional benevolence.

THE GOSPEL OF COMMUNITY

"And all that believed were together, and had all things common; and sold their possessions and goods, and parted them to all men, as every man had need." Acts 2:44-45.

---

[74]"Contemplated Female Orphan School," *M.H.*, 3d S., III (July, 1846), 419.

[75]"Noble Enterprise," *P.U.*, II (August 5, 1846), 130.

[76]"Covington Male Orphan Asylum," *M.H.*, 4th S., V (March, 1855), 156-163.

[77]Little attention was given to interdenominational or secular benevolent movements by church leaders. Such enterprises smacked too much of a usurpation of the authority of the church. See, for a few of the scattered references, "A City Hospital," *P.U.*, III (December 9, 1849), 2; A. C., "Pittsburg Infirmary," *M.H.*, 4th S., I (August, 1851), 465-467; "Deaf and Dumb Asylum," *C.R.*, III (August, 1845), 53-54.

In the first half of the nineteenth century America became a haven for religious and utopian social experimenters.[78] No facet of American life escaped the scrutiny of these crusaders in their search for an American millennium—including the nation's economic institutions. Most of the community experiments of the period were dramatic failures but a few, such as the Shakers and the Mormons, made a permanent imprint on the course of American thought.

"The specific origin of the communitarian ideal, as it developed in America," according to Arthur E. Bestor, Jr., "is to be found in the religious ideology of the radical Protestant sects that arose in the Reformation."[79] In the early years of the nineteenth century many of the radical European Protestant sects were transplanted into America but the Shakers "were more influential than all their sectarian predecessors combined."[80] The clash of the Shakers and the nascent Christian movement in Kentucky in the first decade of the nineteenth century has already been noted. Barton Stone's frantic efforts to stop the spread of Shakerism in the West were motivated by his aversion to their religious, social, and economic radicalism. Apparently, Stone was first repulsed by the Shaker doctrine on celibacy; John Dunlavy, one of the Christian preachers who defected to the Shakers, wrote that Stone was "well pleased" with the testimony of the "three witnesses" until "they came on marriage."[81] But when Stone began his crusade against the Shakers, he also attacked their economic radicalism. He charged that the Shakers were "world-minded, cunning deceivers." "The *Shakers* are come to take people's land—Everyone that joins them must immediately give up his deed to the elders!"[82] Unquestionably one of the effects of the Shaker controversy on the early Christian movement was to drain off that radical element which would have

---

[78]The best general account of the radical community experiments of the first half of the nineteenth century is Arthur Eugene Bestor, Jr., *Backwoods Utopias* (Philadelphia: University of Pennsylvania Press, 1950). See, also, Tyler, *Freedom's Ferment*, pp. 46-224; Everett Webber, *Escape to Utopia* ("American Procession Series"; New York: Hastings House Publishers, 1959).

[79]Bestor, *Backwoods Utopias*, p. 4. For a general description of the American religious community experiments before 1860 see pp. 20-59.

[80]*Ibid.*, p. 33

[81]Andrews, *People Called Shakers*, p. 80.

[82]Richard M'Nemar, *The Kentucky Revival* . . . (reprinted; Albany: E. and E. Hosford, 1808), pp. 95-101. See, also, Rogers, *Biography of Stone*, pp. 62-64.

agitated for, or been receptive to, radical communal schemes.[83]

In 1829 Alexander Campbell debated with perhaps the most significant and widely known socialist reformer of the first half of the nineteenth century, the Scottish philanthropist, Robert Owen.[84] Owen established an outstanding record as a reforming member of the English parliament during this period, and his short-lived and unsuccessful co-operative society at New Harmony, Indiana, established in 1825, was probably the most publicized social experiment in this country. Owen combined his social radicalism with a militant atheism and was under rather constant attack from religious leaders in America as early as 1817. The Campbell-Owen debate was held in Cincinnati as the result of a challenge issued by Owen offering to meet any reputable Christian minister to discuss the merits of Christianity. The debate was primarily concerned with Owen's skepticism rather than his radical social philosophy and significantly Campbell never attacked the New Harmony experiment—in fact, he persistently refused to be put in the position of opposing the social experiment.[85] Several times prior to the debate Campbell predicted the failure of the New Harmony project because of its antireligious basis but, prior to 1840, he never objected to the co-operative plan as such.[86]

During the debate Campbell connected Owen's social ideal with his

[83]There was an extended debate on the subject of Christian communism in the *Christian Messenger* in 1836. Several leading ministers of the Christian movement, including D. Pat Henderson, John T. Jones, and Samuel Rogers, wrote articles with radical economic undertones. But the whole discussion was closed by Barton Stone on a quite moderate tone. See the *Christian Messenger* from February, 1836, to September, 1836.

[84]For general information on Owen and his New Harmony experiment see Bestor, *Backwoods Utopias*, pp. 60-229. This was not Campbell's first experience with economic experimentation. In his early years in this country he had been interested in a cooperative church venture. See Richardson, *Memoirs of Campbell*, I, 459-461; Lunger, *Political Ethics of Alexander Campbell*, p. 181. He also was familiar with the work of a radical religious reformer in Ohio named Henry Kurtz. "Deism and the Social System—No. IV," *C.B.*, V (September, 1827), 27.

[85]See Alexander Campbell and Robert Owen, *The Evidences of Christianity: A Debate Between Robert Owen of New Lanark, Scotland, and Alexander Campbell, President of Bethany Coll., Va. . . .* (5th stereotyped ed.; Cincinnati: American Christian Publication Society, 1854), p. 167; "Deism and the Social System—No. IV," *C.B.*, V (September, 1827), 27-31.

[86]See "Mr. Robert Owen and the Social System," *C.B.*, IV (April, 1827), 186-188.

own Christian concept of the millennium and suggested that God might be using the British philanthropist to hasten the coming of that glorious era.[87] The burden of Campbell's argument on Owen's social system was not that it was bad but that it was based on Christian principles and that the humanitarian impulse behind the experiment came through Owen's philanthropic father-in-law, Mr. Dale.[88]

But if Campbell was tolerant of, and even sympathetic with, the co-operative experiments so prominent in the first few decades of the century, he was never a visionary. During his most radical reforming days before 1830 (which was also the period of his most fervent and optimistic post-millennialism), he considered any attempts to try to introduce communal practices in the church highly impractical.[89] As a matter of fact, in 1830 Campbell completely quashed the only serious attempt to introduce social radicalism in the Disciples movement.

Sydney Rigdon was one of the first Disciples converts in northern Ohio and his spectacular preaching soon made him one of the most widely known and popular Disciples preachers on the Western Reserve. By 1830 Rigdon's church in Kirtland, Ohio, had adopted a system of community property. When the Mahoning Association of reforming churches on the Western Reserve met in 1830, Rigdon "introduced an argument to show that our pretensions to follow the apostles in all their New Testament teachings, required a community of goods." Campbell, who was present at the meeting, was concerned with what effect such a message might have. According to Amos S. Hayden, Campbell successfully countered Rigdon's arguments by demonstrating that there was clear precedent for private property in the New Testament. Rigdon left the meeting "chafed and chagrined" and slightly over two months later became one of the first and unquestionably the most important Mormon convert in Ohio.[90]

Rigdon immediately became an important leader in the Mormon movement and under his leadership there were significant defections among Ohio Disciples churches, especially around Hiram and Kirtland. Rigdon

---

[87]*Campbell-Owen Debate*, p. 108.

[88]*Ibid.*, p. 167.

[89]"Extracts from a Variety of Letters," *C.B.*, IV (July, 1827), 257-260.

[90]See Hayden, *Western Reserve*, pp. 209-222, 298-299; Garrison and DeGroot, *Disciples*, pp. 300-301.

persuaded Joseph Smith to accept a good deal of his scheme of Christian communism and subsequent Mormon history was significantly influenced by the Kirtland church's economic system. Rigdon soon became associated with Joseph Smith in the first presidency of the Mormon church and two other early Disciples preachers, Parley P. Pratt and Orson Hyde, were elevated to the office of "apostle."[91] The lasting effects of the Mormon defections on Disciples churches were not serious and the rapid growth of the movement in Ohio was hardly interrupted. More important, from the point of view of Disciples, was the fact that the radical element in the church, the element which had been prone to accept radical economic schemes, was largely drained off in the process.

In the decades after 1830 there were no further serious attempts to introduce radical economic schemes into the church. Although most of the church leaders retained a good-natured, tolerant attitude toward social experimentation, they generally believed that such utopian schemes were "impractical." Campbell retained a high respect for Robert Owen and when the great Scottish reformer died in 1859 he wrote: "For gentlemanly courtesy, good nature, and general candor and straight-forwardness as a debatant, Robert Owen excelled all other men with whom I have ever argumentatively discussed any religious question."[92] But as the years passed Campbell became more and more skeptical of the worth of co-operative schemes. In 1851, while on a tour of Ohio, he met Robert Dale Owen, the son of his famous antagonist, and wrote: "Even with all the visionary and imaginative aberrations of Robert Owen and Robert Dale Owen, I cherish for them both a melancholy benevolence, along with a deep conviction, that neither of them will leave the world as good and as happy as they found it."[93]

After 1840 the Disciples had little real contact with radical economic experiments and their editors generally dismissed them with an occasional unfavorable excerpt from some exchange newspaper. In 1845, in an article entitled "Associations, Communities, Phalanxes," Campbell wrote: "I regard all such schemes as more or less utopian, unnatural, and

---

[91]See Thomas R. O'Dea, *The Mormons* (Chicago: The University of Chicago Press, 1957), pp. 186-197.

[92]"The Neotrophian Magazine," *M.H.*, 5th S., II (March, 1859), 173.

[93]"Tour of Forty Days," *M.H.*, 4th S., IV (January, 1851), 17.

inexpedient."[94] Disciples were never fertile soil for social radicalism; by 1840 they were not even interested.

RUMBLINGS OF THE FUTURE

"But Philip . . . preached in all the cities, till he came to Caesarea." Acts 8:40.

In his corresponding secretary's report to the American Christian Missionary Society in 1858 Isaac Errett bemoaned the weakness of the Disciples in the cities:

> With scarcely an exception, we are weak, very weak in the great centers of wealth and power. Philadelphia, Cincinnati, St. Louis, Richmond, Nashville, Springfield, Ill., have each but one pastor, and these men, with their churches, alone, with fearful odds against them, with even the jealousies of our own country population to contend against, have to labor with but little of the sympathy to which they are justly entitled. Washington, New York, Baltimore, Lexington, Wheeling, Peoria, and other large cities, have no pastors. In Boston, Buffalo, Pittsburgh, Cleveland, Columbus, the cause has not even a name to live. In New Orleans the church is in ruins. In Chicago it is only within the last year that a house of worship has been erected.[95]

Errett's statement is misleading; by 1865 there were significant Disciples memberships in such cities as St. Louis, Nashville, Cincinnati, Lexington, Louisville, and Indianapolis. The lack of pastors was more the result of deep-seated prejudices against the "pastor system" than an overwhelming absence of churches in these Western cities. If the Disciples were still largely rural in 1865, they were not without a growing urban membership. More significant was the open rift which was already developing between urban and rural congregations.[96] Errett's analysis is prophetic of the bitterness which culminated in the post-Civil War years between "city pastors" and less sophisticated, less educated, and less secure "old fogies."

As a matter of fact, the Disciples had never been uninterested in city evangelization. If the cities were particularly wicked, they were especially in need of evangelization. Alexander Campbell wrote in 1834: "But the

---

[94]*M.H.*, 3d S., II (March, 1845), 136.

[95]*Report of the Proceedings of the Anniversary Meeting of the American Christian Missionary Society, Held in Cincinnati, October 19, 20, 21, 1858* (Cincinnati: C. B. Bentley and Co., Printers, 1858), p. 45.

[96]See "The Idol, Fashion," *M.H.*, N.S., VII (February, 1843), 65-68; "Proposals," *M.H.*, V (April, 1834), 188-192; John R. Howard, "Cities," *Christian Age and Protestant Unionist*, VI (January 4, 1850), 2.

greatest need for evangelical, or what some call missionary labors, appears
to exist in the eastern cities."[97] Such pleas remained scattered during the
years before 1865, but it was becoming obvious by this time that the Disciples were no longer just a rural movement.[98] The interest of Disciples
in urban problems in the post-Civil War period was far greater than a
census of the church's rural and urban membership might indicate. Beginning in the decade of the 1850's city editors, city preachers, and
city churches played an increasingly important part in the molding of the
thought of the church.

In the years before the Civil War, however, only a few of the most informed and most perceptive leaders of the church were concerned about
the rapidly developing social ills connected with urbanization and industrialization. During his 1847-48 trip to the British Isles Alexander Campbell saw some of the great social problems that were to plague post-Civil
War America. Campbell recognized the fact that the class inequalities
generated by the industrial revolution was an explosive problem: "Men
may keep silence for a time, but they will speak at last; after words they
advance to blows; and then, alas for him that has to fight alone against a
thousand!"[99] In 1848 he was not sure that there was "any cure" for these
problems and bluntly advised that "we have, as Christians, little to do
with such matters."[100]

And yet the whole problem of industrial dislocation was disturbing to
the essentially optimistic postmillennial orientation of the reformer. He
believed that the Anglo-Saxon Protestants of England and America were
to lead in the introduction of the millennium and such abject economic
injustice would have to be relieved. "The people must be employed," he
warned shortly after his return from England. The only real attempt that
Campbell made to solve these problems was typical of his agrarian emphasis. He believed that the American West was the only possible safety
valve for chronic unemployment and overproduction. He wrote: "An

---

[97]"Proposals," *M.H.*, V (April, 1834), 190.

[98]For examples of articles stressing city evangelization see A. C., "Letter from
Europe—No. V," *M.H.*, 3d S., IV (September, 1847), 517-526; E. E. Orvis, "An
Important Consideration," *The Disciple*, I (April, 1852), 315-316.

[99]"Letters from Europe—No. V," *M.H.*, 3d S., IV (September, 1847), 526.

[100]"Letters from Europe—No. XXXV," *M.H.*, 3d S., V (December, 1848), 668.

Agrarian spirit has gone abroad, and who can restrain it? . . . Other new settlements must be formed, new outlets for industry must be created, and more security of reward must be guaranteed."[101] But if Campbell failed to come to grips with the real issues of the emerging industrial and urban problems, he was not unconcerned about them and he firmly believed that economic injustice must be alleviated before the kingdom of millennium could commence.

Campbell's agrarian solution to the economic problems of his day probably was typical of the views of most Disciples. Jacob Creath, Jr. made a similar proposal in the *Christian Evangelist* in 1858:

I propose that the Congress of the United States give one of our Territories to the poor men, citizens of the United States, who have FAMILIES. Say that they shall prove or swear that they are not worth more than three hundred dollars in property and money after their debts are paid, they shall be allowed an hundred acres of land in said Territory free of charge, and they and their families shall be required to live on it and cultivate it. . . . Single men not to possess any land in said Territory, nor rich men. It shall be the land of poor men with families.

Creath suggested to Daniel Bates, the editor of the paper, that his plan be forwarded to several of the Western congressmen and that Disciples preachers should agitate for such a reform. While Bates considered Creath's idea "wise and benevolent," he believed that as long as "party interests absorb the entire attention of such a large number of our lawmakers" it would hardly be successful.[102]

But if most Disciples before 1865 remained unaware of the deeper implications of the rising capital-labor antagonism, there were a few prophets with real insight. Probably the most perceptive was Charles L. Loos, widely respected teacher and preacher. Loos, a German immigrant, was fully conversant with the continental currents of radical thought in the early 1860's and warned that the great challenge to the church in the future would be the rising mass of unchurched city workers. Loos early recognized the fact that this was no longer a European problem but that there was already a "great body of very active . . . social agitators . . . in our land." He refused to stereotype the labor leaders as "rabble" but insisted

---

[101]"An Address," *M.H.*, 3d S., VII (May, 1850), 241-272.

[102]"Suggestion," *C.E.*, IX (January, 1858), 30-31. See, also, R. French Ferguson, "Distress," *C.J.*, II (February 10, 1844), 393-394; "The Poor Man's Story," *C.J.*, II (September 30, 1843), 91-92.

that many of them were "very gifted, and talented, and often highly educated" and warned that many of their grievances were just. Loos condemned the "half-secular church establishment, that is busy with its secular interests" and placed a major share of the blame for lower-class discontent on the churches. The only solution he proposed prior to 1865 was "preaching the gospel to the poor" but he was never unaware of the magnitude or the complexity of the problems—and he was interested.[103]

The liberal Kentucky preacher, Lewis L. Pinkerton, also showed keen perception into the failure of American religion to deal with the basic problems of economic injustice in an address in 1858 entitled, "Is the Civilization of Europe and the United States Preferable to Barbarism?" Pinkerton charged that the nation had become enslaved to the industrial and plantation aristocracy. He protested that American religion, instead of attacking these evils, had become subservient to the interests of the capitalist:

I strongly suspect that our civilization and our religion are not separable; and as to Christianity proper, it has nothing to do with our civilization. There is not a well informed, thoughtful man in Europe or America who does not know and feel that our civilization and the religion of Jesus are direct antagonists.[104]

The minority in the church who recognized serious problems in the distribution of wealth in American society prior to 1865 generally believed that the spread of individual Christian ethics was the only solution to these ills. John Campbell suggested that this was the only "safety valve" which could save American society: "The only thing that can save us from the pride, selfishness, avarice and wickedness which the commercial spirit produces, is to engage, heart and hand in the illumination, and improvement, moral and religious, of the world. This is the only safety valve, which will prevent an explosion."[105]

The practical and specific problems of the city worker were seldom encountered by Disciples leaders prior to 1865. In 1845, while living in Pittsburgh, Walter Scott became interested in the fight of the "factory

---

[103]See C. L. Loos, "Infidelity in Our Land—No. 2," *M.H.*, 5th S., VII (May, 1864), 202-207; C.L.L., "Popular Infidelity in London," *M.H.*, XXXVI (June, 1865), 264-270.

[104]John Shackleford, Jr., *Life, Letters and Addresses of Dr. L. L. Pinkerton* (Cincinnati: Chase & Hall, Publishers, 1876), p. 223.

[105]"The Past Year," *Evangelist*, VIII (January, 1840), 17.

girls" of that city for a ten-hour working day. During a strike, Scott attended one of their discussion meetings and was invited to preside. After this experience he wrote an article supporting the women in their efforts. Scott believed that now was the time to establish "right and safe rules" to govern the relationship between employer and employee. He even gave tentative approval to the principle of coercion:

These girls may be blamed for having dared to force their employers into measures; but the fact is that if it is the duty of the masters to do this, we must not be surprised if they require to be compelled to it, for in higher duties than this we all need admonition. "Go compel them to come in," are the words of our Redeemer used in relation to divine things.[106]

Walter Scott was certainly not a social radical in 1845; he accepted the old economic precepts of agrarian, middle-American society as surely as any of his contemporaries, but he was no aristocrat and, when he encountered the struggle of the disinherited on the urban level, there was really no question in his mind about whose side righteousness was on.

THE ECONOMIC PATTERN

"If there come unto your assembly a man with a gold ring, and goodly apparel, and there come in also a poor man in vile raiment; and ye have respect to him that weareth gay clothing; . . . are ye not then partial in yourselves, and become judges of evil thoughts?" James 3:2-4.

The pulse of the Disciples of Christ throbbed in unison with the heartbeat of Christian America in the years before 1865. Disciples were convinced that the Bible taught a Christian to be frugal and industrious but they were just as sure that it was hard for a rich man to enter the kingdom. They were never psychologically radical enough to participate in communal economic experiments but they could be quite disrespectful of established wealth. Throughout the ante-bellum period most Disciples were both ardent supporters and caustic critics of the American economic order.

In the years following 1830, however, the two economic emphases in Disciples thought became more and more obviously involved in the emergence of sectarian and denominational moods in the movement. It

---

[106]"The Factory Girls," *P.U.*, I (September 24, 1845), 166. See, also, "The Needlewomen of Our Great Cities," *Ladies' Christian Annual*, II (August, 1853), 71-73.

became increasingly difficult for leaders of the Disciples to find a Christian message which was compatible with both of these economic emphases. As a matter of fact, as the Disciples slowly divided into three theological camps, "liberals," "conservatives," and "middle-of-the-roaders," they sifted into three economic groups: the rural dispossessed, the rural middle class, and a group of middle-class city members. Although all of these groups were ill-defined before 1865, and the middle-class urban emphasis was just beginning to form, it was becoming increasingly apparent that the trisection of the body was economic as well as theological.

The importance of economic factors in motivating internal strife was clearly evident by 1865. Interchurch organization, church liturgy, meetinghouse standards, the place of men of wealth within the church, and the problem of city evangelization were quite obviously economic as well as theological questions. It is certainly not without significance that "liberal innovations" were spawned in the most sophisticated and wealthiest segments of the movement—in the cities and in Kentucky. The rockribbed conservative emphasis more and more centered around the old pioneer preachers and increasingly gravitated toward the agrarian South. Isaac Errett's 1858 condemnation of the "jealousies of our country population" against the city "pastors" was a perceptive insight into the deep economic tensions within the church.[107] While a large group of moderate Disciples retained the dichotomic, economic philosophy of the "rural church," many church leaders were becoming markedly more sectarian or denominational in their attitudes toward economic problems.[108]

Of course, an economic interpretation of religious history certainly does not explain the motivation of all Disciples leaders. Some men of wealth

---

[107]*Proceedings* of the American Christian Missionary Society, 1858, p. 45.

[108]Although other sociological factors were involved (especially the heritage of sectional bitterness), the two major divisions in the restoration movement obviously have had deep economic undertones. The late nineteenth-century separation of the Church of Christ was, at least in part, a defection of the most radical lower-class element in the stream. But even after this defection the Disciples were by no means a perfectly homogeneous body. The twentieth-century "independent-co-operative" schism within the church unquestionably had rural-urban connotations. The early twentieth-century religious censuses would be a fertile source for county-by-county sociological studies of the first of these divisions. The yearbooks of the independent group could be used as the basis for similar studies of the second schism. See Alfred T. DeGroot, *Church of Christ Number Two* (privately printed, 1956).

and culture were theologically conservative, while some rural churches and uncultured preachers were liberals. The development of diverging theological minds in the movement originated in the personalities of men who acted from a diversity of motives but more and more as the church disintegrated it separated into antagonistic economic groups.

But Disciples leaders were prophets in American society as well as prophets of it—if their environment influenced them, they also tried to Christianize their fellowmen. Throughout the period before 1865, they maintained a constant protest against economic injustice. Sympathy for the poor, humanitarian benevolence, and opposition to unethical business practices were a part of both the sociological and Christian heritage of the Disciples. While the millennium they anticipated was generally an agrarian one and always a capitalistic one, it demanded the abolition of economic injustice. The midnineteenth-century Disciple, like the mid-nineteenth-century American, was almost totally unaware of the cataclysmic economic revolution growing around him; he firmly believed that the conversion of individuals to the spirit of Christianity was the tonic needed by immoral society—but he was never apathetic toward the poor. If pre-Civil War Disciples leaders failed to defend the social rights of the common man adequately, it was a failure of the head and not of the heart.[109]

---

[109]Charles C. Cole, Jr., says of the pre-Civil War Northern evangelists: "Although they could have provided leadership for the lower classes, they were not really interested in the problems of laborers and their message contained a moral solution rather than an economic one." *Northern Evangelists,* p. 191. But Cole's statement is only half true—at least as far as Disciples are concerned. While the solution they offered to the economic ills of the nation was a "moral one," and perhaps an unrealistic one, it was the best they knew how to offer. They were certainly not uninterested in the problems of the poor. H. Richard Niebuhr's summation of the attitudes of evangelical leaders is more accurate: "In all their search for the redeeming word which might direct misery on the way to joy, turn injustice into righteousness . . . Gladden, Rauschenbusch and their colleagues carried with them a vision and a promise which had been written not on stone or paper but on fleshly tables of the heart by a fresh and nation-wide experience of the resurrection." *Kingdom of God,* pp. 162-163. The growing troop of leaders of the Disciples who joined in the liberal Christian protest against industrial economic injustice in the 1880's and 1890's were newly equipped with a firsthand knowledge of these evils and were university trained in such new fields as sociology and economics but their Christian concern for disinherited man was by no means a new development in the history of the movement.

CHAPTER IV

SLAVERY AND SECTIONALISM – AN ENTERING WEDGE
AMERICAN SLAVERY

ON THE EVE of the American Civil War there were about 4,000,000 Negro slaves in the South, concentrated, for the most part, in the areas where Southern staple crops were produced. Legally the slave had few rights and was protected largely by his own economic value or by the humanity of his owner. The life of the slave was hard at best; at worst it could be wretched.[1]

Slaveholders generally had no objections to religious activity among the slaves.[2] Prior to 1830 it was not uncommon to find Negro congregations on the larger plantations and in many of the Southern cities; Negro preachers were found in almost every community. There was always a good deal of local variation in the slave code but increasingly after 1830, as the radical abolitionist campaign gained momentum, the religious privileges of the Negroes were constricted. More and more the Negroes who received any religious instruction were required to attend the white churches.

---

[1]For general surveys of American Negro slavery, see John Hope Franklin, *From Slavery to Freedom* (2d ed. rev.; New York: Alfred A. Knopf, 1956); Kenneth Milton Stampp, *The Peculiar Institution* (New York: Alfred A. Knopf, 1956).

[2]For general accounts of the relationship of the American churches to Negro slavery, see W. D. Weatherford, *American Churches and the Negro* (Boston: The Christopher Publishing House, 1957); Carter G. Woodson, *The History of the Negro Church* (Washington: The Associated Publishers, 1921); William E. Burghardt Du Bois, *The Negro Church* (Atlanta: The Atlanta University Press, 1903).

Antislavery agitation never completely died out after its beginnings in the humanitarian philosophy of the eighteenth century and after 1815 emancipation sentiment increased rapidly in both North and South.[3] This moderate movement culminated in 1817 with the formation of the American Colonization Society.

In the decade 1830-1840 new and militant leaders assumed direction of the abolition movement. The radical abolition impulse which developed after 1830 was dominated in the East by the overpowering personality of William Lloyd Garrison and in the West by a fervent leadership which included Theodore Weld and James G. Birney. The radical abolition crusade was united around one demand—the immediate emancipation of the Negro.

The outbreak of militant abolitionism in the North accelerated the development of a proslavery movement which had been growing in the South since the debate over the Missouri Compromise.[4] A full-blown proslavery philosophy was developed; religious, economic, and anthropological arguments were compounded to demonstrate that slavery was a positive blessing to both whites and Negroes. Although the South never completely accepted the proslavery rationale, it became increasingly unpopular to voice antislavery views in most Southern communities.

The series of crises during the hectic decade that ended with the election of Abraham Lincoln to the presidency in 1860 and included the Compromise of 1850, *Uncle Tom's Cabin,* the Kansas-Nebraska Act, the Dred Scott Decision, and John Brown's Harper's Ferry raid, stirred the slavery issue to increasingly fervent heights. Moderates in both sections of the country slowly lost control. Radical abolitionists in the North and fire-eating secessionists in the South became more numerous and more

---

[3] Two general sketches of the abolition movement are Franklin, *Slavery to Freedom* and Gilbert Hobbs Barnes, *The Anti-Slavery Impulse 1830-1844* (New York: D. Appleton-Century Company Incorporated, 1933).

[4] For general accounts of the development of proslavery thought, see Franklin, *Slavery to Freedom;* William Sumner Jenkins, *Pro-Slavery Thought in the Old South* (Chapel Hill: The University of North Carolina Press, 1935); Clement Eaton, *Freedom of Thought in the Old South* (Durham, N. C.: Duke University Press, 1940).

vocal. By 1861 every major intersectional Protestant denomination had divided. Although moderates remained in both sections, in the churches and in politics, the radicals did their work well; the nation and its churches were choosing between two camps; the country was "a house divided."

BLACK DISCIPLES

"Servants, obey in all things them that are your masters." Colossians 3:22.

Negro slavery preceded the Disciples of Christ to Kentucky by several decades. When the full impact of the restoration movement struck Kentucky in the 1820's and 1830's like a "Baptist plague" it simply gulped down slavery, along with every other social problem in that exuberant and youthful society, to be digested later—when there was time.

The Eleventh Annual Report of the American and Foreign Anti-Slavery Society noted that in 1851 the "Campbellites" owned 101,000 slaves.[5] According to this report only Baptists and Methodists held more slaves than Disciples. This would mean, as recent Disciples historians have pointed out, "Disciples on a per capita basis were the leading slave-holding religious body in the United States."[6] While these statistics are certainly open to question, it is plain that the Disciples, as every other religious group with members in the ante-bellum South, was deeply involved in the slavery dilemma.[7]

---

[5]*The Annual Report of the American and Foreign Anti-Slavery Society* (New York: William Harned, Office Agent, 1851), p. 56. For a general discussion of Negro Disciples before 1861 see Robert O. Fife, "Alexander Campbell and the Christian Church in the Slavery Controversy" (unpublished Ph.D. thesis, University of Indiana, 1960), pp. 102-127.

[6]Garrison and DeGroot, *The Disciples of Christ*, p. 468.

[7]There is, of course, no way to estimate accurately the number of slaves held by ante-bellum Disciples. In 1860 there were about 800 Christian churches in the slave-holding states; a vast majority of these were small congregations in the border states of Tennessee, Kentucky, and Missouri. On the other hand, many of the aristocratic, slaveholding families of Kentucky and Missouri were early converts to the Christian church and there were small but wealthy congregations of Disciples scattered throughout the deep South.

Although Disciples were not extraordinarily active in evangelizing among the Negroes, most of their churches in the ante-bellum South followed the prevalent pattern of having slaves as members.[8] The slaves were listed in the roll books as regular members of the congregation, usually with the comment "slave" or "negro" appended to their names, along with the name of their master. Those who were church members were often subjects of discipline and numerous entries in old church minute books note the exclusion of slaves who "apostatized."[9] "Apostasy" was not the only way the church could lose its slave members. In the minute book of the Canton, Missouri, church the name "Amanda, the slave of H. White" was dropped from the church roll with the remarks: "sold at St. Louis."[10]

Independent Negro congregations were rare in the South among all religious groups, especially after 1830. Almost all of the independent Negro Disciples churches before the Civil War were located either in

---

[8]The Negroes attended services along with the whites and were seated in a segregated section of the building; sometimes galleries were built for their special use. The number of Negro Disciples in the ante-bellum period is very difficult to estimate. The Methodists and Baptists, who pioneered in religious work among the Negroes, each had around 200,000 colored members by 1860. There were only about 20,000 Negro Presbyterians. Carter G. Woodson accounts for this divergence in two ways: the Presbyterians were slower in beginning evangelistic work among the Negroes and their rigid, unemotional doctrinal appeal was less attractive among the slaves. Every indication is that the same factors hindered the work of Disciples in this area. Ten thousand would probably be a liberal estimate of the number of Negro Disciples prior to 1866. See Woodson, *History of Negro Church*, pp 97-99; Du Bois, *The Negro Church*, p. 29; Thomas M. Henley, "For the Christian Examiner," *Christian Examiner*, II (August, 1831), 169-172. Clifton E. Olmstead says that the churches of Disciples were the "most popular" among the Negroes, with the exception of the Baptists and the Methodists, but he gives no hint as to how he reached this conclusion. *Religion in the United States*, pp. 277-280.

[9]Church discipline sometimes served a useful purpose as a part of the slave code. In 1818 the South Elkhorn Church in Kentucky "excluded" a Negro man for "Running away and other Disorderly Conduct." Church Register and Record of the South Elkhorn Church, 1817-1897. For some interesting cases of slave discipline, see Charles Crossfield Ware, *North Carolina Disciples of Christ* (St. Louis: Christian Board of Publication, 1921), pp. 223-229.

[10]Church Record of the Congregation Between Canton and Sully, Missouri, 1850-1866, Disciples of Christ Historical Society, Nashville, Tennessee.

the cities of Kentucky or in the North.[11] A notice of a "very interesting congregation of colored people" in Newtonia, Mississippi, in 1848 is the only reference to a Negro church in the deep South in any of the early Disciples periodicals.[12]

Although there were a few Negro preachers among the Disciples in such cities as Cincinnati, Lexington, Louisville, and Nashville, there was never any concentrated effort to encourage their training or support.[13] The most widely known pre-war Negro Disciples preacher was a Kentucky slave, Alexander Cross. In the late 1840's David S. Burnet became interested in sending a Negro missionary to work among the colonized Negroes in Liberia.[14] As early as 1850 Burnet was feeling out brotherhood sentiment on sending a "colored man" to Liberia; he insisted that it was "not impossible that such a one can be found in Cincinnati."[15]

The man who was finally settled on for the job was Alexander Cross, a slave in Christian County, Kentucky. Arrangements were made for Cross to be freed and the churches of Christian County supported him while he trained for the ministry. In 1853 he appeared before the convention of the American Christian Missionary Society and an appeal was made for the churches to send him to Africa. A collection was taken and then

---

[11]Claude Walker, in his study of Negro Disciples in Kentucky, lists four independent Negro congregations in that state. "Negro Disciples in Kentucky, 1840-1925" (unpublished B. D. Thesis, College of the Bible, 1959), pp. 4-21. There were a few scattered Negro churches in the North. See Shaw, *Buckeye Disciples,* p. 144; Gilbert Lamb and Stephen Burgess, "To the Church of Christ," *Western Reformer,* VI (April, 1848), 378-379; "Editor's Table," *Christian Evangelist,* VII (August, 1856), 385-386.

[12]D. L. Phares, "The Progress of Reform," *M.H.,* 3d S., V (May, 1848), 299. The Nashville, Tennessee, church adopted a Sunday school program which gave the Negroes some independence: "There are also two colored Sunday Schools under the immediate control of colored members; but over which the Church exercises a general superintendence. They number 125 scholars." "The Church of Jesus Christ in Nashville, Tennessee," *Christian Magazine,* II (November, 1849), 422-423. Alexander Campbell was pleased with the Nashville arrangement and commended it to the other Southern churches. "Every Church Ought to Have Its Sunday School," *M.H.,* 3d S., IV (April, 1847), 422-423.

[13]In 1844 R. French Ferguson published in the *Christian Journal* of Harrodsburg, Kentucky, a plea for support for Negro preachers to work among the slaves but such appeals were rare. "Preaching to Slaves," *C.J.,* III (June 1, 1844), 166.

[14]Keith, *Burnet,* pp. 149-151.

[15]D.S.B., "Missions in Africa," *Proclamation and Reformer,* I (November, 1850), 673-674.

in a stirring climax "Cross . . . came forward in the presence of the Assembly, and, whilst, the choir were singing an appropriate hymn, received from the Brethren and Sisters generally, with much feeling, the hand of fellowship and love."[16] Cross departed for Africa almost immediately and arrived in Liberia in January, 1854, but after only two months' work he died suddenly of "immigrant's fever." His death was a tragic blow to what, in many ways, was the most promising missionary enterprise in early Disciples history and a project which might have sharpened and unified the church's interest in the problem of the Negro. Scattered pleas for a reinstitution of the Liberian mission continued through the 1860's but the anemic financial condition of the missionary society, the difficulties involved in finding a suitable missionary, and the general apathy of the church's members toward the Negro forestalled the development of a serious project.[17]

In short, the story of ante-bellum Disciples and the Negro is not essentially different from that of any other religious communion. Although most Disciples unquestionably would have contended that all Christians were equal before God, there is no doubt that the Negro slave was a second-class church member. Most of the Southern churches had Negro members but there was never a concentrated or organized effort to make Disciples among the slaves. The rapidly expanding Disciples apparently did not share in the awakened interest which brought so many Negroes into the Baptist and Methodist churches after 1830. A number of factors were involved in the church's lag in this area: the cold and unemotional character of their doctrine and worship failed to attract large numbers of Negroes; they were almost totally preoccupied with proselyting members from the other frontier sects during this era of expansion; they lacked any effective organizational structure during most of the period; the first attempt by the church to sponsor a Negro mission ended in a tragic and abortive failure. But probably most important, most Southern Disciples

---

[16]Report of the Proceedings of the Convention of Churches of Christ at the Anniversaries of the American Christian Bible, Missionary and Publication Societies: Held in Cincinnati, October 18th, 19th, and 20th, 1853 (Cincinnati: American Christian Publication Society, 1853), pp. 29-45.

[17]See Proceedings of the Convention of Churches of Christ, 1854, pp. 48-49; Report of Proceedings of the Anniversary Meeting of the American Christian Missionary Society, Held in Cincinnati, October 23, 24, 25, 1860 (Cincinnati: H. S. Bosworth, C. B. Bentley and Co., Printers, 1860), p. 16.

shared the apathy of the section's intellectual leaders toward the whole Negro question. Alexander Campbell once made the statement: "Much as I may sympathize with a black man, I love a white man more."[18] What Campbell stated, the church demonstrated.

HUMANITARIAN IMPULSE, 1800-1845

"This is my commandment, that ye love one another." John 15:12.

Religious revivalism, with its strong emphasis on the dignity of the individual, was the seedbed for many American social reform movements. The great Western revivals of the early nineteenth century were a powerful stimulant to antislavery sentiment. Pioneer Baptist, Methodist, and Presbyterian evangelists preached emancipation from slavery as well as emancipation from sin. During the first decade of the nineteenth century manumissions increased 150 percent in the areas of the West where revivalism was most fervent.[19] It was in this incubator of humanitarianism that the early Christian movement was hatched.

In the early years of the revival-spawned Christian stream in Kentucky antislavery sentiment was an important part of the reformers' message. David Purviance, an early Christian church leader, disclosed that after the great revival at Cane Ridge "a majority of the members of Caneridge church that owned slaves, liberated them."[20] It was during this early emotionally charged period that Barton Stone determined to free his slaves.[21] Throughout his life Stone remained true to this commitment and some years later, when he inherited several slaves, he liberated them and arranged for their transportation to Liberia through the American Colonization Society.[22]

Stone remained in the main stream of the humanitarian emancipation and colonization crusade so widespread in the South during the 1820's

---

[18]"Our Position to American Slavery—No. V," *M.H.*, 3d S., II (May, 1845), 234.

[19]See Cleveland, *Great Revival*, p. 158.

[20]Levi Purviance, *The Biography of Elder David Purviance* (Dayton: B.F. & C.W. Ells, 1848), p. 57.

[21]James B. Rogers, *The Cane Ridge Meeting-House* (Cincinnati: The Standard Publishing Company, 1910), p. 165.

[22]See F.P.R., "A Request," and B. W. Stone, "Reply," *Christian Messenger*, IV (December, 1830), 276-277.

and early 1830's. He rejected radical abolitionism as unrealistic: "To free them among us, and let them live among us, is impolitic, as stubborn facts have proved. Were those now in slavery among us to be thus emancipated, I would instantly remove to a distant land beyond their reach."[23] Stone thought the only possible solution to the American slavery problem was the American Colonization Society and he resolutely pressed its claims through the *Christian Messenger*. In 1830 he instigated the formation of a chapter of the colonization society in Georgetown, Kentucky, and was elected its first president. Stone used his paper to urge members of the Christian church to deliver their slaves to the colonization society and under his leadership the Georgetown chapter succeeded in transporting a number of freed Negroes to Liberia.[24]

In the early 1830's it became more and more apparent that the moderate antislavery approach was making no real inroads into the dilemma of American slavery and by 1835 the scheme was suffering its death agonies before a national audience. Lyman Beecher, the die-hard champion of moderate abolitionism and president of Lane Theological Seminary in Cincinnati, was completely routed in 1835 by the radical Theodore Weld in a campaign which resulted in a mass exodus of students from Lane to Oberlin College. The radical abolitionist campaign in the West reopened with unprecedented fervor in the mid-1830's.

From 1831 to 1835 Stone's hopes for emancipation and colonization steadily dimmed. He still urged the support of the American Colonization Society during these years but his enthusiasm was rapidly turning to disillusionment.[25] In 1835 Stone wavered between the alternatives of becoming a radical abolitionist or accepting the permanence of slavery and becoming a supporter of moderation and compromise. In April, 1835, he made a move toward the abolitionist position by beginning the serial publication in the *Christian Messenger* of a tract issued by the Garrisonian New

[23]"An Humble Address to Christians, on the Colonization of Free People of Color," *C.M.*, III (June, 1829), 199.

[24]See "Georgetown Colonization Society," *C.M.*, IV (June, 1830), 163-164; "Slavery," *C.M.*, V (January, 1831), 10-11; "Notice," *C.M.*, V (October, 1831), 236-237.

[25]See "Liberia," *C.M.*, VII (February, 1833), 62-64.

England Anti-Slavery Society advocating "the immediate abolition of slavery."[26] But by the end of 1835 all discussion of the slavery question had disappeared from the *Christian Messenger* and another notice of the subject did not appear for nearly nine years. In June, 1844, an editorial notice of the sectional division of the Methodist church appeared, along with a promise of some comments on the action in a later issue—but the comments never appeared.[27] In a few months Stone died, but it is obvious that he had no heart to discuss the question even if he had lived. By 1845 the slavery issue had become too dogmatic and divisive for the expansive and tolerant mind of Barton Stone.

The broad humanitarianism which characterized the thinking of Barton Stone on the slavery question was typical of most of the early preachers of the Christian movement. Practically the whole roster of first-generation leaders was actively engaged in antislavery agitation. In fact, in its early years the Kentucky Association of Christian Churches refused membership to slaveholding preachers.[28] At a meeting of the conference of Christian churches in Northern Kentucky in 1827 a resolution was passed expressing "deep interest in the colonization society."[29]

Many of the early Christian church preachers were politically active abolitionists. David Purviance, who served in the Kentucky legislature from 1797 to 1803 as a representative of Bourbon county, campaigned vigorously for "gradual emancipation." Purviance, following a pattern of many of the early preachers of the movement who left Kentucky because of their aversion to slavery, moved to Ohio in 1809 and was immediately elected to two terms in the state senate in 1810 and 1812. His outspoken protests against the "black laws" of that state, which required "bail" from all free Negroes to assure that they would not become

---

[26]"Address to the People of the United States on Slavery, cont.," *C.M.,* IX (May, 1835), 97-103.

[27]"Notice," *C.M.,* XIV (June, 1844), 61.

[28]N. Summerbell (ed.), *The Autobiography of Elder Matthew Gardner* (Dayton, Ohio: Christian Publishing Association, 1874), p. 44.

[29]"The Elders and Brethren of the Church of Christ, North of Kentucky, assembled in Conference, to the Christian churches in Kentucky," *C.M.,* I (April 25, 1827), 139-141.

"township charges," led to his defeat in 1814.[30]

The antislavery impulse in the Christian movement had deep roots both in the equalitarian frontier tradition of its native Kentucky and in its humanitarian religious heritage from the Great Revival. The most fervent devotees of the abolitionist philosophy took their religion with them to the new states of the Northwest; those who remained in Kentucky settled into a disillusioned acceptance of a seemingly insurmountable social problem.[31] The Indiana and Illinois abolitionists among the Disciples of the 1850's were in a very real sense the spiritual descendants of the early Christian preachers. Equally as important, the moderate, passive attitude of most Kentucky Disciples leaders toward slavery in the critical decade of the 1850's was, in part, an inheritance from Barton Stone.

CAMPBELL AND COMMON SENSE, 1800-1845
"Let your moderation be known unto all men." Philippians 4:5.

Although antislavery sentiment probably was not as universal among the early reforming Baptists of the Campbell movement as it was among the Christians, it was nonetheless widespread. Some of the early Baptist churches in Kentucky were so fervently antislavery that they formed an independent association in 1807 called "Friends of Humanity."[32] This

---

[30]Purviance, *David Purviance,* pp. 17-38. William Kincaide was an antislavery leader in the Illinois state senate. Samuel Kyle moved from Kentucky because of his antislavery sentiments and was elected to the Ohio legislature. Other early Christian preachers who moved from Kentucky into the states of the Northwest because of their aversion to slavery included John B. New, Elijah Goodwin, S. G. Mitchell, and Daniel Travis. See Summerbell, *Autobiography of Gardner,* p. 44; N. Dwight Harris, *The History of Negro Servitude in Illinois* (Chicago: A. C. McClury & Co., 1904), p. 41; Madison Evans, *Biographical Sketches of the Pioneer Preachers of Indiana* (Philadelphia: J. Challen & Sons, 1862), pp. 79-80, 184; S. G. Mitchell, "An Oration," *C.M.,* III (May, 1829), 163-165; B. W. Stone, "Extracts of a Letter from Bro. Daniel Travis of Ill.," *C.M.,* VIII (March, 1834), 94-95. As late as the 1850's there was a considerable migration of antislavery Disciples preachers out of Kentucky. T. M. Allen to J. A. Gano, November 10, 1851, John Allen Gano Papers, Disciples of Christ Historical Society, Nashville, Tennessee.

[31]William Warren Sweet notes this same pattern among the frontier Methodists. See *Revivalism in America,* p. 155.

[32]See Cleveland, *Great Revival,* p. 157; Sweet, *Revivalism in America,* p. 156; Sweet, *Baptists,* pp. 77-102.

group supplied some of the first Kentucky congregations to join the Disciples.[33]

The personal convictions of Thomas and Alexander Campbell were strongly antislavery. Thomas Campbell was conducting a flourishing frontier school in Burlington, Kentucky, in 1819, but suddenly abandoned the enterprise when he was mildly reprimanded by a friend for violating the state law prohibiting teaching a public assembly of Negroes. Campbell, "dumbfounded and well-nigh heartbroken," refused to continue to live in a state where he could not teach the Bible to a part of the population and resettled in Washington County, Pennsylvania.[34] In his own personal relation to slavery, he remained until his death ardently antislavery and as late as 1845 was considered by James G. Birney and other western abolitionists as a valuable asset to their cause in Virginia.[35] Alexander Campbell shared his father's aversion to the institution and freed "the two or three slaves he had under his control, as soon as they were sufficiently grown to provide for themselves."[36]

In the first issue of the *Christian Baptist* in 1823 Campbell attacked the injustices of a social system which separated "the wife from the embraces of her husband" because "his skin is a shade darker than the standard color of the times."[37] But Campbell had little time for social issues during the iconoclastic days of the *Christian Baptist.* However, when he published the prospectus of the *Millennial Harbinger* in 1829 he listed among the subjects which "shall be attended to:" "Disquisitions upon the treatment of African slaves, as preparatory to their emancipation and exaltation from their present degraded condition."[38]

The first issue of the *Harbinger* indicated that Campbell meant what he said. In the opening number he commended to his readers a recent speech made by Henry Clay before the American Colonization Society in which the Kentucky statesman devoloped his well-known philosophy of

---

[33]Evans, *Pioneer Preachers*, p. 128.

[34]William Herbert Hanna, *Thomas Campbell* (Cincinnati: The Standard Publishing Company), pp. 142-143.

[35]Dwight L. Dumond (ed.), *Letters of James Gillespie Birney 1831-1857* (2 vols.; New York: D. Appleton-Century Company Incorporated, 1938), II, 934-935.

[36]Richardson, *Memoirs of Alexander Campbell,* I, 502.

[37]"The Christian Religion," *Christian Baptist,* I (August, 1823), 18.

[38]"Proposals," *C.B.,* VII (October 5, 1829), 67.

gradual abolition.[39] Clay, in common with many prominent Southerners, maintained throughout his career the antislavery temperament of a pre-Garrisonian moderate and periodically promoted plans for gradual abolition and colonization. Campbell, who was personally acquainted with Clay and shared with him a relationship of high mutual respect, consistently agreed with the politician's views on slavery and on more than one occasion brought them to the attention of the Disciples of Christ.

In the same issue of the *Harbinger* Campbell condemned a move in the Georgia legislature designed to prohibit teaching slaves to read and write. He considered the action ample provocation for the most outspoken attack he ever made on slavery: "Knowledge and slavery are incompatible. . . . Let this barbarous law of Georgia be out-Heroded by any enactment of any age or country. Produce its superior who can."[40] An unsuccessful attempt by the Virginia legislature to pass a similar law just a few weeks later prompted Campbell to reflect on the problem with more moderation and concern. Such laws were to him "tyrannical, unjust, and impious" and the fact that the Southern whites considered them necessary was emphatic proof that it was the slaveholders who were the slaves. But even when the editor was most concerned and indignant, he was not a radical; he assured his readers that he had not become a "visionary on this subject." Before closing the article he added that "the relation of master and servant . . . has been found in all ages and countries" and that it would probably exist in the millennium.[41]

A bloody slave insurrection in Southampton, Virginia, led by the Negro preacher, Nat Turner, in late 1831, ignited an extended debate in the state legislature in Richmond on the whole problem of slavery. Emancipation schemes were openly advocated by many leading Virginia statesmen.[42] In the first two issues of the 1832 *Millennial Harbinger* Campbell

[39]"Kentucky Anti-Slavery," *M.H.*, I (January 4, 1830), 36-37.

[40]"Georgia Slaves," *M.H.*, I (January 4, 1830), 47.

[41]"Emancipation of White Slaves," *M.H.*, I (March 1, 1830), 128-132. Despite his assurances that he was not a "visionary," Campbell's outspoken criticism of slavery brought an immediate plea for silence from an Essex, Virginia, Disciple. *M.H.*, I (April, 1830), 188-190; "Response to 'T'," *M.H.*, I (April, 1830), 191.

[42]See Theodore M. Whitfield, *Slavery Agitation in Virginia 1829-1832* (Baltimore: Johns Hopkins Press, 1930), p. 63.

predicted with exuberant enthusiasm and optimism that Virginia was about to free herself from the evils of slavery. "Often is good educed from evil," he wrote in January. He confidently addressed the legislators of the state:

It is in the power of Virginia, AS WE WELL KNOW, *and, were it our business,* COULD EASILY DEMONSTRATE, *to free herself from this evil without loss of property.* . . . But it is in her power, and the East may, doubtless, without waiting petitions from the West, rely that whatever the legislature can do to deliver us and our brethren in the East from all the curses, direct and indirect, which are found hanging upon that vine brought from Africa, they will have the countenance, support, prayers, and thanks of every *Virginian* in all the hills and valleys of the West.[43]

Campbell's interest was so intense that he revealed to his readers the emancipation plan he had intended to present as a delegate to the Virginia constitutional convention of 1829-30 until persuaded by other members of that body that such a course would be unwise at the time. His plan was simply to use the politically embarrassing government surplus to compensate slaveholders and finance the colonization of freed Negroes in Africa. Editorially he urged Henry Clay to champion such a project in Washington. He believed that "an appropriation of ten millions per annum, for 15 to 20 years, would rid this land of the curse."[44]

The Virginia debates on the slavery question in 1831 and 1832 proved disastrous to the antislavery cause in Virginia. The antislavery forces were too weak to win a victory and the upheaval solidified the proslavery forces in the state into a repressive element determined to squelch any further attempts to discuss the question publicly.[45] During the period of discussion Campbell, with many other prominent Virginians, had his whole heart in the emancipation cause—in Virginia emancipation by Virginians—and he was crushed into nearly three years of silence by its complete failure.

---

[43] "Slavery in Virginia," *M.H.,* III (January 2, 1832), 15.

[44] "The Crisis," *M.H.,* III (February, 1832), 88-93.

[45] Whitfield, *Slavery in Virginia,* pp. 133-142. Clement Eaton writes: "The turning point in the Southern attitude to slavery came about the year 1831." *Freedom of Thought,* p. 30. The theme of Eaton's book is the transition of Southern thought. The early liberal tradition became less and less acceptable to the intellectual leaders of that region.

By 1835 the same disillusionment which was so apparent in Barton Stone and other moderate antislavery leaders was becoming more and more marked in Campbell's thought. In December of that year Campbell again wrote commending his plan of compensated emancipation but not with the same exuberant optimism which marked his earlier articles— he was simply pushed into saying something. He reported that he had received "numerous and various communications on the subject of slavery" but bluntly explained that he had little heart to discuss it:

A person might as rationally expect a candid hearing in a Methodist Chapel in defense of Calvinism, or an impartial audience in a Calvinian Tabernacle in defense of Arminianism, as in this moment of feverish excitement, bordering on insanity, to expect in the South or in the North a fair and impartial, and liberal and magnanimous consideration of any question arising out of the rival interests of free and slave labor.[46]

The abolitionist element within the church grew more and more restless and in 1836 Campbell reported that he was being "assailed both in East and West at one and the same time for not 'coming out' with all decision in favor of the cause of *immediate emancipation*."[47] In an adroit article which dodged the main issue, he said that he was determined simply to work for that greatest of all reforms—Christianity.[48] In 1836 Campbell was trying to be gentle with all the sectional factions within the church; he was trying to reach some rational and moderate middle ground around which the whole church could stay united.

In the years that followed, as it became more and more apparent that the really dangerous divisive element within the Disciples was the radical abolitionists, Campbell began to turn his heavy artillery increasingly toward the North. By 1840 he was sufficiently concerned about such "rash and ultra dogmas" as the assertion that slavery was "always a sin" to draw closer than ever before to writing a slavery apologetic. He gently laid a religious framework which would accommodate both slavery and the church: "The South has said much on the patriarchial character of this institution. It was, indeed, in Abraham's time a very happy institu-

[46]"Slavery and Anti-Slavery," *M.H.*, VI (December, 1835), 587.
[47]"Abolitionism," *M.H.*, VII (June, 1836), 282.
[48]*Ibid.*, 283.

tion; and it is to be hoped that it will yet become so in the South."[49]

In an extended series of articles in 1845 Campbell elaborated his fully developed, moderate, Biblical interpretation of the slavery question. The editor's decision once again to bring the subject into open discussion was not without ample motivation. By this time the Baptists and Methodists, the two largest intersectional religious groups in the country, had either formally divided or were obviously in the process of sectional schism. The annexation of Texas in 1844 had invigorated the national abolitionist movement and, even more important to Campbell, radical abolitionism among the Disciples was increasing both in extent and intensity.[50] By 1845 Campbell was rapidly developing into a mature denominational leader and he was keenly aware of his responsibilities; he unquestionably sensed that the force of his personality in a stand for moderation might be the sole influence capable of maintaining brotherhood unity. It was time to speak: "We must, then, all submit to the new order of things and do homage to his Majesty FREE DISCUSSION."[51] He felt that the liberal and rational character of the restoration movement ought to preserve it from sectional division: "We are the only religious community in the civilized world whose principles (unless we abandon them) can preserve us from such an unfortunate predicament."[52]

The long series of *Harbinger* articles beginning in January, 1845, with a letter from Thomas Campbell and continuing through eight articles by Alexander Campbell, entitled "Our Position to American Slavery," is in sum a detailed Biblical defense of the institution of slavery. The

---

[49]"Morality of Christians—No. XVIII," *M.H.*, N. S., IV (March, 1840), 97-103. Almost immediately Campbell's article was attacked as "pro-slavery" by Gamaliel Bailey in James G. Birney's abolitionist paper, *The Philanthropist*. Bailey's onslaught only intensified Campbell's fear of radical abolitionism. "The Philanthropist and Morality of Christians—No. XVIII," *M.H.*, N. S., IV (May, 1840), 234.

[50]Campbell wrote his old friend Philip Fall of Frankfort, Kentucky: "We are passing through an ordeal of calumny and jealousy and rivalry I little thought of from several quarters—I expected a little more candor and liberality and respect for services rendered." Campbell to Fall, September, 1843, Philip Fall Papers, microfilm copy, Disciples of Christ Historical Society, Nashville, Tennessee.

[51]"Our Position to American Slavery," *M.H.*, 3d S., II (February, 1845), 50.
[52]*Ibid.*, 51.

burden of the whole Campbell *magnum opus* was that slavery was not scripturally condemned. In his fifth article he summarized his position:

Whether clearly and definitely stated or not, in what has already appeared, our position, however it may be regarded or sustained, is based on three propositions— rather, indeed, on three well established facts, viz.—1. Roman slavery, certainly no better than American slavery, pervaded all the countries in which those churches existed to which the apostolic epistles were addressed, and in which the relation of master and servant is at all alluded to.

2. In the primitive church there were masters and slaves while they were yet under the personal inspection and guidance of the Apostles themselves.

3. From a particular and full induction of every passage in the New Testament that alludes to the relation of master and slave, or to their relative duties of master and slaves, there is not any indication of the unlawfulness of the relation; but simply a recognition of it, with very clear and specific directions to the parties, how they should conduct themselves to each other in the discharge of those duties.[53]

It seemed to Campbell that such clear-cut Biblical evidence ought to preclude all radicalism among the Disciples: "AS CHRISTIANS, WE CAN LAWFULLY UNDER CHRIST, GO NO FARTHER THAN TO EXACT FROM CHRISTIAN MASTERS AND CHRISTIAN SERVANTS ALL THAT IS COMPREHENDED IN THOSE PRECEPTS."[54]

Throughout his discussion Campbell made an important distinction between what was lawful as far as the Christian was concerned and what was desirable as far as American citizens were concerned. As citizens, individual Disciples had the right to take any position on the question which they felt was expedient—so long as it was not religiously unlawful:

As American citizens, the members of our churches have the same political rights with the members of all communities. They may become 'Whigs' or 'Democrats,' 'Liberty' or 'Pro-Slavery men,' according to their views of political expedience and propriety. On these views we all have our opinions.[55]

This was Campbell's formula of union. American slavery was not a religious problem but a political one and the fundamental principle of the reformation which recognized the right to differ on nonessential, nonreligious matters ought to prevent division. He again pointed out that he personally was antislavery in sentiment but insisted that this was a

---

[53]*Ibid.*, No. V, *M.H.*, 3d S., II (May, 1845), 232.
[54]*Ibid.*, No. III, *M.H.*, 3d S., II (March, 1845), 109.
[55]*Ibid.*, No. V, *M.H.*, 3d S., II (May, 1845), 234.

political opinion and could certainly not become the basis for religious nonfellowship.[56]

Campbell obviously hoped that his discussion would close the door on the subject as an issue among the Disciples. He had given a scriptural treatment to the subject; he had devised a formula which would avoid division; he hoped the brethren would agree to relegate the whole slavery question to a position of political expediency. In actual fact, Campbell's series of articles pried open the floodgates which were already bulging under the pressure of disgruntled and impatient brethren on both sides of the momentous question—even the enormous influence of Alexander Campbell could not hold back the deluge.

ABOLITIONISM AND CONTROVERSY, 1845-1861
"If thy brother sin, rebuke him." Luke 17:3.

By 1845 extremists within the Disciples were impatiently chafing under the ban of silence imposed on them by the leaders of the movement. Belligerent abolitionism seethed through the churches of the North from two emerging centers of Disciples radicalism—the Western Reserve in northern Ohio, and central Indiana. The radical abolitionists in Ohio in the 1840's were led by Cyrus McNeely of Hopedale and Matthew S. Clapp of Mentor, while in Indiana the leadership increasingly centered around the personality and influence of an outstanding layman, Ovid Butler. By 1850 North-Western Christian University had been founded in Indianapolis and, while it was never completely under the control of the abolitionists, it was at least partially motivated by the desire for a "sound" institution on the slavery question and was the first real institutional expression of radical abolitionism within the Disciples. In 1854 the fiery abolitionist John Boggs began the publication of the *North-Western Christian Magazine,* which, with its successor the *Christian Luminary,* served as the much needed newspaper organ for radical Disciples.

The transformation in the character of the antislavery crusade during the 1830's opened a clear radical-moderate rift in the Disciples churches of the North. While it is impossible to determine the exact strength of the radicals in the churches in the North, it is obvious that they were both

---

[56]*Ibid.*

considerable and influential. Henry Shaw, in his book, *Buckeye Disciples,* estimates that "for the most part" church members in the Western Reserve "leaned toward the abolitionist view."[57] Bogg's militant abolitionist publications received a reasonably healthy patronage during these years when it was no mean trick to keep any religious publication alive.[58] The contributors to the *North-Western Christian Magazine* and *Christian Luminary* included some of the ablest and most influential preachers in the North. In short, by the 1830's radical abolitionists were a marked minority within the church, but, as in the nation as a whole, they were an energetic, determined, and vocal minority. Although they were sometimes attacked by their brethren in the North (the rumor was circulated among the Northern churches that the editor of the *North-Western Christian Magazine* was a "nigger"),[59] they often had the genuine sympathy of individuals in the much larger group of moderate antislavery Disciples in the North.

There was never any real battle between radical abolitionists and proslavery agitators among the Disciples.[60] Geography, utter disgust, and a buffer group of moderates in between them made the radicals in both North and South appear almost oblivious to one another. Disciples abolitionists trained their guns almost completely on their moderate brethren so numerous in the churches of the North and border states of Kentucky and Missouri.[61]

---

[57]Shaw, *Buckeye Disciples,* p. 142.

[58]See J.B., "Valedictory," *North-Western Christian Magazine,* IV (June, 1858), 377-379; J. B. Allan, "Solid Sympathy," *N.W.C.M.,* IV (February, 1858), 253-254; J. B., "Wayside Sketches—No. 14," *N.W.C.M.,* IV (November, 1857), 134-135; Robert E. Barnes, "An Analytical Study of the Northwestern Christian Magazine" (unpublished B.D. thesis, Butler School of Religion, 1951).

[59]J. B., "Wayside Sketches—No. 22," *N.W.C.M.,* IV (March, 1858), 276.

[60]The closest thing to a real public exchange between a Disciple abolitionist and a Southerner was a discussion between John Boggs and John R. Howard. But their exchange was limited and Howard was a moderate proslavery advocate. See *North-Western Christian Magazine,* I, beginning February, 1855, for the start of the series, "Discussion of the Slavery Question."

[61]Gilbert Barnes notes that this was a "fundamental quality" of the whole antislavery movement. *Anti-Slavery Impulse,* p. 25. See, also, Eileen Gordon Vandegrift, "The Christian Missionary Society: A Study in the Influence of Slavery on the Disciples of Christ" (unpublished M.A. thesis, Division of Graduate Instruction, Butler University, 1945), pp. 14-15.

From 1845 until the outbreak of the Civil War a series of incidents, some within the church and others national, ignited almost continuous verbal skirmishes between the abolitionists and moderates. Campbell's long series of articles on "Our Position to American Slavery" in 1845 had immediate repercussions. The *Harbinger* editor was swamped with criticism of his views and several staunch abolitionists cancelled their subscriptions. Milton Short, an old and respected Ohio Disciple, referring to the title of the Campbell series, wrote: "When you write on slavery again, say *my* position instead of *our* position."[62] Campbell had no intention of allowing a general discussion of the subject and hastily banned all articles on slavery from the *Harbinger*.[63] It had again become apparent to the mellowing editor that the most effective deterrent against a brotherhood explosion was a policy of studied suppression.[64]

In 1849 the rift between the abolitionists and Campbell momentarily narrowed when he publicly urged the citizens of Kentucky to vote for the inclusion of provisions for the gradual abolition of slavery in the new constitution which was being drafted in that state. Campbell followed closely the arguments used by Henry Clay in a similar open letter to the voters of Kentucky. Both men compared the economic progress of Ohio and Kentucky in an attempt to show that slavery was an economic liability to the Southern state. Campbell urged the Disciples of the state to support the candidates for the convention who were committed to emancipation: "By a single clause in a new Constitution you may put an end to it beyond a given day. . . . The Ruler of nations, in his providence, is now conferring this power on every voter in the State."[65]

Two years later one of the most extended and ablest brotherhood debates on the slavery question was published in the *Millennial Harbinger*.

---

[62]A. C., "Abolition, Masonic, and Odd-Fellow Intolerance," *M.H.*, 3d S., II (July, 1845), 313.

[63]A. C., "American Slavery," *M.H.*, 3d S., II (August, 1845), 355,358.

[64]In 1847, in a bizarre incident in Edinburgh, Scotland, Alexander Campbell was imprisoned on a libel charge by the antislavery leaders of that city. The affair caused considerable discussion but had little lasting impact on views of Disciples on slavery. See Thomas Chalmers, *Alexander Campbell's Tour in Scotland* (Louisville: Guide Printing & Publishing Co., 1892); Richardson, *Memoirs of Campbell*, II, 552-566. Also the November and December, 1847, numbers of the *Millennial Harbinger* and the *Protestant Unionist*.

[65]"A Tract for the People of Kentucky," *M.H.*, 3d S., VI (May, 1849), 247.

The discussion was triggered by the passage of a new and stringent Fugitive Slave Law as a part of the Compromise of 1850. To every ardent
abolitionist the law was an unthinkably wicked enactment. Campbell wrote
two articles in the January, 1851, edition of the *Harbinger* in an attempt
to cut short any radical demonstrations on the part of Disciples abolitionists. He insisted that the law was "perfectly constitutional" and ought
to be obeyed.[66] The reaction of "many" of the Northern brethren to Campbell's defense of the obnoxious law was not unpredictable.[67] Ovid Butler
wrote Campbell that he had "hoped" the *Harbinger* would not again stir
up the issue as it was obvious that their views were "irreconcilable."[68]
The church at Berrien, Michigan, sent Campbell a copy of resolutions
they had passed (the resolutions were directed to the President of the
United States) declaring the congregation's allegiance to the "higher
law" and its determination to "feed the poor, panting fugitive."[69]

Isaac Errett, already a powerful writer although still a young man in
his early thirties, wrote the ablest and most challenging attack on Campbell's views. Errett, insisting that there was a "higher law," systematically
countered Campbell's arguments for civil obedience with biblical examples of civil disobedience. He forcefully pointed out that Campbell's
appeals to patriotism were meaningless as "this nation was born in revolution against injustice." The question to Errett and the radicals was
one of justice—not obedience.[70]

In his attempt to answer his critics Campbell pretty largely offered a
restatement of what he had written before. The Bible was the "highest
law" and it unquestionably authorized the institution of slavery. Aboli-

---

[66]"The Fugitive Slave Law," *M.H.*, 4th S., I (January, 1851), 27-35; "Summary," *M.H.*, 4th S., I (January, 1851), 52-53. For a general discussion of the
controversy in the church over the Fugitive Slave Law see Fife, "Slavery Controversy," pp. 182-207.

[67]A. C., "Slavery and the Fugitive Slave Law—No. II," *M.H.*, 4th S., I (May,
1851), 247.

[68]A. C., "Slavery and the Fugitive Slave Law—No. V," *M.H.*, 4th S., I (August,
1851), 425-435.

[69]A. C., "Slavery and the Fugitve Slave Law," *M.H.*, 4th S., I (March, 1851),
171-172.

[70]"Queries Touching the Fugitive Slave Law," *M.H.*, 4th S., I (April, 1851),
224-228.

tionism was based on the "morbid, sickly" doctrine that all men are created equal:

I am fully aware, that there is a text in some Bibles that is not in mine. Professional abolitionists have made more use of it than of any passage in the Bible. It came, however as I trace it, from Saint Voltaire, and was baptized by Thomas Jefferson, and since almost universally regarded as canonical authority—"*All men are born free and equal.*"[71]

This was Campbell's last real flurry on the slavery question. He barely noticed the passage of the Kansas-Nebraska Bill in 1854[72] and completely ignored the numerous other nationally momentous events that slowly led to secession and war. The impression seeps through that with regard to the slavery question Campbell was a weary, disillusioned warrior by November, 1851. As a humanitarian he had always hated the institution and yet in his effort to find a Biblical basis for brotherhood solidarity he had been forced to defend it. This burden rested heavily on his shoulders; he never ceased to disavow the appellative "proslavery." The emotionally motivated abuse heaped on him by his abolitionist brethren was equally distressing to him. He was actually refreshed by Isaac Errett's attempt to justify abolitionist doctrine logically and scripturally. For over twenty years the leader of the Disciples had followed a calculated stop-and-go policy in discussing the slavery issue—publishing articles on the subject when he felt that they might help and closing the columns of the *Harbinger* when he thought the times too tender for useful discussion. The fact that his policy never really accomplished anything to bring the warring factions together is less the responsibility of Campbell than simply the inevitability of the times. In spite of Campbell's efforts, the 1850's proved to be a decade of hardening in party lines and a slowly emerging pattern of abolitionist withdrawal from the institutional complex of the moderate-dominated Christian church.

The June, 1850, *Millennial Harbinger* included a notice of the announcement of the opening of North-Western Christian University in Indianapolis with Ovid Butler as the Chairman of the Board of Directors.

---

[71]"Slavery and the Fugitive Slave Law—No. II," *M.H.*, 4th S., I (May, 1851), 252.

[72]"The Protestant Clergy of New England and Chicago Versus the Nebraska Bill," *M.H.*, 4th S., IV (June, 1854), 349-351.

This school, which had strong abolitionist backing, remained a constant
source of friction between moderates and radicals for the next decade.[73]
In a letter to Campbell, Butler explained that "many" Indiana Disciples
were convinced "that, in religion as in politics, the south claims and re-
ceives the principal attention of our leading brethren." Campbell did little to conceal his chagrin. He bluntly denounced the new school as an
open manifestation of "sectional Christianity" and declared the project a
direct attack on him and Bethany College. He loosed a scathing tirade
which was a virtual declaration of war: "I hope the brethren will hasten
leisurely, and hear all the premises and arguments before they act in such
a way as to create half-a-dozen of ill-begotten, misshapen, club-footed,
imbecile schools, under the name and title of Colleges and Universities."[74]

The response to Campbell's vituperative attack on the new school un-
doubtedly was violent because by August he was engaged in a full-scale
tactical withdrawal. He wrote: "Instead of attacking the project of a
North-Western Christian University, I simply aimed at defending the institution at Bethany from any imputation of subserviency to one section
of the Union." Almost meekly the lion of Bethany added that he wished
"every State in the American Union had at least one Christian College."[75]
The editor's unguarded attack on "imbecile schools" had probably offended a number of powerful church leaders who were interested in such
projects in other areas.

In 1856 the Bethany-Indianapolis feud erupted again after an abolitionist student rebellion at Bethany College. Led by A. B. Way and
Harvey W. Everest of Ohio and Philip Burns from Scotland, a number
of abolitionist students caused a near riot at the college by preaching in
the Bethany church on the sinfulness of slavery. The ultimate result of the
affair was the expulsion of five of the students and the resignation of five

---

[73]Although all the supporters of North-Western Christian University were not
ardent abolitionists, Ovid Butler, the financial backbone and largest stockholder
of the institution, was a full-fledged radical. The climate of the school was sufficiently extreme for John Boggs to endorse it as a "safe" place for abolitionists to
send their children. See "N.W. Christian University," Christian Luminary, I
(September 1, 1858), 74.

[74]"The North-Western Christian University," M.H., 3d S., VII (June, 1850),
329-335. Campbell's early objections to the new school were not motivated solely
by his fear of abolitionism, but the sectional factor was important.

[75]Ibid. (August, 1850), 454-458.

others.[76] The disciplined students were immediately hailed as martyrs to the cause of slavery in the North and were dramatically dubbed the "immortal ten."[77] By February Campbell had learned that several of the expelled students had matriculated at North-Western Christian University. He was incensed that the Indiana school would accept those "dismissed for immoral and unchristian conduct here."[78] The incident ended with the exchange of bitter notes between the faculties of the two schools. The disenchanted Indianians insinuated that Campbell's actions in the affair could most kindly be attributed to his growing senility. The Bethany group labeled this stunning charge a "reckless outrage" and coldly warned the radicals: "The brotherhood have not come to that degree, that God hath given children to be their princes, and babes to rule over them. Nor will they submit to have the youth behave himself proudly before the ancient, and dishonor the hand that has nourished him."[79]

The brew simmered but did not boil over again until December, 1859, when William K. Pendleton in surveying the educational institutions of the movement in the *Millennial Harbinger* caustically remarked of North-Western Christian University: "There is, too, at Indianapolis, a North-western Christian University, but we fear it is too much tinctured with the fanatical sectarianism of politico-religious abolitionism to be of any service to the Christian church or cause."[80] Pendleton's note brought indignant replies from some of the moderate stockholders of the school. The discussion that followed revealed that there was a moderate element, as well as a radical, connected with the college but the really significant feature of the whole exchange was that it took place between Indiana

[76]See A.C., "Disturbances in Bethany College," *M.H.*, 4th S., VI (January, 1856), 54-60; Philip Burns *et al.*, "Disturbances at Bethany, Virginia," *N.W.C.M.*, II (January, 1856), 213-218. A good account of the incident by one of the Northern students involved is in the Butler Manuscript Collection. H. W. Everest to Isaac Errett, February 20, 1856.

[77]T. J. Newcomb, "Discussion at New Philadelphia," *N.W.C.M.*, IV (January, 1858), 221.

[78]"Reported Troubles in Bethany College," *M.H.*, 4th S., VI (February, 1856), 115.

[79]"College Etiquette and the Faculty of the N. W. Christian University," *M.H.*, 4th S., VI (April, 1856), 226-229.

[80]"Our Progress and Prospects," *M.H.*, 5th S., II (December, 1859), 713.

moderates and the *Harbinger*—by 1860 the abolitionists were not even interested in answering Pendleton's charges.[81]

Before the establishment of the *North-Western Christian Magazine* in 1854, the abolitionists in the church were without a periodical organ of expression. Campbell and the other moderate editors could and did ignite and squelch discussion of the slavery issue according to their own dispositions. But after 1854 the abolitionists were in the writing business.

A withering stream of argument and invective poured off their Cincinnati press. Campbell, and other moderate preachers, the American Christian Missionary Society, and other moderate institutions, were under almost constant attack by Boggs and his corps of able contributors. Sometimes they were sharp and logical; usually they were intense and emotional; occasionally they were vituperative and abusive. The Disciples abolitionists were a tenacious breed of Christian preachers—they were prophets obsessed with a sense of mission. The injunction to "do unto all men as you would they should do unto you" became to them the all-consuming design of Christianity.

Disciples abolitionists were a colorful lot: John G. Fee, one of the Lane rebels, established an interracial school in Berea, Kentucky, with the support of Henry Ward Beecher and the Tappan brothers; he was mobbed twenty-two times, disowned by his family, and finally driven from the state in 1859.[82] J. O. Beardslee was an early disciple of Charles G. Finney and a member of the first graduating class at Oberlin College; Cyrus McNeeley made his pioneer Hopedale, Ohio, school interracial; George Campbell, John B. New, Love H. Jameson, and Alanson Wilcox were all active in the birth of the Republican party in Indiana;[83] James A. Butler, an aristocratic Southerner, fought slavery in Alabama and Mississippi

[81]See Jer. Smith, "Northwestern Christian University," *M.H.*, 5th S., III (January, 1860), 50-52; B. K. Smith, "N. W. Christian University Again," *M.H.*, 5th S., III (March, 1860), 169-174; E. G., "The N. W. C. University," *Christian Record*, 3d S., IV (January, 1860), 13-14.

[82]See John G. Fee, *Autobiography of John G. Fee* (Chicago, Illinois: National Christian Association, 1891); Tyler, *Freedom's Ferment*, p. 521; "Editorial Items," *Christian Standard*, XXXVII (January 19, 1901), 73; J. S. Hughes, "John G. Fee and the Holy Spirit," *Christian Oracle*, XVI (September 21, 1899), 8.

[83]See J. B., "A Week in Indiana," *N.W.C.M.*, I (August, 1854), 59; Alanson Wilcox, "A Pioneer's Experience," *Christian Standard*, XXXIII (February 6, 1897), 167; Hayden, *Western Reserve*, pp. 398-401.

until forced to leave the South just prior to the Civil War.[84] There were others of the same mold but none was more colorful or influential in the church than a spirited Kansas preacher—Pardee Butler.

Like so many social reformers, Butler's psychological composure was that of a restless, uncompromising combatant.[85] His calling in life was to crusade and he thrived on opposition and persecution. He enlisted first in the cause of abolition and later in the crusade for prohibition and battled them both to their death in Kansas—one wonders how it could have been otherwise.

Butler was one of the troop of "two-ideaed" preachers who went to the territory of Kansas in 1855 to keep the devil out of the young churches and to keep the slaveholders out of the young territory. The turbulent territory deservedly earned the title "bleeding Kansas" in the five riotous years from 1855 to 1860 and Pardee Butler was a catalytic part of the ferment. Butler's son reminisced that "in those days it took a man with sand in his craw to come to Kansas and stay."[86] Pardee Butler not only went to Kansas to stay but shortly after his arrival bought a farm in Atchison County, the center of Southern strength in the territory.

Butler soon began relentlessly to attack the slave element in the territory from the pulpits of the scattered Christian churches, by writing voluminously in the free-soil papers of the territory, and by sending occasional reports to the New York *Tribune*. The outspoken preacher quickly became a marked man in his home county and on scores of occasions his life was threatened by the Southern "border ruffians" who roamed Atchison County. He was warned not to enter the town of Atchison but, not to be intimidated by threats, he boldly walked into the Southern stronghold on several occasions.

Twice Butler was mobbed in Atchison. On one occasion he was tarred and feathered (cotton was used because of the inavailability of feathers).

---

[84]See B. F. Manire, *Reminiscences of Preachers and Churches in Mississippi* (Jackson, Miss.: Messenger Company, 1892), pp. 6-10; "A Letter from Dr. H____ of Tuscaloosa, to J. A. Butler of Lowndes Co. Ala.," *The Morning Watch*, I (May, 1838), 220-221.

[85]For general information on Pardee Butler, see Rosetta B. Hastings, *Personal Recollections of Pardee Butler* (Cincinnati: Standard Publishing Company, 1889); Charles P. Butler, "Pardee Butler: Pioneer Minister and Statesman," *Shane Quarterly*, III (January, 1942), 78-83.

[86]Butler, "Pardee Butler," *Shane Quarterly*, III, 79.

On another visit to the town he had the unique experience of being "rafted." His assailants tied two logs together, deposited Butler on this rude and unseaworthy craft, towed him into the middle of the treacherous Missouri River, and cut him adrift. In large print they marked an "R" on his forehead to signify that he was a "rogue" and commissioned his tiny vessel with a colorful pennant: "Greeley to the rescue: I have a nigger. The Rev. Mr. Butler, agent for the underground railroad." Outwardly unperturbed by the harrowing experience, Butler, as he recalled the incident, admonished his antagonists as they towed him away from the bank of the river: "Gentlemen, if I am drowned I forgive you; but I have this to say to you: If you are not ashamed of your part in this transaction, I am not ashamed of mine. Good-by."[87] The fiery abolitionist escaped with his life and when the story of his persecution was published Butler became a national martyr in the free-soil cause.[88]

In 1859 Butler became the central figure in the agitation for the formation of an antislavery missionary society among the Disciples of Christ.[89] Disciples abolitionists had criticized the American Christian Missionary Society from its inception because of the appointment of Dr. James T. Barclay as a missionary to Jerusalem at the first meeting of the society in 1849. Barclay was a Virginia slaveholder and although he disposed of his slaves when he received his missionary appointment, he was never acceptable to Disciples radicals. Throughout the decade of the fifties the abolitionists in the church continued to attack the Barclay mission as an example of the " 'Legree' theology" which dominated the missionary society.[90]

The corresponding secretary of the American Christian Missionary Society remained under almost constant fire from the abolitionist press. The various secretaries who were in the unenviable position of trying to raise

---

[87]Hastings, *Butler,* pp. 71-72.

[88]For additional information see Emory Lindquist, "Religion in Kansas During the Era of the Civil War," *Kansas Historical Quarterly,* XXV (Winter, 1959), 412-414; Abby Huntington Ware, "Dispersion of the Territorial Legislature of 1856," Kansas State Historical Society, *Transactions,* 1905-1906, IX, 540-545.

[89]One of the better theses done in the area of Disciples history deals with this movement. Vandegrift, "Christian Missionary Society."

[90]The *Northwestern Christian Magazine* contains repeated attacks on the Barclay mission. See, for instance, J. B., "Dr. Barclay, and Slavery," *N.W.C.M.,* I (October, 1854), 108-110.

operating funds in both Northern and Southern churches, tried to steer a nonpartisan, unoffensive middle course. But by 1857 relations between the abolitionists and the society were nearing a breaking point. John Boggs was editorially lambasting Benjamin Franklin, then the corresponding secretary of the society, because Franklin had advised J. O. Beardslee, a missionary to Jamaica, to be moderate in his public statements on the slavery question. Boggs accused Franklin of "servility to the slavery power" and, not without good reason, charged that he was trying to "carry water on both shoulders."[91]

Just when it seemed that a complete rupture between the society and the radical abolitionists was imminent, a shakeup in the organization of the society brought Isaac Errett into the corresponding secretary's office. Even the disgruntled John Boggs accepted the appointment of such a good "antislavery" man as a token of conciliation. He assured his fellow radicals that the abolitionists now had a man in the society "who we know where to find."[92] But almost immediately the spell of enchantment was broken and the hopes of any real reconciliation between the two groups were shattered.

In April, 1858, Pardee Butler appealed to the missionary society for financial support in his work in Kansas and the controversy which ensued ended in the institutional separation of the abolitionist element from the main body of the Disciples of Christ. Errett's reply to Butler was optimistic but contained a qualifying provision which proved to be explosive:

It must, therefore be distinctly understood, that if we embark in a missionary enterprise in Kansas, this question of slavery and anti-slavery must be ignored; and our missionaries must not be ensnared into such utterances as the "Northwestern Christian Magazine" can publish to the world, to add fuel to the flame already burning in our churches on this question.[93]

Butler retorted that slavery was a "Bible question" and that Errett was dictatorially trying to proscribe his "freedom of thought and speech."[94]

---

[91]"The Mission to Jamaica," *N.W.C.M.*, IV (November, 1857), 142-144.

[92]"American Christian Missionary Society," *N.W.C.M.*, IV (November, 1857), 156-157.

[93]J. S. Lamar, *Memoirs of Isaac Errett* (2 vols.; Cincinnati: The Standard Publishing Co., 1893), I, 215.

[94]Hastings, *Butler*, p. 320.

John Boggs was incensed by what he felt was a betrayal by Errett: "We can stand anything from avowed enemies, but we confess it grieves us to be stabbed in the house of a friend."[95] He charged that Errett had become "the pliant tool of slave-holding aristocracy, ready to explain away his former position and cringingly deny that he ever considered slave-holding of sufficient importance to disturb church fellowship."[96] Errett

had fallen from anti-slavery grace. . . . He was denounced from the pulpit, and the press waged bitter, relentless war against him. His Michigan field of labor was flooded with documents attacking his honesty, and calling him hard names. . . . As a matter of course, the Society could not be countenanced nor supported.[97]

Nor was Errett alone; by the end of 1858 abolitionist pressure was on the moderates all along the line. James A. Garfield, the young president of Eclectic Institute in Hiram, Ohio, wrote his besieged friend, Errett: "There has been an attempt to throw the abolition stench around us, and I have resisted successfully, though not without bringing down upon me the small thunder of a few rampant ones. . . . I know you can sympathize with me."[98]

The Butler-society episode was significant not only as the beginning of a new and vigorous abolitionist attack but also because for the first time these radicals met a determined and uncompromising opposition. Young and outspoken moderate leaders stood toe-to-toe and swapped argument for argument, abuse for abuse, and name-calling for name-calling. Isaac Errett and Benjamin Franklin blasted away at the radicals week after week through Franklin's new weekly paper, the *American Christian Review*. Errett ridiculed the whole abolitionist attack as a "farce" which, "if it were not linked with things sacred, would be funny."[99] It was obvious by the end of 1858 that the moderates were ready to fight back—even if it meant a division in the church. The abolitionists faced a choice between two alternatives: they either had to accept the leadership of a new and militant moderate group which had little patience with their idiosyncrasies, or they had to take steps to create an organizational

[95]"The General Missionary Society," *N.W.C.M.*, IV (April, 1858), 314.

[96]Lamar, *Errett*, I, 217.

[97]*Ibid.*, 219.

[98]*Ibid.*, 220.

[99]"Pardee Butler—Mission to Kansas," *A. C. R.*, I (November 23, 1858), 186.

structure which they could dominate—it was a choice between submission and secession.

During 1859 the abolitionists moved rapidly in the direction of an independent convention and missionary society. Early in the year Pardee Butler set out on a tour of the free-state churches in an effort to raise funds for his Kansas mission. Although his efforts were not especially successful financially (Errett reported that after "five months of sweating, spouting, lecturing, and undisturbed denunciation of the American Christian Missionary Society," Butler, with the part-time help of Boggs and Hartzell, had raised only $255),[100] Butler's excursion served the purpose of locating and uniting the abolitionist churches of the Northern states. In July, 1859, Butler made a public report of his trip which included the first open recommendation for separate abolitionist organization:

> We have three pressing wants: 1. A *sustained* paper that will not bow the knee to the image of this modern Baal. Such a paper we have, but it can only be sustained by the timely effort of its friends. 2. We need a convention made up of men who regard slavery as a moral evil, and are disposed to make their own consciences the rule of their action. 3. We need a missionary fund, which shall be placed in such hands that it shall not be prostituted to the vile purpose of bribing men into silence on the subject of slavery.[101]

In May, 1859, Ovid Butler and John Boggs began mailing to a select group of Northern church leaders circulars proposing the meeting of an antislavery convention in Indianapolis. Within a few months over 800 signatures had been received favoring such a convention and in the September issue of the *Christian Luminary* a public call was made for delegates to meet in Indianapolis, November 1, 1859.[102]

The publication of the call shocked the moderates in the brotherhood. Errett, in an article entitled "The Secret Circular," charged that it was now evident that the abolitionists were intent on dividing the church over a "difference of opinion" and that they would use every "shameful" means at their disposal to accomplish that end.[103] Franklin tried to limit the influence of the convention by advising the brethren to ignore it: "We again advise the brethren to have nothing to do with it in any way.

---

[100]"Sectional and Factious Movement," *A. C. R.*, II (August 23, 1859), 135.

[101]Hastings, *Butler*, p. 327.

[102]See Vandegrift, "Christian Missionary Society," pp. 30-39.

[103]*A. C. R.*, II (September 20, 1859), 150-151.

. . . In one word, there will be no convention that need to disturb any-body."[104] In the North there was a general ferment; many of the churches were seriously divided;[105] many of the old pioneers of the movement were torn between their loyalty to the church and their unyielding commitment to abolitionism.[106]

The convention that met in Indianapolis, November 1, 1859, was more than an impulsive gathering of dissatisfied fanatics; it was the natural and considered fruition of a long and tortuous period of conflict and was attended by able and determined men.[107] After some discussion, the Christian Missionary Society was chartered and the convention set about the task of drafting a constitution and electing officers for the new missionary organization. The new society was organized on a clear antislavery basis and the convention resoundingly elected Ovid Butler its first president.

The activities of the new missionary society were never very extensive, but neither was it simply a figurehead.[108] It supported the preaching of an "ungagged" Pardee Butler in Kansas for a time and during 1860 and 1861 sponsored a mission in Minnesota. After the outbreak of the Civil War the natural course seemed to point toward the reunion of the In-dianapolis group with the American Christian Missionary Society. In 1862 Boggs editorially regretted that there had ever been a need for the "divi-sion of efforts in the missionary labors" and expressed the hope that the Cincinnati society would "speak in reference to slavery" at its next annual meeting so that the Christian Missionary Society could conscientiously dis-band.[109] The failure of the American Christian Missionary Society to pass suitable resolutions in 1862 was a bitter disappointment to the Indian-apolis group and the radicals doggedly continued their separate organiza-tion. The following year, however, the American Christian Missionary

---

[104]"The New Movement Again," *A. C. R.*, II (October 25, 1859), 170.

[105]For example, the church in Indianapolis; see "Reply of Ovid Butler to Elder Isaac Errett," *A. C. R.*, II (September 13, 1859), 147.

[106]See Ovid Butler, E. G., and Archippus, "A Call for a Northwestern Christian Convention," *A. C. R.*, II (September 6, 1859), 143; L. H. Jameson to Isaac Errett, August 25, 1859, Butler Manuscript Collection.

[107]See Vandegrift, "Christian Missionary Society," pp. 40-51; J. J. Moss, "In-dianapolis Convention—No. I," *A. C. R.*, II (November 22, 1859), 186-187.

[108]See Vandegrift, "Christian Missionary Society," pp. 52-77.

[109]*Ibid.*, p. 74.

Society passed a set of stringent loyalty resolutions and at its 1863 convention the Christian Missionary Society was dissolved.[110]

JAMES SHANNON
FIRE-EATING PREACHER

"Cursed be Canaan; a servant of servants shall he be unto his brethren."
Genesis 9:25.

Many of the outstanding Disciples preachers in the South were slaveholders. While they all agreed that the relationship of "master and slave" was one authorized and provided for by the Scriptures, most of the leaders in the Southern churches were moderates in their defense of slavery. There was a group within the Southern churches, however, which, on occasion, militantly defended the institution.

As Alexander Campbell became more and more critical of abolitionism in the 1840's, he became an increasingly attractive figure to the churches of the South.[111] The editor's 1849 *Tract to the People of Kentucky* momentarily estranged some of his Southern admirers. One disgruntled Kentuckian ordered Campbell to "discontinue" his *Harbinger* and requested that in the future the editor keep his advice to himself as the citizens of Kentucky were "as intelligent as any people on the subject of abolition."[112]

But this 1849 tiff marked the last real conflict between Campbell and Southern slavery apologists. As the feeling between Campbell and Northern radicals became more and more bitter in the decade of the fifties, he turned increasingly to the South for support. His frequent tours in search of endowment for Bethany College swung preceptibly southward. Never again did the Bethany editor give serious offense to the sensitive defenders of slavery.

---

[110]See A. R. Benton to Isaac Errett, November 3, 1863, Butler Manuscript Collection.

[111]After Campbell's misfortune with the abolitionists of Scotland in 1847, R. A. Clark of Jackson, Mississippi, urged that the reformer make an immediate tour of the South: "I need not suggest that the ardent feelings and generous friendship of the South will insure him the most cordial reception by all men; the more so, since his recent persecution on account of Southern institutions." "Tour by A. Campbell," *B.A.*, VI (May 1, 1848), 69.

[112]Abraham Smith, "Letter from Brother Smith," *M.H.*, 3d S., VI (July, 1849), 413.

During the 1850's the unchallenged leader among Disciples proslavery advocates was James Shannon. Probably no other man in the first-generation history of the Disciples came as close to rivaling Alexander Campbell in education, intellectual capacity, and sheer force of personality as Shannon.[113] He was a graduate of the classical course at the University of Belfast. After receiving bachelor's and master's degrees from that institution (where, according to William C. Rogers, he had "an unsurpassed record for brilliancy and scholarship"),[114] he migrated to America in the 1820's and began an impressive career as an educator in the South. He was for a time Professor of Ancient Languages at the University of Georgia in Athens and then, from 1835 until his death in 1859, served successively as president of the College of Louisiana in Baton Rouge; president of Bacon College, in Harrodsburg, Kentucky, the oldest Disciples of Christ college; president of the University of Missouri, in Columbia; and president of Christian University in Canton, Missouri. During this period he was also active as a preacher and was regarded by Campbell and many other Disciples leaders as the most brilliant speaker in the brotherhood.

Shannon was cast in the traditional mold of Southern fire-eaters. A recent historian has described him vividly: "Not all Irishmen are contentious but as the record will show Shannon fulfilled all the requirements of the conventional type. He was positive and colorful to the full meanings of these terms."[115]

Shannon traveled widely among the Christian churches of the South preaching his religious and political views. While serving as president of Bacon College in the late 1840's he wrote extensively in defense of slavery and engaged the president of neighboring Centre College, an outstanding Presbyterian leader in Kentucky, John C. Young, in a public debate on the slavery question. Shannon utilized most of the ultra proslavery arguments in his discussions. He believed that "some are incapable

---

[113]For general information on Shannon, see W. C. Rogers, *Recollections of Men of Faith* (St. Louis: Christian Publishing Company, 1889), pp. 15-18; George L. Peters, James Shannon—Christian Educator, typed biographical sketch, James Shannon Collection.

[114]Peters, James Shannon—Christian Educator, typed biographical sketch, James Shannon Collection.

[115]Jonas Viles, *The University of Missouri* (Columbia, Missouri: University of Missouri, 1939), p. 54.

of making a proper use of freedom; and, that, for all such, bondage is a blessing, and freedom an unmitigated calamity." He fortified his arguments with a mass of Biblical material. He argued that human bondage had always been a part of God's plan, "benevolently instituted" as a "cure for sin." Slavery had been provided for by Jewish law and was accepted without protest by Christ and his apostles. The doctrine that all men are created equal he considered a "wild and mischievous delusion" which had repeatedly proved disastrous to those who tried to build national governments on it.[116]

In 1850 Shannon moved to Missouri to accept the presidency of the young state university and remained a key figure in the turbulent politics of the state until his death in 1859. During the 1850's both of the major political parties in Missouri split into warring factions on the slavery question. Senator Thomas Hart Benton's opposition to the annexation of Texas and the Compromise of 1850 divided the Democratic party into Benton and anti-Benton factions and by 1854 the Missouri Whigs also were divided into radical and moderate elements over the slavery question. As president of the University of Missouri, Shannon was perched atop a political powder keg, and he was just the man to light the fuse.[117]

Proslavery sentiment was riding a high tide in Missouri in the years from 1850 to 1855 and the combination of an anti-Benton Democratic university board with the influence of Christian church leaders in Columbia was responsible for the selection of Shannon for the presidency of the university.[118] Shannon was drawn almost immediately into the political imbroglio. He made flaming proslavery speeches throughout the state and deluged the anti-Benton Columbia papers with inflammatory material. Former Senator Benton bluntly accused him of fomenting a "conspiracy" against the Union.[119] Shannon became the prime target of moderate concern. James S. Rollins, an influential Boone County Whig leader, wrote

---

[116]James Shannon, The Philosophy of Slavery as Identified with the Philosophy of Human Happiness, unpublished address, James Shannon Collection.

[117]For a discussion of Missouri politics in the 1850's, see Anthony Trexler Harrison, *Slavery in Missouri* (Baltimore: The Johns Hopkins Press, 1914), pp. 134-170.

[118]See Viles, *University of Missouri*, pp. 52-83; T. M. Allen to J. A. Gano, December 26, 1850, John Allen Gano Papers, University of Missouri.

[119]Viles, *University of Missouri*, p. 59.

his friend George R. Smith: "Let me tell you that no man is doing more to corrupt the public mind of Missouri, on these exciting questions than the aforesaid Shannon."[120] Dubbed the "damned Campbellite Democrat,"[121] and the "old Hibernian Gander"[122] by his antagonists, his possession of the president's office at the university soon became a major political issue. As early as 1853, Thomas M. Allen wrote his friend John Allen Gano that Shannon had escaped being dismissed by the legislature by the "skin of his teethe" [sic] as the result of a coalition of "Benton and his allies, and all the Sects."[123]

The passage of the Kansas-Nebraska Act in 1854 keyed the proslavery agitation in Missouri to a feverish pitch. Led by Governor Sterling Price and Judge William B. Napton a proslavery convention met in Lexington, Missouri, in July, 1855, to discuss the whole question of slavery.[124] On the second day of the convention Shannon delivered a lengthy keynote address.

Shannon's speech was electrifying. After amassing an elaborate array of proslavery arguments, he loosed a resounding and thunderous challenge:

And if, as we have seen, right of property in slaves is sanctioned by the light of Nature, the Constitution of the United States, and the clear teaching of the Bible, a deliberate and persistent violation of that right, even by government, is as villainous as highway robbery; and, when peaceable modes of redress are exhausted, IS A JUST CAUSE OF WAR BETWEEN SEPARATE STATES, AND OF REVOLUTION IN THE SAME STATE. . . . Proclaim it aloud, then, in the hearing of my enemies; publish it, if you please, to the ends of the earth, that I have said it;—and if this be treason, let free-soil traitors and abolition negro-thieves, leagued with British tories in an unholy conspiracy to dissolve the Union, make the most of it.[125]

---

[120]Harrison, Slavery in Missouri, p. 199.

[121]Viles, University of Missouri, p. 70.

[122]C. B. Rollins, "Letters of George Caleb Bingham to James S. Rollins," Missouri Historical Review, XXXII (January, 1938), 189.

[123]T. M. Allen to J. A. Gano, May 21, 1853, John Allen Gano Papers.

[124]For information on this convention, see Address to the People of the United States, Together with the Proceedings and Resolutions of the Pro-Slavery Convention of Missouri, Held at Lexington, July, 1855 (St. Louis: Republican Office, 1855); Harrison, Slavery in Missouri, pp. 190-201; Floyd C. Shoemaker, "Missouri's Proslavery Fight for Kansas, 1854-1855," Missouri Historical Review, XLVIII (July, 1954), 324-335.

[125]Address to the People, p. 24.

The address so pleased the proslavery leaders of the convention that they ordered it printed with the proceedings and requested him to repeat the address throughout the state.[126] President Shannon immediately took to the stump and delivered his address in most of the major towns of the state.[127] Shannon's escapades during the summer of 1855 led to his estrangement from all but the most avid proslavery fire-eaters in the state. Thomas M. Allen, probably the leading Disciples preacher in the state and one who from the beginning had been Shannon's most loyal and most influential supporter, wrote his friend John Allen Gano in August, 1855, that Shannon was "chin deep in politics" and that his actions would almost certainly "lead to his removal from his present position."[128] Under extreme pressure Shannon resigned his office in 1856 and accepted the presidency of a new school established by Disciples in Canton, Missouri, Christian University, where he remained until his death in early 1859.

The impact of James Shannon's career as a proslavery agitator on the history of the Disciples probably was not great. Although there were some other radical agitators among Disciples preachers in Missouri,[129] it seems that most of the church leaders were more moderate proslavery men. For the most part the radical Southerners were quietly tolerated by the moderates among the Disciples (although the Sycamore Street congregation in Cincinnati refused Shannon the use of its building in 1845 because of the pressure applied by the abolitionist Gamaliel Bailey through his local paper the *Philanthropist*).[130] Generally the idiosyncrasies of the fire-eaters were judged to be in the area of "opinion" and the tradition of the church was to be tolerant on such questions.

---

[126]See *Address to the People*, p. 28; Harrison, *Slavery in Missouri*, p. 201; Rollins, "Letters of George Caleb Bingham to James S. Rollins," XXXII, 191-192.

[127]See T. M. Allen to J. A. Gano, August 10, 1855, John Allen Gano Papers, University of Missouri; Rollins, "Letters of George Caleb Bingham to James S. Rollins," XXXII, 193-194.

[128]T. M. Allen to J. A. Gano, August 10, 1855, John Allen Gano Papers, University of Missouri.

[129]Hastings, *Butler*, pp. 194-195; J. W. Hawkins (ed.), *Speeches and Lectures of Dr. M. C. Hawkins* (Canton, Missouri: Canton Press Job Print, 1874), pp. 25-36.

[130]See the *Christian Journal*, III, November and December, 1844, and March, 1845. There was quite a disturbance in the church over the episode.

THE MODERATE MOLD

"But foolish and ignorant questionings refuse, knowing that they gender strifes."
II Timothy 2:23.

Eva Jean Wrather, biographer of Alexander Campbell, lavishly praises
him for his moderate stand on the slavery issue: "Campbell was an
eighteenth-century rationalist, fundamentally opposed to fanaticism; and
he never showed his sanity, his tolerance, his straight thinking more
clearly than in defining his position on the proper attitude of the Christian toward the abolition crusaders."[131] The same moderate, nondivisive
attitude which characterized the thinking of Alexander Campbell on the
slavery issue was shared by a large majority of the leaders of the church.
The spectrum of moderates in the church spanned from slaveholding,
slavery defenders in the South to staunch antislavery men in the North
who united around the central conviction that the slavery question ought
not to disturb the unity of the church.[132]

A few leading Disciples editors followed an unwavering course of
absolute neutrality. Aaron Chatterton, editor of the Davenport, Iowa,
Evangelist, bluntly reported in 1859 that he had not "taken much interest
in these shots fired across Mason's and Dixon's line."[133] In noticing John
Boggs's radical *Christian Luminary,* Chatterton dispassionately wrote: "It
is distinguished for its radical anti-slaveryism. Some blame Bro. Boggs
for the course he pursues; others pet him. We do neither. He can do just
as he pleases, without let or hindrance from me; and if anybody wants
the *Luminary* we wish them to have it."[134]

---

[131]Eva Jean Wrather, "Alexander Campbell and Social Righteousness," *Christian Standard,* LXXIII (September 17, 1938), 912.

[132]Most evangelical Protestant leaders took a moderate stand during the slavery
controversy. See Niebuhr, *The Kingdom of God,* pp. 121-122; Olmstead, *Religion
in the United States,* pp. 362-383; Cole, *Northern Evangelists,* pp. 192-220. It was
difficult for all of the nation's religious leaders to decide "at what point the
solidarity of national religious and benevolent societies became less important than
a clear witness against human bondage." Smith, *Revivalism and Social Reform,*
p. 81. See, also, pp. 178-224. Disciples were not unique in their moderate stand
which attempted to stave off division. Disciples moderates were perhaps slightly
more successful but they were no more determined, and probably no more numerous, proportionately, than in other similar groups.

[133]"Editor's Table," *Evangelist,* X (November, 1859), 528.

[134]"Periodicals of the Reformation," *Evangelist,* XIII (May, 1862), 225.

But such studied neutrality was the exception rather than the rule. Most of the moderate preachers of the South believed that slavery was a scriptural institution; many of them owned slaves and contended that when the relationship between masters and slaves was humanely regulated, it was a benevolent social system.

Scattered moderates in the South supported the American Colonization Society into the decade of the fifties[135] but for the most part they either lapsed into a sullen silence or became defensive of the South and its peculiar institution. After Alexander Campbell virtually ceased to write on the subject of slavery in the *Harbinger* in 1851, his son-in-law, William K. Pendleton, directed the paper on a moderate proslavery course. The conservative Virginian was an ardent admirer of President James Buchanan. Pendleton and Campbell, while making a tour of the East, had a personal audience with President Buchanan. Pendleton lavishly praised the President's "enlarged and conservative policy on the stormy questions of sectional differences."[136]

The influential moderate pro-Southern editors among Disciples included Tolbert Fanning of Tennessee, Benjamin Franklin of Ohio, John R. Howard of Missouri, and John T. Walsh of North Carolina. All of these men generally accepted the racist conviction that the Negro was mentally and morally inferior—the inheritor of the "curse of Canaan."[137] Occasionally, during the early years of the movement, articles appeared in the Southern church papers defending slavery but more and more the few notices the institution received were joined with efforts to arrest all discussion on the subject.[138] John Howard summed up the Southern policy of nonintervention:

---

[135]See "The Republic of Liberia," *E.R.*, III (March 30, 1850), 212.

[136]"Notes of a Tour for Bethany College," *M.H.*, 5th S., I (March, 1858), 158. The man who arranged the presidential audience was Attorney-General Jeremiah Sullivan Black, distinguished Pennsylvania lawyer, and probably the most prominent Disciples layman before the Civil War. Black was a moderate on the slavery question. See William Norwood Brigance, *Jeremiah Sullivan Black* (Philadelphia: University of Pennsylvania Press, 1934), pp. 76-81.

[137]See T. F., " 'The Higher Law,' " *G.A.*, VII (March, 1861), 65-70; J. M. M., "Prophecy—II," *C.R.*, V (August, 1847), 45-47; A. C., "Conversations at the Carlton House," *M.H.*, N. S., IV (November, 1840), 493-501.

[138]See "Letter from Thomas M. Henley," *Christian Publisher*, II (June, 1838), 178-180; J. R. H., "Treatment and Duties of Servants," *M.H.*, 4th S., II (December, 1852), 668-673.

It comes not within the scope of our design, to discuss the subject of slavery, as to whether it is right or wrong. Slavery is a *political* institution; and we find it and leave it just where the New Testament does. It belongs to the *civil* government . . . to say whether it shall be retained or abolished.[139]

Many of the most powerful Disciples preachers in the North, while staunch antislavery advocates, refused to identify with the radical abolition movement.[140] Some of these Northern moderates continued to support colonization schemes long after the radical abolition movement began sweeping the nation.[141]

Walter Scott was a typical and important member of this large group of Northern moderates. Scott, like Campbell and Stone, was committed to emancipation and colonization during the early years of the movement and until the end of his life remained a bitter critic of slavery. Scott's first printed encounter with radical abolitionism appeared in his paper, the *Evangelist*, during the years 1834 and 1835. In October, 1834, he was jarred by a letter from a radical Disciple from Jeffersonville, Indiana, Nathaniel Field, who wrote: "I have fears that the leaders of the reformation are wanting in moral honesty as well as moral courage. . . . They show a willingness to compromit [*sic*] the truth with 'oppressors and robbers' for such are slave holders when weighed in the balance."[142] Scott's answer to his assailant is a good summary of moderate disillusionment and their logical explanation for refusing to join the radical abolition campaign:

The manumission of our slave population can be accomplished now only by a means which, heaven alone knows—I know it not. You are pleased to resolve the silence of certain of us on this great subject into a "want of moral honesty." I

---

[139]J. R. H., "Family Religion—No. 8," *B.A.*, VII (September, 1849), 75-76.

[140]See "Querist's Department," *C.R.*, 2d S., II (July, 1851), 28-29; A. C., "The Robertson Case," *C.R.*, V (May, 1848), 347-348; ["Letter from W. Baxter"], *P.U.*, III (October 20, 1847), 182; "The Crisis of the Union," *C.A.P.U.*, VI (March 8, 1850), 38; Lamar, *Errett*, I, 85-88; W. W. Wasson, *James A. Garfield: His Religion and Education* (Nashville: Tennessee Book Company, 1952), pp. 81-82; Pillsbury, *Anti-Slavery Apostles*, pp. 443-444.

[141]See Ed., "Liberia," *Evangelical Inquirer*, I (December, 1830), 158; "Improvement of Africa," *C.R.*, V (September, 1847), 69; "How to Abolish Slavery—No. 2," *N.W.C.M.*, IV (March, 1858), 277-279; Elmira J. Dickinson (ed.), *A History of Eureka College* (St. Louis: Christian Publishing Company, 1894), pp. 217-219; Fife, "Slavery Controversy," pp. 139-141.

[142]"Letter from Nat. Field, Jeffersonville," *Evangelist*, III (October, 1834), 233.

think if wit and charity combined to judge us in the case they would soon discover that our silence is susceptible of a very different explanation. I am no friend to slavery, like you and the good men to whom I have alluded I deprecate its commencement . . . but I am silent because I think to speak would be folly. What ought to be said I cannot say, and what ought not to be said I will not say.[143]

In short, Southern and Northern moderates reached the same conclusion —that silence was the best check on the divisive tendency of the whole slavery problem.

It was not until the last few hectic years of the 1850's that some of the moderates abandoned this philosophy of suppression. Something has already been said in this chapter on the development of the militant moderate movement during these years. Under constant attack from radical abolitionists, some of the moderates, both Southern and Northern, led by Benjamin Franklin and Isaac Errett, began to strike back beginning around 1856. Franklin wrote in 1856: "We have been scolded, bemeaned, threatened, and called a 'coward,' a 'time server,' a 'dumb dog,' and a 'popularity seeker,' not because of what we *have* said, but because of what we have *not* said—because of our silence."[144] The editorial battle that followed was both extensive and bitter—the unity of the church tottered in the balance.

THE SECTIONAL PATTERN

"Moreover if thy brother shall trespass against thee, go and tell him his fault. . . . But if he will not hear thee . . . tell it unto the church: but if he neglect to hear the church, let him be unto thee as a heathen man and a publican." Matthew 18:15-17.

The story of the Disciples of Christ and the institution of slavery in the nineteenth century is an American saga. Planters, one-horse farmers, college professors, country schoolmasters, budding industrialists, crossroads storekeepers, cultured preachers, pioneer exhorters, Northerners and Southerners—Disciples were Americans. The nation and the church were "houses divided" in the decades preceding the Civil War. Somehow the centrifugal force of habit and tradition crowded fire-eating Southerners, abolitionists, and moderates in North and South all into the same bucket

---

[143]"Answer to the Above Letter," *ibid.*, 236.

[144]"Where Is the Safe Ground," *A.C.R.*, I (February, 1856), 35.

until the irrepressible explosion of 1861. The difficulties faced by the church during the hectic decade preceding 1861 were the same ones that faced the nation. If it was a problem to keep James Shannon and John Boggs in the same nation, it was no less a problem to keep them in the same church. What the Disciples did to ease the travail of the nation is an intriguing subject. The question is equally as fascinating and even more significant when the principles are reversed: What was the lasting impact of the great slavery controversy on the Disciples of Christ?

A number of Disciples played significant roles in their respective camps during the slavery debate. Pardee Butler and John G. Fee were nationally known abolitionists; James Shannon was a key figure in the proslavery party in Missouri; Campbell, Stone, Scott, and a number of other moderate leaders were of more than local importance. But more pertinent than an assessment of the contributions of individual Disciples is the question of the impact of the movement on the troubled American scene.

The humanitarian impulse inherent in the sectarian message of Christianity, remained an important element in Disciples thought. Before 1830 many Disciples followed the examples of Stone and Campbell and emancipated their slaves. At the local level church members were often zealous and effective leaders in gradualist emancipation schemes—as late as the decade of the fifties. Among those church members who retained their slaves, such as John Allen Gano and Thomas M. Allen, the humanity of their religion unquestionably did a good deal to ease the most brutal facets of the slave system.

During the early years of the movement this spirit of benevolence joined with an activistic and optimistic postmillennialism as the basis of widespread attacks on slavery. Before 1830 most Disciples thought the millennium near at hand and they relentlessly attacked every social evil—including slavery—which blocked its introduction. Kentuckians, Virginians, and Carolinians, as well as Northerners, shared the vision of a nation with all men equal and a world with all men good.

But as the nature of the abolition crusade changed in the decades following 1830, the Disciples also changed. Radical abolitionists determined not only to pray for the freedom of the slaves but to fight for it; they not only loved the Negro, they also hated the slaveholder; their proposition was no longer that slavery should be abolished but that it must be abolished. Some Disciples made this transition. They became political activists and fanatics in the cause of love. The fullblown fruit of Disciples fervor was humanitarian sons of thunder.

And yet, most Disciples, like most Americans, were unwilling to accept the uncompromising conclusions of militant abolitionism. Disciples leaders shared the aversion of most American Protestant churchmen to the excesses of the abolitionist attacks of the post-1830 era. Men such as Tolbert Fanning, Philip Fall, and James S. Lamar in the South; Isaac Errett, David S. Burnet, and Elijah Goodwin in the North; and Alexander Campbell, Thomas M. Allen, and John T. Johnson in the border areas were unemotional, rationalistic moderates. Abolitionism smacked of a social fanaticism essentially out of step with the tolerant mind of much of the movement.

After 1830 the Disciples gospel of the millennium became less intolerant of slavery. As the early optimistic dreams of postmillennialist Disciples became less urgent, they more and more conceived of social reform as a long and gradual historical process. Most moderates in the church remained concerned about slavery but by the mid-1830's they were by no means sure that the solution to the problem was either obvious or imminent. As a matter of fact, the sheer magnitude of the dilemma led some of the church's leaders to the conclusion that a slave system might not be incompatible with the reign of Christ on earth. The moderate postmillennialism which developed in the church after 1830 predicted an evolution rather than a revolution in American society.

Another factor which hindered the spread of radical antislavery activity among the Disciples was their sectarian aversion to "preaching politics." The Protestant left-wing tradition of separation of church and state, the restoration emphasis on the all-sufficiency of the church, and the fine theological distinction between matters of "faith" and "opinion" were strong bulwarks against the inroads of radical abolitionism. As moderate church leaders became more and more obsessed with the fear of division in the decade of the fifties, they leaned heavily on these intellectual presuppositions.

Perhaps more than anything else, Biblical literalism was the core of the moderate case among the Disciples. If the benevolence of the gospel message motivated many of the early leaders of the church to free their slaves, the letter of the New Testament surely taught that slaveholding was not a sin. Within a group dedicated to the literal "restoration of primitive Christianity," Paul's letter to Philemon was an almost insurmountable obstacle to mass conversion to abolitionism.

In short, the voice of the Disciples was as the voice of the nation. Out of the diversity of the Disciples mind came the testimony of prophets and peacemakers. Abolitionists, fire-eaters, and moderates all had roots in the Christian message of the movement. If uncompromising and un-selfish prophets filled the American wilderness with demands for universal liberty, Disciples were among them. If men of good will and broad minds worked valiantly to stem the bloody ordeal of a fratricidal war, Disciples were among them. If men of Christian conviction wrestled desperately with the insoluble dilemma of a nation in travail, Disciples were among them.

Although it is obvious that the Disciples Christian ethos was mold-ing American society, it is at least equally as obvious that the church's message was influenced by the sectional severing of the nation. The schizoid personality of the movement slowly parted in the years after 1830 into liberal and activistic, and conservative and politically non-active groups. The relationships between these divergent theological emphases and the sectional philosophies of the dividing nation are ob-vious. The roots of Disciples schism reach deeply into the slavery con-troversy.[145]

---

[145]Many factors are involved in the schisms of the restoration movement in the late nineteenth and early twentieth centuries. The role of economics has already been discussed. It is also obvious that sectionalism was an important factor in these divisions. The Church of Christ–Disciples of Christ rupture was basically a North-South division (although rural-urban and other factors are important). More is said of this in the chapter on war—the pattern becomes increasingly clear after 1870. Equally as interesting is the sectional nature of the co-operative-independent schism in the history of the Disciples in the twentieth century. Independent strength in East Tennessee, Kentucky, and other regions which were border areas in slavery days and the Civil War is suggestive of the moderate pro-South group in the earlier history of the movement (although, once again, urban-rural considerations are obviously extremely important). In short, Disciples were sectionally divided during the slavery controversy and the Civil War into three groups—Southern, middle, and Northern. The theology of these three groups tended more toward conservatism the further South its strength lay. Once again, it might be suggested that the religious censuses of the nineteenth century would furnish the material for some valuable local studies in this area. See Harrell, "Sectional Origins of the Churches of Christ," *Journal of Southern History*.

The impact of the sectional division of the United States on American religion was momentous. H. Richard Niebuhr writes:

> In few instances have schisms been so obviously due to the operation of social factors as in the case of the break which the Civil War and its antecedents effected in the churches of America. Rarely have the causes of schism been less obscured by rationalization, for the sister churches of the North and South, whether Presbyterian, or Methodist, or Baptist, or Lutheran continued to confess their creedal unity while maintaining their ecclesiastical separation.[146]

For an obvious reason Niebuhr omits the Disciples of Christ in his discussion of the denominational divisions of this period of national crisis.[147] Almost unanimously Disciples historians have taken considerable pride in the truism that the Christian church did not divide during this critical period. Robert Richardson, the father of Disciples historiography, wrote in 1868: "Mr. Campbell's conservative course in regard to this disturbing question [slavery], while it preserved the reforming churches from division, excited against him the animosity of many individuals."[148] Winfred E. Garrison, the very able dean of modern Disciples historians, wrote of Campbell over sixty years later: "It cost him much criticism from both sides, but it established the general lines of an attitude which not only saved the Disciples from a division in 1845, but enabled them to go through the Civil War still undivided."[149] This interpretation of Disciples history has long needed reevaluation.

The abolitionist defection among the Disciples of Christ in the late 1850's was too sizable a group to be ignored. It is almost impossible to estimate what might have been the eventual breadth of its appeal. The movement was still in its infancy when the war triggered a complete readjustment of sectional alignments within the church. But enough is obvious to indicate that it was more than an insignificant splintering. The abolitionist leadership was determined, able, and comparatively widespread. When compared in size to the early stages of the antiorgan move-

---

[146]Niebuhr, *Social Sources*, pp. 187-188.

[147]The omission is significant because Niebuhr deals extensively with Disciples in the preceding chapter. *Ibid.*, pp. 135-164.

[148]Richardson, *Memoirs of Campbell*, II, 534.

[149]Garrison, *Religion Follows the Frontier*, pp. 179-180. Most general histories reflect this interpretation. See Olmstead, *Religion in the United States*, p. 383.

ment which led to the formation of the Church of Christ, this early separatist surge had markedly more potential. They had an organ of periodical expression, were the dominant influence in one school, and had the sympathy of several others. It is impossible to know the number of churches which supported the bolting abolitionists when they established the Christian Missionary Society, but Pardee Butler reported in 1859 that he "found the masses of the people [in the free-state churches] with such convictions as will constrain them to treat slavery in the United States as a moral evil, and to patronize only such societies as assume toward it a similar position."[150] The Christian Missionary Society, although its beginnings were small, and although it lived less than five years, was more than a figurehead organization—it had an air of permanency. In summary, the abolitionist separation which solidified in the founding of the Christian Missionary Society in 1859 unquestionably was a minority movement even among Northern Disciples; it was in the formative and chaotic stage of organizing when the Civil War broke out; but it was more than the "little faction" Benjamin Franklin called it.

The process of division was a bewildering unknown to the Disciples in the 1850's. It took most of the remainder of the nineteenth century to demonstrate the localized, time-consuming process necessary for a permanent schism in the loosely knit movement. The basic ingredients which proved necessary were the solidification of factions around opposing sets of institutions such as papers, schools, and societies and the development of an "issue" of sufficient importance to be regarded as a "test of fellowship." By 1860 abolitionist Disciples were rapidly uniting around separate institutional loyalties and many of them were prepared to make the slavery issue a "test of fellowship."

Almost from the beginning the Disciples included those who believed that slaveholding was an offense worthy of "disfellowshiping." Nathanial Field wrote Walter Scott in 1834 that he had "resolved not to *break the loaf* with slaveholders or in any way to countenance them, as Christians."[151] In 1851 John Kirk of Ohio wrote Alexander Campbell: "If I am correctly informed, our brethren generally in the slave States are

[150]Hastings, *Butler*, p. 326.
[151]"Letter from Nat. Field, Jeffersonville," *Evangelist*, III (October, 1834), 234.

slaveholders, and that you fellowship them as Christian brethren. I think this altogether wrong."[152] This sentiment rapidly expanded in the Northern churches during the 1850's. By 1857 numerous congregations in the North were organized on an antislavery basis and John Boggs editorially gave his approval to the development: "Every congregation built on the Bible, and the Bible alone, would . . . prohibit the reception as members those who practise . . . slavery."[153]

By 1859 the Disciples of Christ were organizationally divided at both the congregational and the national level. But perhaps as important as this practical division, for some of the congregations had been exclusively antislavery for years, was the prevailing feeling in the brotherhood that a general division was in progress.

Although Pardee Butler, John Boggs, Ovid Butler, and other abolitionist leaders sometimes made uncertain sounds on whether slaveholding was a "test of fellowship," their hesitancy was always based on the condition that the Southern churches would reform.[154] The growing awareness among the abolitionists in the last years of the 1850's that such a hope was unrealistic led them increasingly to the conviction that a clear-cut division was inevitable. In his 1859 report Pardee Butler discussed both the process and the imminence of division:

Discipline is special to each congregation, but that sense of justice which always stands as the basis of discipline, is common to all the churches in one communion. This public opinion is created by a mutual interchange of sentiment—the books we read and the preachers we hear. For years past slaveholders have ceased to hear those suspected of abolitionism or to read their writings. I will bear very long with error where mutual discussion and free interchange of sentiment promise

---

[152]"Our Position to American Slavery," *M.H.*, 4th S., I (January, 1851), 49.

[153]"Querist's Department," *N.W.C.M.*, IV (September, 1857), 90.

[154]Until the end some of the Disciples abolitionists protested that they did not intend to divide the church. John Boggs wrote in 1854: "Our object, then, is not to 'cause division,' and to make two parties among us, but, on the contrary, to call the attention of our slave holding brethren to the subject; show them the sinfulness, and we have faith enough in their piety to believe they will renounce it." "What They Say of Us in Kentucky," *N.W.C.M.*, II (August, 1854), 54. Every student of Disciples history who has seriously considered the divisive influence of the abolitionist element has accepted this interpretation. See Barnes, "Analytical Study of Magazine," pp. 126-130; Vandegrift, "Christian Missionary Society," p. 81; Fife, "Slavery Controversy," pp. 255-273.

ultimately to bring all to be of the same mind. . . . There must and will be a reform; it has become a public necessity. . . . The people will not follow those who
have been accustomed to lead, notwithstanding those leaders will have power
greatly to embarrass the action of those who do not follow them.[155]

Jasper J. Moss and Elijah Goodwin, two moderate Indianians who attended the abolitionist convention in 1859, reported that the leadership
of that meeting was determined to create a permanent schism. Moss
wrote:

P. Butler said they were prepared for division, that is, they were prepared to declare non-fellowship with slave-holders, or to refuse them membership in their
society, but they did not want it now; that is they must be divorced, but they
wanted us to sue for the bill . . . because they would then have the sympathy of
the people with them.[156]

There was a widespread conviction among moderates in both North
and South that the abolitionist defection would end in permanent division. The aging Love Jameson wrote Isaac Errett in August, 1859: "I
feel that there is much to discourage those who are toiling for the up-
building of the Cause. How or when the matter will end, I don't pre-
tend to predict[.] In schism I fear."[157] Benjamin Franklin's and Isaac
Errett's attacks on the abolitionist movement as "sectional and factious,"
although partly tactical attempts to prompt an abolitionist retreat, were
expressions of a genuine and growing fear.[158] In a rare and significant
notice of the radical abolition movement in 1861, William Lipscomb,
writing in the Nashville, Gospel Advocate, accepted division as an accomplished fact: "Beyond the circle of a pitiable clique in the Northwest, our brethren are still united and must remain so as long as they
are content to adhere faithfully to the simple order of Heaven."[159]

If one divides the Disciples moderate group, four significant ideological and sectional factions emerge in ante-bellum Disciples history:

---

[155]Hastings, *Butler*, p. 327.

[156]"Indianapolis Convention—No. III," *A.C.R.*, II (December 13, 1859), 200;
E. G., "The N. W. C. Convention (?)," *C.R.*, 3d S., III (December, 1859),
150-151.

[157]L. H. Jameson to Isaac Errett, August 25, 1859, Butler Manuscript Collection.

[158]See "Where Is the Safe Ground?" *A.C.R.*, I (February, 1856), 35-39; Isaac
Errett, "Sectional and Factious Movement," *A.C.R.*, II (August 23, 1859), 135.

[159]"The Duty of the Hour," *G.A.*, VII (March, 1861), 85.

abolitionists, antislavery moderates, proslavery moderates, and proslavery radicals. Disciples historians have generally failed to recognize the potency of the sectional slavery issue in the history of the movement because of the tireless efforts of Disciples moderates to minimize the internal tensions in the church. What actually did happen among the Disciples between the years 1855 and 1860 was a general defection of the most radical Northern group. But the church did divide and the tenuous union of the remaining three groups was not so permanent as appeared on the surface.

The lasting effect of the pre-Civil War sectional splintering of the church may only be suggested here but some important insights into the future sociological pressures on church solidarity were apparent by the end of the slavery controversy. The reunion which took place at the end of 1863 between the abolitionists and the American Christian Missionary Society was not a surrender of Northern radical sectionalism. The reunion was simply a merging of the two Northern groups in the church which had been estranged in 1859. The passage of loyalty resolutions by the society in 1863 was in essence a capitulation to the radical Northern position[160]—a great national war succeeded in breaking down the moderate resistance in the North where antislavery sentiment had failed.

Furthermore, the reunion between abolitionists and Northern moderates in the American Christian Missionary Society in 1863 was a decidedly sectional achievement. What the reaction of the South would be to the Northern-dominated society was by no means certain in 1863. Some Southerners had revealed that they had serious doubts about a national organization that tried to accommodate varying sectional interests. Tolbert Fanning, powerful church leader in Middle Tennessee, wrote in 1858: "For many years we have felt but little confidence in any missionary operation founded in human wisdom. We need not fear a northern or southern spirit while the Bible remains the supreme authority. . . . Hence we have preferred missionary operations by church authority alone."[161]

---

[160]See A. R. Benton to Isaac Errett, November 3, 1863, Butler Manuscript Collection; Vandegrift, "Christian Missionary Society," pp. 83-85.

[161]"Jamaica Mission," *G.A.*, IV (May, 1858), 149. See, also, T. M. Allen to J. A. Gano, January 17, 1849, John Allen Gano Papers.

In the troubled years following the Civil War new divisive issues arose among the Disciples of Christ but the sectional alignment of factions was, at least in part, a heritage from the slavery controversy. After 1859 the restoration movement was never without a major element opposed to the operations of the American Christian Missionary Society—the sectional pattern had emerged.

CHAPTER V

PACIFISM AND PATRIOTISM – THE CLEAVAGE DEEPENS

PRELUDE

"To everything there is a season, and a time for every purpose under the heaven.
. . . A time to love, and a time to hate; a time of war, and a time of peace."
Ecclesiastes 3:18.

IF THE CHRISTIAN MESSAGE has been repeatedly perverted into nationalistic propaganda in modern Western history, it has also been this culture's most persistent and fruitful ideological source of pacifism. When local and state peace societies began to emerge in the United States after the close of the War of 1812, clergymen and church leaders were their most important supporters and the New Testament was their major source of authority. Although the ante-bellum peace movement never gained the momentum of a major crusade, and certainly never commanded the loyalty of most of the American people, by 1828 pacifist agitators had succeeded in establishing a national organization, the American Peace Society. The peace campaign was most successful in the East, where the War of 1812 and the Mexican War were unpopular, and it gained at least nominal support from numerous influential reformers.[1]

Although Disciples leaders were not outspoken pacifist crusaders during the years prior to 1846, they were both aware of and in sympathy with the organized efforts of American reformers. Alexander Campbell early made his pacifist convictions known; he spasmodically reported the actions of the peace reformers and occasionally reprinted their articles in

---

[1]For general discussions of the peace movement to 1865, see Merle Eugene Curti, *The American Peace Crusade 1815-1860* (Durham, North Carolina: Duke University Press, 1929); Merle Curti, *Peace or War: The American Struggle 1636-1936* (2nd ed.; Boston: J. S. Canner & Company Publishers, 1959), pp. 16-73; Devere Allen, *The Fight for Peace* (New York: The Macmillan Company, 1930).

the *Millennial Harbinger*.[2] Barton Stone followed a similar course in his *Christian Messenger* and as early as 1827 coupled "war and slavery" as the "greatest evils in the world."[3] Although Disciples leaders were not deeply involved in the peace crusade in the years preceding the Mexican War, they were interested in it and were unanimously in sympathy with its aims.[4]

In general, the reaction of American churches to the Mexican War in 1846 reflected the geographic distribution of their membership.[5] The most vigorous protests against the war came from the Northeast. On the other hand, as Clayton Sumner Ellsworth points out, "No church with its members concentrated in the Southwest or with a strong stake there opposed the war."[6] Such social issues as slavery, manifest destiny, and anti-Catholic feeling were important influences in determining the attitudes of the churches.

The outbreak of war with Mexico in May, 1846, was the first real test of Disciples' devotion to the principles of pacifism and it triggered the first major discussions of the war question in the church's periodicals. In November, 1846, Alexander Campbell published a long pacifist

---

[2]For examples of Campbell's early interest in the peace movement, see "Duty of Laboring Assiduously and Praying Unceasingly for the Abolition of War," *M.H.*, V (July, 1834), 306-309; "War and Christianity Antipodal," *M.H.*, 3d S., VII (September, 1850), 523-524. For a good summary of Campbell's early pacifist contributions, see Lunger, *Political Ethics of Alexander Campbell*, pp. 242-247. Campbell occasionally reported on the workings of the peace movement in Europe. See "Peace Congress," *M.H.*, 3d S., VI (December, 1849), 703-706; "A Cry from London," *M.H.*, 5th S., IV (June, 1861), 334-335.

[3]"Queries Proposed for Investigation by a Worthy Brother," *C.M.*, II (December, 1827), 36.

[4]Even at this early period, however, there apparently was a significant gap between the leaders and the mass of the church's membership. Colby Hall concludes from his study of Texas Disciples that many of the church members in that state were active in the Texas Revolution. See *Texas Disciples* (Fort Worth, Texas: Texas Christian University Press, 1953), pp. 64-74.

[5]See, for general accounts of the churches' reactions to the Mexican War, Clayton Sumner Ellsworth, "The American Churches and the Mexican War," *American Historical Review*, XLV (January, 1940), 301-326; Anson Phelps Stokes, *Church and State in the United States* (3 vols.; New York: Harper & Brothers, 1950), II, 75-83; John R. Bodo, *The Protestant Clergy and Public Issues 1812-1848* (Princeton, New Jersey: Princeton University Press, 1954), pp. 216-223.

[6]"Churches and the Mexican War," XLV, 326.

article in the *Harbinger* after being urged "from all quarters" to give his views "of war in general and of the present American Mexican Republican war in particular." After pointing out that he consistently had opposed war in his public writings since the first issue of the *Christian Baptist*, Campbell began a long scriptural defense of the principles of pacifism. Supported by his dispensational concept of biblical history, Campbell dismissed the precedent of Old Testament Jewish wars and emphasized such strongly pacifist New Testament texts as Jesus' statement: "My kingdom is not of this world. If my kingdom were of this world, my servants would have fought."[7] In an 1848 address before the Lyceum of Wheeling, Virginia, Campbell further developed his pacifist philosophy. His conclusions were clear and uncompromising: "The precepts of Christianity positively inhibit war."[8]

Many other influential Disciples leaders were outspoken in their condemnation of the Mexican War. Immediately after the hostilities began Walter Scott urged "feelings of forgiveness and compassion" toward the enemy and counseled Christians to use their influence to "allay the

---

[7]"War—No. I," *M.H.*, 3d S., III (November, 1846), 638-642.

[8]"An Address on War," *M.H.*, 3d S., V (July, 1848), 361-368. Harold Lunger analyzes this important speech in detail, *Political Ethics of Alexander Campbell*, pp. 247-257. The impact of Campbell's pacifist articles was considerably weakened by his refusal to deal with the real problem—not war in the abstract but the Mexican War. He wrote: "I must, for more reasons than one, decline the task of scrutinizing the existing war either in its object, character, or tendency." "War—No. I," *M.H.*, 3d S., III (November, 1846), 638. The reformer's millennial confidence in the destiny of Protestantism and the American nation and his moderate views on slavery made him unwilling to condemn the expansionistic war with Mexico. He was also influenced by his growing determination to keep sectional issues out of the church. Samuel Rogers records an interesting example of Campbell's reticence to discuss the subject: "President Shannon, in speaking of their talks, remarked that he had failed to provoke Mr. Campbell into a controversy as to the justness or unjustness of the late war with Mexico. Mr. Campbell, however, did say to him with considerable emphasis that he could not believe that one Christian nation, so-called at least, could wage just war against another Christian nation. He would not discuss the merits of the question—but this was his view, in short, and here the matter ended. But President Shannon did believe that the United States was justifiable in going to war against Mexico, and was as well prepared to defend this view as any statesman in the Union." Rogers, *Recollections*, pp. 16-17.

exasperation of national strife, and promote pacific counsels."[9] In 1847
Scott again advised his readers to "use all their influence, to bring the
war in which we are engaged to a close."[10] The caustic Benjamin U.
Watkins sarcastically remarked that it was a strange "new method of
praying for enemies" which implored "that our most *christian cannon*
may tear the entrails out of thousands of Mexicans!—that our most *pious
bomb shells* may dash to pieces thousands of women and children!"[11]

If the Mexican War provided the occasion for the first general pacifist
assault by Disciples leaders, it also revealed that the church was far from
united on the subject. In 1846 William Baxter protested that "many of
the professed followers of the peace loving and peace speaking Saviour,
have taken up weapons and sought the battle field." Even "some of the
ministers," according to Baxter, "betrayed a most unseemly anxiety to
leave the pulpit . . . to seek on the fields of the far South, a sphere of
action totally at variance with the spirit and precepts of that religion of
which they are the professed teachers."[12] James Shannon, president of
Bacon College and ardent defender of slavery, supported the war as a
benevolent attempt to extend and improve the slave system.[13] Michael
Mavity, in a series of articles in the *Western Reformer,* argued that Christians were bound by the doctrine of civil obedience to support national
wars.[14] But probably the most important ideological justification for the
war was anti-Catholic prejudice. Robert Forrester, coeditor with Walter
Scott of the *Protestant Unionist,* thought that the struggle was both inevitable and righteous: "Popish intolerance standing opposed to the popular
current of the age, if it refuse to yield, must be swept away by its overwhelming force."[15]

When faced for the first time with the practical problem of war, the
Disciples demonstrated an ominous lack of agreement. While some of the

---

[9]"War—Duty of Christians," *P.U.,* II (June 10, 1846), 106.

[10]"Peace," *P.U.,* III (February 17, 1847), 42.

[11]"War and Christianity," *G.P.,* I (August, 1847), 64.

[12]"The War," *P.U.,* II (November 18, 1846), 198.

[13]See Rogers, *Recollections,* pp. 16-17.

[14]See "War and Christianity," *W.R.,* V (May, 1847), 421-422.

[15]"The War," *P.U.,* II (September 23, 1846), 166. See, also, "Lectures on
Genesis," *C.Mag.,* I (August, 1848), 229.

church's leaders, in all sections, vigorously denounced the struggle, others militantly defended it as a Christian effort.[16] But, in general, the Mexican War created little lasting concern among the Disciples.

Perhaps the most significant impact of the Mexican War was its ignition of the first brotherhood-wide periodical debate on the war question. The *Gospel Proclamation* published monthly articles by George Pow and Benjamin U. Watkins for almost two years beginning in December, 1847. There were other such debates in the years before 1860 and a rash of them in the decade from 1860 to 1870 but none was more extended than the Pow-Watkins discussion—the pattern it set was pretty generally followed for half a century. Both writers accepted the Scriptures as authoritative and their examination of pertinent texts was virtually exhaustive. As the discussion progressed it became apparent that the answer to this question in Christian ethics turned, among Disciples at any rate, on the problem of whether or not some of the Christians of New Testament times were soldiers.[17] Pow argued that some New Testament Christians, such as the Roman centurian, Cornelius, were soldiers and that this evidence conclusively proved that Christians could fight. Watkins countered that it was imperative to assume that Cornelius and other such Christians resigned their military offices just as it was natural to assume that any man engaged in sinful practices would reform when he became a Christian. A stalemate developed before the antagonists had written two articles. What had been proved by the end of the discussion was that both sides could be scripturally fortified. A supply of ammunition had

---

[16]This was the reaction of most American churches. Ellsworth's summary of Disciples is substantially correct. See "Churches and the Mexican War," XLV, 323.

[17]This was consistently the crucial question in Disciples debates on the war question. The strict dispensationalism of the group made it impossible for either side to draw authoritative conclusions from the examples of the Old Testament. While most of the prowar writers would cite the examples of the Jewish wars, in the final analysis both sides would turn to the New Testament to try to justify their conclusions. The pacifists simply would not admit that Old Testament examples had any pertinence in the Christian age. John R. Bodo points out that all of the early Christian pacifists used this stratagem: "The pacifists stressed the dichotomy between the 'two covenants' and the supremacy of the New Testament." *Clergy and Public Issues*, p. 228. Disciples theology was fertile soil for such New Testament pacifism. But the prowar advocates were not without a New Testament case.

been stockpiled for future use on both sides of the question. It was to be exploited.[18]

As the stricken nation lumbered toward its 1861 rendezvous with tragedy the mind of Disciples of Christ was unsettled and unsure. Probably most of the leaders of the church were moderate pacifists. There was much in the common mind of the movement to support such a view. Sectarian disdain for the affairs of the world and New Testament primitivism were powerful stimuli for pacifist convictions. The moderate and rational mood of the Disciples mind was not well suited to the climate of fanatical times. But there were other factors at work by 1860.

The church was by no means united as it approached the national crisis. It was questionable in 1860 whether the unbending sectarian pacifism widely evident in 1848 extended far beneath the surface of a few outspoken leaders. Furthermore, the Mexican War had demonstrated the fact that prowar advocates were not without intellectual justifications from the storehouse of the common mind of the movement. They fortified their position with New Testament proof texts just as pacifist Disciples did. Above all, these militant Disciples were obsessed with visions of the millennial destiny of Protestant, Anglo-Saxon America. If some were slow to accept war as a means of fulfilling this providential mission, others were not.

CRISIS

"And when Joshua heard the noise of the people as they shouted, he said unto Moses, There is a noise of war in the camp." Exodus 32:17.

During the hectic decade of the 1850's the organized peace movement in the United States rapidly declined; by 1860 it had virtually collapsed. This by no means meant that most Americans in 1860 were determined

---

[18]By the end of the discussions during and after the Mexican War almost every pacifist argument which was to be used for half a century had been developed. Merle Curti points out that this was perhaps the outstanding contribution of the early pacifist movement: "Perhaps the most striking contribution of early organized pacifism was the development of a body of brilliant arguments against war. By 1860 practically every argument against war now familiar had been suggested, and almost every current plan for securing peace had been at least anticipated." *American Peace Crusade*, p. 225.

to settle the momentous national problems by a test of arms. As a matter of fact, on November 6, 1860, two fifths of the American people voted for candidates committed to the peaceable preservation of the Union— fully as many as voted for Abraham Lincoln. In the months that followed the election of President Lincoln, as the nation trudged slowly toward the bloody harvest of a half century of internal discord, there were frantic efforts to halt the disintegration of the country and to consummate a new and lasting sectional compromise. But somehow the cries of the prophets of peace could not compete with the crescendo of bellowing demagogues, galloping hoofs, and clattering caissons as the nation converged on Bull Run.[19]

Two momentous questions loomed in the minds of the leaders of the Disciples: what should Christians do if war came and what would be the impact of a great civil struggle on the church? Through most of 1860 Disciples periodicals were shrouded in portentous silence, but by the beginning of 1861 the old policy of suppression of the controversial was abandoned and the editors of the church one by one published appeals for moderation. Above all, they urged that whatever course the nation might take, Christians should remain united. Elijah Goodwin, a staunch Union man, wrote:

But let what come that may, in the political affairs of our country, we hope, and pray that these matters may be kept out of the church of God; and that even if the States should sever the ties that have so long bound them together, the christian brotherhood will still remain a unit.[20]

Alexander Campbell remained silent until June, 1861. By this time the nation was divided into two armed camps; Fort Sumter had been seized two months previously; before another month passed the first major battle of the American Civil War would be fought at Manassas Junction in northern Virginia. Campbell pleaded with the two sides to submit to

---

[19]See Mary Scrugham, *The Peaceable Americans of 1860-1861* (Columbia University Studies in History, Economics and Political Science, XCVI; New York: Columbia University, 1921), pp. 23-104, for a good summary of the efforts to compromise on the eve of the Civil War.

[20]"The North and the South," *C.R.*, 3d S., V (January, 1861), 25.

"arbitration." The tired old man, who had abruptly returned home in the midst of one of his long tours when he heard the news of the outbreak of hostilities, made an impassioned appeal to the nation:

Civilized America! civilized UNITED STATES! boasting of a humane and Christian paternity and fraternity, unsheathing your swords, discharging your cannon, boasting of your heathen brutality, gluttonously satiating your furious appetites for fraternal blood, caps the climax of all human inconsistencies inscribed on the blurred and moth eaten pages of time in all its records.[21]

During the stormy months from the fall of 1860 to midsummer, 1861, there was frantic and fervent private communication among the leaders of the church. Out of this ferment emerged the most important public statement of neutrality by Disciples leaders in 1861, a circular signed by fourteen of the outstanding preachers of Missouri. While the circular was not a pacifist statement, it urged neutrality in the strongest terms:

Whatever we may think of the propriety of bearing arms in extreme emergencies, we certainly can not, by the New Testament, which is our only rule of discipline, justify ourselves in engaging in the fraternal strife now raging in our beloved country.[22]

The neutrals, however, by no means completely dominated the fervent behind-the-scenes activity. Walter Scott wrote a militant article supporting the forcible preservation of the Union which his old comrade of so many battles, Alexander Campbell, refused to publish in the *Harbinger*.[23] William T. Moore used his strategically located pulpit in Frankfort, Kentucky, to try to swing wavering Christian church state legislators into the Union camp.[24] On the other side, Thomas W. Caskey, probably the lead-

---

[21]"Wars and Rumors of War," *M.H.*, 5th S., IV (June, 1861), 348.

[22]"Circular from Preachers in Missouri," *M.H.*, 5th S., IV (October, 1861), 583-584. Church leaders in other localities also worked feverishly to maintain peace in the nation and in the church. See Philip Fall Papers; John Allen Gano Papers; Butler Manuscript Collection; Lamar, *Errett*, I, 238-248.

[23]Scott wrote: "The government . . . that will not, with all its *force*, in defiance of all obstacles, put down anarchy and the doctrine that leads to it, ought itself to be put down." Stevenson, *Walter Scott*, p. 220. Scott's intense nationalism triumphed over his pacifism. During the Mexican War he had been one of the most courageous and outspoken pacifists within the movement but he could not believe that the great and providentially prepared American nation should be destroyed without a struggle.

[24]Moore reports his actions as follows: "At this juncture it came to my knowledge that a careful canvass had been made with the result that the legislature was about equally divided for and against 'armed neutrality,' with five or six members

ing Disciples minister in Mississippi, was touring his state with the Attorney-General "to talk the people out of the Union."[25]

In sum, as the national crisis ripened in the early months of 1861, the Disciples reacted chaotically. There were theoretical pacifists, practical neutralists, and militant Northern and Southern war hawks within the church. By the summer of 1861 it was impossible to tell which group was most numerous or most influential in the councils of the church. Nor was there more than a semblance of stability within the groups. In May, 1861, Dr. John P. Robison, who a few months earlier had written an anti-war letter to Isaac Errett, informed his correspondent that he was "out of the woods and in for the fight."[26] In the months that followed such transitions were common.

PACIFISTS AND NEUTRALS

"But I say unto you, Love your enemies." Matthew 5:44.

By and large, American churches in both North and South rallied to the support of their sections when the war began. The Baptists and the Methodists, the two largest Protestant denominations in the country, had already been divided for years. Shortly after the secession of the Southern states had been completed, Southern Presbyterians, Episcopalians, and

---

classed among the doubtful. Now it happened that all but one, I believe, of these doubtful legislators were members of the Christian Church. I immediately announced that I would preach the next Sunday morning on the 'Duty of Christians in the Present Crisis.' Some forty or fifty members of the legislature heard the sermon, and among them those who had been reckoned as doubtful with respect to the vote which would be taken the early part of the week. The vote was taken, and 'armed neutrality' was defeated; and this defeat was secured, in the opinion of some of those who are acquainted with the facts, by the influence of the sermon which I preached. It was an appeal to the Christian conscience against embarking in an enterprise which meant only evil for that fellowship which had been so strong between the Christians residing in the respective hostile sections. It was known before the sermon that the doubtful voters leaned toward the 'armed neutrality' measure, but when the time of final decision came they voted against that measure, and thereby secured its defeat, and at the same time saved Kentucky to the Federal Union." W. T. Moore, "Reformation of the Nineteenth Century," *Christian Evangelist*, XXXVI (May 18, 1899), 617.

[25]B. F. Manire, ed., *Caskey's Last Book* (Nashville: The Messenger Publishing Co., 1896), pp. 29-30.

[26]J. P. Robison to Isaac Errett, May 31, 1861, Butler Manuscript Collection.

Lutherans formed independent organizations. As Clifton E. Olmstead says: "Few wars in history have received such overwhelming approval from religious institutions as the Civil War."[27]

There were, however, considerable and important segments in the nation which disapproved of the war. Although most religious groups turned from the altar of peace to the altar of Mars, there were those, such as the Quakers and several German sects, which persistently preached and practiced pacifism. Furthermore, there were elements in both sections who disapproved of the conflict and who worked throughout the struggle for peace. There were many motivations for such practical neutrality: political, ideological, economic, and humanitarian. While these Civil War peace movements were largely unfruitful, they remained strong throughout the war, especially in the border states.[28]

---

[27]Olmstead, *Religion in the United States,* p. 384, see pp. 384-390. Consult, also, Sweet, *Religion in America,* pp. 312-317; Stokes, *Church and State,* II, 203-245; Edward McPherson, *The Political History of the United States of America During the Great Rebellion* (Washington, D. C.: Solomons & Chapman, 1876), pp. 461-554; Chester Forrester Dunham, *The Attitude of the Northern Clergy Toward the South 1860-1865* (Toledo, Ohio: The Gray Company, Publishers, 1942), *passim.* All of these general studies omit the Disciples in their analyses of the reaction of American religion to the Civil War. For accounts of the reaction of specific denominations, see William Warren Sweet, *The Methodist Episcopal Church and the Civil War* (Cincinnati: Methodist Book Concern Press, n.d.); Lewis G. Vander Velde, *The Presbyterian Churches and the Federal Union, 1861-1869* (Cambridge: Harvard University Press, 1932); Joseph Blount Cheshire, *The Church in the Confederate States* (New York: Longmans, Green, and Co., 1912); Ralph Ernest Morrow, *Northern Methodism and Reconstruction* (East Lansing: Michigan State University Press, 1956).

[28]Edward Needles Wright's study, *Conscientious Objectors in the Civil War* (Philadelphia: University of Pennsylvania Press, 1931), is the best study of pacifism during the War, although he deals almost totally with the Quakers and German sects. He does not mention the Disciples. Wright is concerned solely with Christian pacifism in his study and does not deal with the neutralist movement. Disloyal and peace movements within the two sections are dealt with in Elbert J. Benton, *The Movement for Peace Without Victory During the Civil War* (*Collections* of the Western Reserve Historical Society, No. 99; Cleveland: n.p., 1918) and Georgia Lee Tatum, *Disloyalty in the Confederacy* (Chapel Hill, N. C.: University of North Carolina Press, 1934). Jeremiah Sullivan Black, outstanding Disciple layman, was one of the leading moderate Peace Democrats during the war years. As a former member of President Buchanan's cabinet, he played an important role in the abortive peace negotiations of 1864. See Edward Chase Kirkland, *The Peacemakers of 1864* (New York: The Macmillan Company, 1927), pp. 117-124.

Among a sizable group of Disciples leaders, the frantic neutrality of the early months of 1861 deepened into a firm commitment to peace. The motivations of this influential group were diverse. Some of them were New Testament pacifists, imbued with a sectarian distrust of civil government and determined not to become involved in the gigantic sins of the nation. Others were practical neutrals, men of moderation who believed that the war was a national disaster and that only the greatest prudence could keep it from becoming a disaster to the church as well. There were Southern sympathizers in the North who believed that the South had the constitutional right to secede; there were Northern sympathizers in the South who believed that the South had no right to resort to arms. Disciples motivated by all of these factors formed an antiwar coalition within the church during the war years—it is never easy, and sometimes impossible, to determine the motivation of any one man.

The still powerful influence of Alexander Campbell (although he became less and less active after 1861) was solidly behind the neutral position. Although he rarely wrote on the subject, he remained firm in his commitment to pacifism. The "Preface" of the 1864 volume of the *Millennial Harbinger* is perhaps the most moving passage in the voluminous Campbell writings. The aging and failing old warrior (in the same issue of the magazine he announced his resignation as its editor) called for a rededication by Disciples to the great principles of the restoration movement. At best, the church was on the brink of schism; at worst, it was in the midst of a wholesale defection to the world. Calling on the great reservoir of courage which had seldom failed him and rallying his fading giant intellectual power, the sage of Bethany wrote with real pathos:

Many seem to have passed, we trust but for a time, under the "power of the world," and to have forgotten the spirit and service of the gospel. The times are full of corruption, and the church is contaminated with the times. We all need to be reminded, in tones of tenderness, coming as from the world-renouncing agonies of the cross, that *we, the people of the living God, are not of the world. . . .* Brethren, we are in the midst of appalling tokens of this very defection—and who is faithful and fearless! Shall we see our long labors go down in the storm of an hour, and give ourselves and our sacred charge, without an effort or struggle, up to the devouring elements? . . . Shall we forget this ourselves, or fail from false policy or treasonable cowardice to warn and admonish those whom we see departing from this only legitimate work of our high and noble calling? Who are the faithful ones, that stand ready to hold up our hands in this work? Our present volume asks this question and holds out its hands for the answer.[29]

---

[29]"Preface," *M.H.*, 5th S., VII (January, 1864), 4.

In all, the *Millennial Harbinger,* which increasingly was directed by
William K. Pendleton, remained remarkably pacifistic during the war
years.[30] Probably more important, however, was the outspoken neutrality
of Benjamin Franklin and his powerful Cincinnati weekly, the *American
Christian Review.* Franklin was a pacifist, although he admitted that the
whole question was a "difficult one,"[31] and he unbendingly refused to
publish any remotely partisan articles. The editor's policy enraged the
Northern war advocates within the church but received strong support
from the border-state areas.[32]

In September, 1861, John R. Howard and David T. Wright, editors of
the Missouri paper, the *Christian Pioneer,* reported that "every paper published and recognized by our brethren, both North and South, have [*sic*]
come out, and are [*sic*] now coming out, in even stronger terms than
we have, against Christians going to war."[33] While the *Pioneer's* editors'
estimate was unquestionably overly optimistic, and was immediately challenged by Northern radicals, it was true that most Disciples periodicals
remained at least nominally neutral. The two editors also believed that
"almost every preacher we have of any note" was with them "as a unit

---

[30]Harold Lunger says: "The editorial policy of the *Millennial Harbinger* throughout the War was thoroughly pacifist," *Political Ethics of Alexander Campbell,*
p. 259. This is generally true. On the other hand, Pendleton showed a decided
tendency to drift into the Union camp. Prowar articles did appear in the *Harbinger* and Pendleton refused to publish a pacifist article written by Robert Richardson on the grounds that it was "inopportune." "Address," *M.H.,* XXXVIII
(June, 1867), 277. A wartime Bethany student reported that at the "commencement of this war" Pendleton was "in sympathy with the rebellion" but that
"long before the war closed, he saw the folly of his course, and has ever since
manifested the true spirit of loyalty and a profound regret that he had ever
sullied his character by that misguided step." J. F. Berry, "Letter from Bethany,"
North-Western Christian Proclamation, I (April, 1866), 345.

[31]B. F., "What Is Political Preaching?" *American Christian Quarterly Review,*
II (1863), 277.

[32]Franklin, with characteristic color, charged that those who disagreed with him
were under the influence of "one-ideaism, hobbyism and ultraism." "N. W. C.
University," *A.C.R.,* V (August 12, 1862), 2. See, also, John F. Rowe, "Little
Men with Pet Notions," *A.C.Q.R.,* I (1863), 262-265; B. F., "What Is Political
Preaching?" *A.C.Q.R.,* I (1863), 276-278. Franklin's paper apparently had a con-
siderable circulation among the peace groups of the North. "The Genesis of the
Independent Monthly," *Independent Monthly,* I (October, 1869), 331.

[33]"A Vindication of Ourselves and the Christian Pioneer," *C.P.,* I (September,
1861), 170.

on this question."[34] Howard and Wright listed the names of twenty-three outstanding Disciples ministers whom they believed to be firm neutrals. Three of these men, Alexander Campbell, William K. Pendleton, and Robert Richardson, were from Bethany. Three—Robert Milligan, Aylette Raines, and Winthrop H. Hopson—lived in Kentucky, and two more, Benjamin Franklin and David S. Burnet, lived just across the Ohio in Cincinnati. Two, Tolbert Fanning and Philip Fall, were from Tennessee. Eleven were Missouri preachers—Thomas M. Allen, Benjamin H. Smith, Butler K. Smith, Josiah W. Cox, Thomas P. Haley, H. H. Haley, Moses E. Lard, John W. McGarvey, Alexander Procter, Francis R. Palmer, and Jacob Creath, Jr. The only Northern church leaders named were Isaac Errett and Silas Shepard and not a single Disciple from the deep South was listed. The *Pioneer's* list was inaccurate. Certainly the two Northern preachers named, if they had ever given any real indication that they were going to be neutrals, soon clearly demonstrated that they were ready for the fight. Burnet and Hopson, and possibly some of the others named eventually deserted the ranks of the neutrals. But what the *Pioneer's* list does emphasize is that there were concentrations of pacifist and neutral strength within the church. The strongholds of this position throughout the war were in the border areas of West Virginia, Kentucky, Missouri, and Tennessee.[35]

---

[34]*Ibid.*

[35]This is not to say that there were no pacifist Disciples outside of these border areas. Carroll Kendrick continued to preach in Texas throughout the war, as did B. F. Manire in Mississippi, John T. Walsh in North Carolina, Justus M. Barnes in Alabama, and William Baxter in Arkansas. A number of leading preachers in the North remained firmly in the pacifist camp. See C. Kendrick, "Good Words From Our Correspondents," *M.H.*, XXXVI (December, 1865), 573; Justus M. Barnes, "Good Words From Our Correspondents," *M.H.*, XXXVII (January, 1866), 45-46; Manire, *Reminiscences*, pp. 34-35; William Baxter, *Pea Ridge and Prairie Grove* (Cincinnati: Poe and Hitchcock, 1864), pp. 24-25; S. T. Meng, "The Church and the World Powers," *G.A.*, XII (January 28, 1869), 76-78; Delbert Dayton Keesee, "The Churches of Christ During the War Between the States" (unpublished M.A. thesis, Division of Graduate Instruction, Butler University, 1954), pp. 23-65. The most clearly pacifist element within the Disciples was in middle Tennessee where virtually every major church leader refused to participate in the war. See David Edwin Harrell, Jr., "Disciples of Christ Pacifism in Nineteenth Century Tennessee," *Tennessee Historical Quarterly*, XXI (September, 1962), 263-274. Glen W. Mell says: "There can be no doubt as to

There were two major motives behind Disciples neutrality. Some of the church's members were Christian pacifists, dedicated to the sectarian theory of separation of the Christian from the problems of the world. Probably the larger group, however, were not doctrinaire pacifists but were simply opposed to the Civil War. The 1861 Missouri Circular was a frank practical protest against the war rather than a pacifist declaration.[36] Northern Disciples often charged that neutralism was a Southern device to abet secession, as silence had been a Southern stratagem to defend slavery. After the war, Isaac Errett bluntly accused some of the wartime pacifist Disciples of disloyalty: "With many, this [pacifism] is a new-born faith, unknown before the recent civil war, and chiefly prevailing among those who were in sympathy with a lost cause."[37] In 1869 the rabid Unionist Lewis L. Pinkerton charged that the *American Christian Review* had received the bulk of its support from Northern Copperheads: "It is to be expected therefore, that Indianians and Ohioans . . . who desired the success of the rebellion . . . during our struggle for national existence, read the *American Christian Review*."[38]

It is also difficult to evaluate the impact of neutralism and pacifism on the movement in general. Unquestionably some of the churches in the border states were held together because of the moderating influence of neutralist leaders—but there were also some that were not held together. Some young Christians were probably influenced not to enter the conflict by a pacifist minister—and yet, Campbell, Richardson, Gano, and a host of other pacifist preachers had sons in the war. The truth of the matter is that the Disciples reacted to the war about the same as the na-

---

the position taken by the leaders of the Disciples in regard to the Civil War and war in general. They opposed it, almost to a man." "A Study of the Opinions of Some Leading Disciples Concerning Pacifism" (unpublished B.D. thesis, College of Religion, Butler University, 1936), p. 53. W. T. Moore also concludes that "moderately disposed brethren were in a large majority during the whole period of the Civil War." *Comprehensive History*, p. 491. While many Disciples leaders were moderates throughout the war, these estimates are certainly exaggerations.

[36]"Circular from Preachers in Missouri," *M.H.*, 5th S., IV (October, 1861), 583. Disciples historians have repeatedly and incorrectly labelled this document a "Pacifist Manifesto"—which it is not.

[37]"Religion and Politics," *Christian Standard*, I (October 20, 1866), 228.

[38]"The Genesis of the Independent Monthly," *Independent Monthly*, I (October, 1869), 331.

tion did. They reacted sectionally. If some Kentucky and Missouri preachers and church members among the Disciples refused to become involved in the cataclysm, many of them did not refuse the call. Some of the Christians of Tennessee were persuaded by the fervent pacifism of their preachers not to become involved in the sins of the world but most young Disciples in North and South carefully packed their Bibles into saddlebags and rode off to war.

CHRISTIANS GO TO WAR

"And Moses said unto the children of Gad and to the children of Reuben, Shall your brethren go to war, and shall ye sit here?" Numbers 32:6.

Most influential Disciples editors either ignored or condemned the Civil War but neither North nor South suffered a total lack of editorial endorsement. By the fall of 1861 Elijah Goodwin's *Christian Record,* located in the hotbed of Disciples abolitionism and prowar feeling, Indianapolis, had given tacit approval to the war.[39] By 1862 the *Christian Record* had become a weekly, mainly because of the dissatisfaction of the loyalists in the church with the *American Christian Review,* and it bristled with militant articles from Disciples Unionists.[40] The *Record* soon began to "wage war on the *Review's* mum position."[41] The loyalist editor scathingly attacked the policy of neutrality—an assault which unquestionably was aimed specifically at Benjamin Franklin and the *American Christian Review:*

Now, who can be neutral on this awful subject, while this tremendous struggle is in progress? . . . The man who will not define his position and let his contemporaries know where he stands, is justly suspected by every true patriot, and should be watched; for he that is not for us is against us. It is impossible for any man, in these trying times, to be neutral in *fact.* He may talk neutrality, but in his heart, he sympathizes with the rebellion.[42]

---

[39]"Remarks," *C.R.,* 3rd S., IV (September, 1861), 279-280. Editor Goodwin began to make the transition to the prowar position early in the fall of 1861.

[40]See the 1862 volume of the *Weekly Christian Record* for numerous prowar articles. J. Harrison Jones became the paper's regular "Army Correspondent."

[41]W. R. Jewell, "Miscellaneous," *Independent Monthly,* II (February, 1870), 60.

[42]"He That Is Not For Us Is Against Us," *W.C.R.,* I (April 15, 1862), 2. The *Christian Record's* prowar policy was supported by John Boggs's militant abolitionist paper, the *Christian Luminary,* until its demise in 1863, and by the *Weekly Gospel Echo,* begun in 1863 by E. L. Craig of Carrollton, Illinois.

There is no reason to believe that Disciples laymen in the Northern states reacted much differently to the call to arms than members of other religious groups. Large numbers of the young men in the church enlisted in the Union army.[43] Disciples colleges were virtually deserted; the students, often accompanied by their teachers, flooded into the mushrooming volunteer regiments. Nathaniel S. Haynes, in his history of Disciples in Illinois, writes of Eureka College: "It is a fact significant of the loyalty of the Disciples of Illinois to our flag that, in the awful period of storm and strife, the college graduated only three men."[44]

Disciples were not particularly prominent in the chaplaincy of either side during the conflict but they were represented in both armies. J. Harrison Jones, a promising young preacher on the Western Reserve, joined James A. Garfield's regiment as the chaplain.[45] Several other Disciples ministers served as chaplains in the Union army, and a number worked with the humanitarian Federal agencies spawned by the war.[46]

At least one Disciples periodical supported the cause of the South throughout the war. John G. Parrish's *Christian Intelligencer,* published in Richmond, Virginia, was militantly committed to the cause of the Confederacy. Parrish accused the North of "waging an unprovoked, unholy, and unjustifiable war against us."[47] The *Christian Intelligencer* remained doggedly faithful to the cause of the Confederacy until the end.[48]

---

[43]See Keesee, "Churches During the War," pp. 66-101; Nathaniel S. Haynes, *History of the Disciples of Christ in Illinois* (Cincinnati: Standard Publishing Company, 1915), pp. 42-43; J. Ed Stevens and Vernon Rose, *Historical Sketches of the Christian Churches of Kansas and of Representative Workers* (Newton, Kansas: Journal Print, n. d.), p. 21; Dickinson, *Eureka College,* p. 62; William D. Dorris to I. T. Reneau, December 26, 1866, Isaac Tipton Reneau Papers.

[44]Haynes, *Disciples in Illinois,* pp. 42-43.

[45] See Wasson, *Garfield,* pp. 80-81.

[46]See Stevens and Rose, *Churches of Kansas,* p. 21; Hastings, *Butler,* p. 220; Giovannoli, *Kentucky Orphan School,* pp. 139-144; D. R. Lucas, "Personal Retrospect," *Christian Oracle,* VIII (February 19, 1891), 6; C. O. Denny, "Misc., Elder James P. Roach," *Christian Oracle,* IX (February 11, 1892), 95.

[47]Quoted in H. Jackson Darst, *Ante-Bellum Virginia Disciples* (Richmond: Virginia Christian Missionary Society, 1959), p. 165, see pp. 165-168.

[48]Parrish wrote in January, 1864: "We are now entering upon the year 1864— a momentous year for the people of the Confederate States. . . . On our ability to resist the unprecedented effort which will be made, the present year, to enslave us, depends, in a large measure, our future destiny. The alternatives are freedom and slavery; *there is no middle ground."* "The Times," *Christian Intellingencer,* XIX (January 15, 1864), 2.

Every indication is that the Disciples in the South reacted to the war in the same patriotic manner as those in the North. In 1866 a pacifist Texas preacher reported that "many of our able Preaching brethren went wild on the war question, and caused many a brother to apostatize."[49] The larger part of a company of the 6th Texas Cavalry was composed of members of the Christian Church of Grayson County, Texas. The captain and first lieutenant of the company were elders of the church, the orderly sergeant was the senior deacon, the preacher, Benjamin F. Hall, was regimental chaplain, and the regimental commander was Barton W. Stone, Jr., the son of the revered religious reformer.[50] The colleges of the South also suffered crippling losses of students when the war began.[51]

A number of the most prominent Disciples preachers in the South supported the war. John G. Parrish, George W. Abell, and, late in the war, Winthrop Hopson preached among the Army of Northern Virginia although none of them was a chaplain.[52] The two most colorful Disciples Confederate chaplains were Benjamin F. Hall and Thomas W. Caskey. Hall, chaplain of Barton W. Stone, Jr.'s regiment of the Sixth Texas Cavalry, was immortalized in William Baxter's *Pea Ridge and Prairie Grove*. Baxter and Robert Graham, Disciples ministers who had been operating a college in Fayetteville, Arkansas, visited Hall when his unruly outfit passed through their village shortly after the opening of the war. Baxter wrote of the visit:

I had known him [Hall] in former years and was not prepared for the change, which a few hours' intercourse was sufficient to convince me had taken place. He boasted of his trusty rifle, of the accuracy of his aim, and doubted not that the

---

[49]R. Green, "From Texas," *North-Western Christian Proclamation*, II (July, 1867), 122.

[50]See Hall, *Texas Disciples*, p. 60; Baxter, *Pea Ridge*, pp. 113-122.

[51]See Scobey, *Franklin College*, pp. 321-322; Baxter, *Pea Ridge*, pp. 31-35.

[52]See John G. Parrish, "Preaching in the Army," *C.I.*, XIX (January 15, 1864), 2; Peter Ainslie, *Life and Writings of George W. Abell* (Richmond: Clemmitt & Jones, Publishers and Printers, 1875), pp. 130-135; Darst, *Virginia*, pp. 165-168; Hopson, *Hopson*, pp. 114-161. Early in the war Hopson served as regimental chaplain for Morgan's Raiders. See Hopson, *Hopson*, p. 118. In his study of the Confederate chaplaincy, Herman Norton points out that low wages and lack of religious interest often caused a shortage of chaplains. See "The Organization and Function of the Confederate Military Chaplaincy, 1861-1865" (unpublished Ph.D. thesis, Vanderbilt University, 1956), pp. 242-289. Few Disciples preachers became chaplains but many of them sometimes preached among the troops.

weapon, with which he claimed to have killed deer at two hundred yards, would be quite as effectual when a Yankee was the mark. . . . I ventured to ask what were his views concerning his brethren with and for whom he had labored in other years in the North and West. He replied that they were no brethren of his, that the religionists on the other side of the line were all infidel, and that true religion was now only to be found in the South. . . . Once during the evening he wished that the people of the North were upon one vast platform, with a magazine of powder beneath, and that he might have the pleasure of applying the match to hurl them all into eternity. Elder Graham was a man of fine social qualities, gifted in conversion and repartee; but that evening he was speechless. . . . To argue was not only useless, but dangerous, and we prudently . . . said but little in reply.[53]

Thomas W. Caskey, probably the outstanding prewar Disciples preacher in Mississippi, was appointed chaplain of the Eighteenth Mississippi Regiment of Volunteers at the beginning of the war. He was at the First Battle of Manassas, actively participated in the fighting, and earned the name, "Fighting Parson."[54] Caskey soon retired from his chaplain's office, was appointed director of hospital facilities for the Army of the West, and organized a convalescent center in the buildings of the University of Mississippi at Oxford.[55]

In sum, the Disciples behaved little different from most other religious groups during the Civil War. Christians North and Christians South prayed as they fought. They shared the hates and hopes and hardships and labors of their kinsmen and neighbors. In the heat of human passion Disciples killed their brethren.

THE CHURCH GOES TO WAR

"My soul hath long dwelt with him that hateth peace. I am for peace: but when I speak, they are for war." Psalm 120:6-7.

More significant than the activities of individual members of the church was the wartime course of the young co-operative organizations of the movement. The future unity of the church was seriously threatened by

---

[53]Baxter, *Pea Ridge*, pp. 114-116.

[54]Manire, *Caskey's Last Book*, p. 34.

[55]See, for general information on Caskey, Harmon, *Churches in Mississippi*, pp. 95-96; Manire, *Caskey's Last Book*, pp. 34ff; Chas. Carlton, "Our Budget," *Christian Evangelist*, XXVII (February 13, 1890), 104; F. D. Srygley, *Seventy Years in Dixie* (Nashville: Gospel Advocate Publishing Co., 1891), pp. 350-353.

the mass participation of Disciples on both sides in the conflict and the outspoken partisanship of several periodicals but more important was the policy of the American Christian Missionary Society. In 1861 the society was the group's only semblance of national organization. Its effectiveness was already seriously threatened on the eve of the war by the sectional defection of Northern abolitionists and a lack of support from important conservative church leaders. Whether or not any compromise could have saved the society from further entanglement in the interchurch sectional tensions is doubtful—that the course which was followed was disastrous to the future hopes for a national society is unquestionable.

When the American Christian Missionary Society met in Cincinnati in October, 1861, the air was charged with excitement. Conspicuously present at the convention were a number of former preachers in recently tailored Union uniforms, including Colonel James A. Garfield. The most immoderate Northern sympathizers came to the convention determined to pass a resolution expressing the loyalty of the society to the government in this crisis. The statement published in the Missouri *Christian Pioneer* that every Disciples preacher "of note" was taking a neutral position had been reprinted by the Cincinnati daily press and had infuriated the prowar element.[56] Aside from the emotional intensity generated by the war there were practical considerations for desiring the passage of loyalty resolutions at the convention. The abolitionist Christian Missionary Society, established in Indianapolis two years previously, had announced that it would disband if the American Christian Missionary Society passed suitable resolutions. The strong group of moderate antislavery men in the North, who had been unwilling to support the bolting abolitionist society, were now determined to heal this organizational schism.

It was obvious, however, that the war faction was not to control the convention in 1861 without a struggle. In the first place, to pass such resolutions was a distinct departure from such strong Disciples traditions as absolute separation of church and state, the right to disagree on non-

[56]One of the prowar leaders later wrote that it was directly due to "such unwarranted statements" as the one in the *Pioneer*, which resulted in the Disciples "being assailed by the press," that loyalty resolutions were introduced at the 1861 Convention. See One of the Men, "A Reply to 'Vindication of Ourselves and the Pioneer,'" *C.P.* I (December, 1861), 322-334.

scriptural subjects, and the impropriety of Disciples organizations issuing anything that smacked of an official pronouncement. No such resolution on any major social question had ever been passed at a convention of the church. In addition, the strong neutralist Northern and border state church leaders were intent on keeping the organization uninvolved in the great national struggle. Not only did they believe that the church had no scriptural right to speak on the subject but they were convinced that such a step would mean the financial ruin of the American Christian Missionary Society, which had traditionally received a large portion of its support from the South, especially from the seriously divided churches of Kentucky. The scene was set for bitter struggle.

Although no major church leaders from the deep South were present, the 1861 convention in Cincinnati was the largest meeting of the society since its founding. Over eight hundred prominent Disciples ministers and laymen from the North and border-states crowded into the bustling wartime city. The crucial moment in the convention arrived when John P. Robison[57] of Bedford, Ohio, offered the following resolution: *"Resolved,* That we deeply sympathize with the loyal and patriotic in our country, in the present efforts to sustain the Government of the United States. And we feel it our duty as Christians, to ask our brethren everywhere to do all in their power to sustain the proper and constitutional authorities of the Union." The resolution was seconded by the avid Kentucky Unionist, Lewis L. Pinkerton, who the next year became a surgeon in the Union army. The effect of the motion was electric. David S. Burnet, Cincinnati minister, immediately raised the question of whether it was constitutional for the body to entertain such a resolution. Isaac Errett, presiding for the aging society president, Alexander Campbell, who sat in the audience, ruled that the motion was in order. The venerable Kentucky pioneer preacher, "Raccoon" John Smith, even though he was a staunch Unionist, appealed the decision of the chair but, apparently after a heated discussion, withdrew his appeal. The appeal was then reentered

---

[57]Robison, an early Western Reserve preacher turned businessman and politician, was an influential member of the Ohio State Senate. He was also a leader of the Bedford, Ohio, Christian Church, one of the largest congregations in the state. See M. C. Tiers, ed., *The Christian Portrait Gallery* (Cincinnati: Stereotyped at the Franklin Type Foundry, 1864), pp. 23, 198.

by Richard M. Bishop, prominent Cincinnati layman,[58] and sustained by a vote of the convention. Apparently according to prearranged strategy, Pinkerton then called for a ten-minute recess. During the recess David S. Burnet was called to the chair, Robison's resolution was again introduced, and, after a short speech by Colonel Garfield, was passed by the extralegal assembly with only one dissenting vote.[59]

The convention of 1861 ended without a clearcut victory. The war sympathizers were dissatisfied and irritated at the obstinate refusal of the moderates to relent under pressure (the abolitionist Christian Missionary Society was deeply disappointed and refused to disband). On the other hand, while the moderates tried to belittle the recess session, they obviously had tacitly compromised with the war hawks. The neutralists had mustered sufficient strength to keep the resolution out of the convention proceedings but they remained in the auditorium and did not vote against the resolution during the rump session. The meaning of this compromise of 1861 was a matter of significant debate in the months that followed.

Almost immediately after the convention the *Christian Pioneer* received a letter from one of the preachers whom it had listed as opposed to the war. The letter was simply signed "One of the Men" but it was apparently written either by Isaac Errett or Silas Shepard.[60] The author attacked the *Pioneer's* statement that every preacher "of note" in the brotherhood had endorsed the antiwar position. He cited himself and Garfield as specific exceptions and insisted that "several of those whom you mention are positively misrepresented."[61] The disgruntled correspondent added that it was the *Pioneer's* statement which led to the introduction of the loyalty resolution:

[58]Bishop was at the time mayor of Cincinnati and was an elder in Robert Graham's Eighth and Walnut Street congregation in the city. See Tiers, *Portrait Gallery*, pp. 213-215.

[59]See *Report of Proceedings of the Thirteenth Anniversary Meeting of the American Christian Missionary Society, Held in Cincinnati, October 22, 23, 24, 1861* (Cincinnati: E. Morgan and Son, Printers, 1861), pp. 19-20. For further insight, see Keith, *Burnet*, pp. 161-163; One of the Men, "A Reply to 'Vindication of Ourselves and the Pioneer,'" *C.P.*, I (December, 1861), 322-334.

[60]This is the guess of a contemporary, who also included David S. Burnet. "One of the Men," *C.P.*, I (April, 1862), 511. Shepard seems the most logical of the three.

[61]One of the Men, "A Reply to 'Vindication of Ourselves and the Pioneer,'" *C.P.*, I (December, 1861), 322-334.

This state of the case, led to the introduction of a resolution of sympathy with those brethren of the Army of the U.S. now in the field . . . and though Bro. Burnet raised the point of order, that it could not be entertained by the Society; yet the whole concourse, in a recess of ten minutes granted for that purpose, Bro. Burnet in the Chair, passed the resolution without dissent, by a rising vote. Alexander Campbell, W. K. Pendleton, John Smith, A. Raines, B. Franklin, Isaac Errett, Elijah Goodwin, S. E. Shepard of those you name, and 800 others were present.[62]

But if the early neutralist estimates of the *Christian Pioneer* were exaggerated, its loyalist attacker also claimed too much. The presence of many of the leading preachers at the rump session of the convention by no means meant that they approved of the resolution. Disciples moderates were certainly not prepared to allow the loyalists to claim the 1861 compromise as a triumph.

Benjamin Franklin led the neutralist counterattack. The caustic editor emphatically denied that there was any significance in the silent acceptance of the rump session resolution by the moderate church leaders. Had they known that this was the purpose of the recess, they would have stopped it:

It is not true that a recess of ten minutes was granted *for that purpose.* . . . Had the purpose been understood, the recess would not have been granted, not that many were opposed to the contents of the resolution; but *they were opposed to introducing it into our missionary meeting.* Still, it is true, that A. Campbell, W. K. Pendleton, over whom "One of the Men," makes such a flourish, and others had nothing to do with the political meeting—they did not act at all.—They looked upon the thing as a farce, and one of the warmest men in favor of introducing it, in a letter to us, calls it, "a farcical meeting."[63]

In short, the convention compromise of 1861 had not really satisfied any of the factions in the church. Disciples leaders in the lower South were displeased at the only partial success of the neutralists. On the other hand, in the North the result was certainly far from satisfactory. The radicals of the Christian Missionary Society had not been pacified. Although the loyalists could claim something of a triumph, the only action they had gotten was obviously extralegal and the outspoken editorial chief of the

---

[62]*Ibid.,* 324.

[63]"Remarks," *A.C.R.,* VI (January 14, 1862), 2. See, also, J. R. H., "The 'Review's' Correction of 'One of the Men,'" *C.P.,* I (February, 1862), 430-431; J. R. H., "Reply to 'One of the Men,'" *C. P.,* I (January, 1862), 371-376.

neutralist block had ridiculed their efforts as "a farce." Pushing a resolution through the American Christian Missionary Society remained a major objective of a large group of Northern preachers.

Benjamin Franklin wrote feverishly for the next few months trying to forestall any such development in the future meetings of the convention. He was joined in his efforts by John R. Howard and David T. Wright in the *Christian Pioneer*. Wright wrote:

Hence the urgent necessity of guarding against the introduction of political issues into the church or our other christian organizations, gotten up for the spread of the Gospel, in both of which the unity of the brethren is paramount to every earthly consideration.[64]

A new crisis arose in the summer of 1862 when the Indiana state meeting passed a resolution of "loyalty to the government, and sympathy with the suffering soldiers."[65] Franklin immediately attacked the resolution, the Indiana convention, and the Disciples of Indiana in general. He charged that the churches of that state were under the "influence of *hobbyism* and *ultraism* of every sort."[66] Franklin's tirade brought an immediate reaction from the Indiana loyalists. Elijah Goodwin, in his *Weekly Christian Record*, retorted that Franklin seemed "determined to make a schism" and warned that if the *Review's* editor was trying to make a "party" it would be "a very small one."[67]

For the most part the neutralists succeeded in keeping the church conventions gagged through 1862. The meeting of the American Christian Missionary Society in October, 1862, passed almost without incident. The war sympathizers were in control of the convention but they made no effort to pass resolutions. David S. Burnet's corresponding secretary's report, which referred to the crippling effects of the "rebellion," led to a brief exchange on the floor of the convention. John W. McGarvey, Kentucky pacifist and Southern sympathizer, moved that the phrase "attempt at revolution" be substituted for "rebellion" but his motion was

---

[64]"A Reply to 'Vindication of Ourselves and the Pioneer,' " *C.P.*, I (December, 1861), 327.

[65]"Indiana Semi-Annual State Meeting," *A.C.R.*, V (June 24, 1862), 2.

[66]*Ibid.*

[67]"The Review on the Rushville Meeting," *W.C.R.*, I (June 26, 1862), 2. See, also, P. Hall, "Communication," *A.C.R.*, V (July 15, 1862), 2.

defeated. McGarvey caused another stir when he submitted a report adopted by the Kentucky state society which reprimanded the church members of that state who were participating in the war. A general committee of the convention, headed by Elijah Goodwin, submitted a supplementary report which commended "those faithful brethren who are suffering on account of their devotion to the law of Christ, which commands Christians to 'be subject to the powers that be.' "[68]

Benjamin Franklin was elated by the successful avoidance of open hostilities on the question at the 1862 convention. He wrote: "It is a grand triumph for Christianity at such a time as this, for the people of God to meet . . . and attend to the things of the kingdom of God . . . in such kindness, love and harmony, and at the same time keeping the terrible issues of the world out."[69] But sentiment in favor of loyalty resolutions had not died. Elijah Goodwin revealed in the *Record* that many of the preachers at the meeting felt that such resolutions ought to be passed but "for the sake of peace, the matter was not pressed."[70]

As the year 1863 progressed it became increasingly apparent that the Disciples war enthusiasts were becoming impatient with compromise. The state meeting in Pennsylvania passed loyalty resolutions which drew only a slight reprimand from Benjamin Franklin.[71] In the summer of 1863 the state meeting in Ohio passed a set of stringent resolutions—in spite of the presence of Alexander Campbell and Benjamin Franklin.[72] The loyalists were prepared for a showdown.[73]

The 1863 General Convention opened on an ominous note for the neutralists when David S. Burnet, in his corresponding secretary's address, made his sympathies with the cause of the Union armies resound-

[68]*Report of Proceedings of the Fourteenth Anniversary Meeting of the American Christian Missionary Society, Held in Cincinnati, October 20, 21, 22, 1862* (Cincinnati: E. Morgan and Sons, Printers, 1862), pp. 6, 15. See, also, Keith, *Burnet*, pp. 103-104.

[69]"The General Missionary Meeting," *A.C.R.*, V (November 4, 1862), 2.

[70]"A. C. Missionary Society," *W.C.R.*, I (November 4, 1862), 2.

[71]"Co-Operation Meeting in Pa.," *A.C.R.*, VI (January 13, 1863), 6.

[72]See A. S. H., "Missionary Convention at Shelby Ohio," *A.C.R.*, VI (July 14, 1863), 110; Alanson Wilcox, *A History of the Disciples of Christ in Ohio* (Cincinnati: The Standard Publishing Company, 1918), pp. 114-119.

[73]"Course of the Christian Record," *A.C.R.*, VI (September 22, 1863), 150.

ingly apparent.[74] The war sympathizers, who had long been convinced that the society's silence aligned the Disciples with the South,[75] were determined to act. The crisis came when Randall Faurot introduced the following preamble and resolutions:

Whereas, "there is no power but of God," and "the powers that be are ordained of God;" and whereas, we are commanded in the Holy Scriptures to be subject to the powers that be, and "obey magistrates," and whereas an armed rebellion exists in our country, subversive of these divine injunctions; and whereas, reports have gone abroad that we, as a religious body, and particularly as a Missionary Society, are to a certain degree disloyal to the Government of the United States; therefore—

Resolved, That we unqualifiedly declare our allegiance to said Government, and repudiate as false and slanderous any statements to the contrary.

Resolved, That we tender our sympathies to our brave and noble soldiers in the fields, who are defending us from the attempts of armed traitors to overthrow our Government, and also to those bereaved, and rendered desolate by the ravages of war.

Resolved, That we will earnestly and constantly pray to God to give our legislators and rulers, wisdom to enact, and power to execute, such laws are [as] will speedily bring to us the enjoyment of a peace that God will design and bless.[76]

As soon as the resolution was introduced, the floor of the convention came alive with confusion. A motion was made to adjourn, but was defeated. The question was raised as to whether the resolutions were in order and Isaac Errett, who was presiding at the session, ruled that they were not according to the vote of the convention two years previously but publicly stated that he thought this ruling was in error. An appeal was made from the decision of the chair and after a debate the appeal was sustained. Another motion to adjourn was lost, as was a motion to lay the question on the table. Finally, the resolutions were voted on by the convention and resoundingly passed.[77] The moderates had been routed. Northern radicals and their sympathizers in the border states were now clearly in con-

[74]Report of Proceedings of the Fifteenth Anniversary Meeting of the American Christian Missionary Society, Held in Cincinnati, October 20, 21, 22, 1863 (Cincinnati: E. Morgan and Sons, Printers, 1863), p. 13.

[75]This view was widespread in the North. See "The Letter from Georgia," Christian Standard, I (June 16, 1866), 84.

[76]Proceedings of American Christian Missionary Society, 1863, p. 24.

[77]Ibid.

trol of the missionary society.[78]

The passage of the resolutions was a stunning blow for the neutralists. Immediately after the close of the convention Benjamin Franklin wrote: "We do not feel as full of hope for the Society as we have done on some former occasions."[79] Franklin predicted that the society had almost certainly ruined its future usefulness in the South and border areas.[80] The most ferocious attack on the society, however, came from the powerful Lexington preacher, John W. McGarvey. He wrote: "I have judged the American Christian Missionary Society, and have decided for myself, that it should now cease to exist." McGarvey insisted that the society had permanently estranged a large segment of the brotherhood by its action and if it continued to exist, it would be "a source of untold trouble."[81] The influential Kentucky pacifist's article ripped wide open the festering sores of sectional bitterness. Opposition to the society spread throughout Kentucky. Aylette Raines tersely scribbled in his diary: "Bro. McGarvey has taken the position that the A. C. Missionary Society is dead!"[82]

EVIL OMENS

"Destroy, O Lord, and divide their tongues: for I have seen violence and strife in the city." Psalm 55:9.

While all Disciples moderates were not as pessimistic as Franklin and McGarvey about the lasting impact of the loyalty resolutions on the unity of the church, they were all deeply concerned. William K. Pendleton

---

[78]For evaluations of the 1863 convention, see William Baxter, "Bro. McGarvey and the Missionary Societies," *A.C.R.*, VI (December 22, 1863), 201; "The Way It Is Done," *Independent Monthly*, I (October, 1869), 327-329; Alfred Martin Haggard, "Isaac Errett and Our Later History." *Christian Quarterly*, VII (October, 1898), 517-518; W. T. Moore, "Reformation of the Nineteenth Century, The Turbulent Period," *Christian Evangelist*, XXXVI (May 25, 1899), 648-649; Keith, *Burnet*, pp. 168-169. Earl West calls it the "War Convention," *Ancient Order*, I, 225.

[79]"The General Missionary Meeting," *A.C.R.*, VI (November 10, 1863), 178.

[80]"The General Missionary Meeting," *A.C.R.*, VI (November 10, 1863), 178; D. S. Burnet, "The A. C. Missionary Society," *A.C.R.*, VI (November 24, 1863), 186.

[81]"Missionary Societies," *A.C.Q.R.*, II (1863), 342-345.

[82]Diary, December 27, 1863, Aylette Raines Collection, College of the Bible, Lexington, Kentucky.

voiced the Bethany community's concern:

It ought not to be disguised, that the fortunes of the American Christian Missionary Society have for a year or two been under a cloud. . . . The fact that the Society violated her constitution, in introducing and forcing to a willful vote a set of political resolutions, cannot be denied or explained away.[83]

The heir of Campbell's mantle issued a fervent plea for peace but he was fully aware that these troubled waters ran deep.

In his plea for reconciliation, Pendleton wrote: "Many . . . we know there are who are abandoning the Society."[84] He continued: "In a spirit, I fear, of local sensitiveness, not a few are for isolating the co-operation of our brotherhood by the boundaries of States."[85] Early in 1865 Moses E. Lard protested against similar symptoms of sectional disintegration: "Many so-called brethren in our ranks now actually refuse to meet with and fellowship their brethren of the adverse political faith."[86]

Ominous symptoms of a three-way division had become increasingly clear in the years from 1861 to 1865. The churches in the North, the border areas, and the South became more and more insistent that the message of the Disciples show deference to their sectional prejudices. The result was a reorientation of institutional loyalties around sectional interests.

By 1863 the loyalists of the North had won control of the American Christian Missionary Society and had several periodicals under their direction but they were determined to launch a new prestige weekly to challenge the middle-of-the-road policy of the *American Christian Review*. As early as 1861 several of the leading loyalist preachers, including D. Pat Henderson, Silas E. Shepard, and Isaac Errett were corresponding about the possibilities of "the publication of a weekly sheet for the advocacy of *Truth*."[87] By 1863 most Northern church leaders, joined by some bor-

---

[83]"American Christian Missionary Society," *M.H.*, 5th S., VII (September, 1864), 419.

[84]*Ibid.*, 420.

[85]*Ibid.*, 422.

[86]"The Work of the Past—The Symptoms of the Future," *L.Q.*, II (April, 1865), 259.

[87]D. Pat Henderson to Isaac Errett, November 21, 1861, Butler Manuscript Collection.

der state loyalists, were openly critical of the *American Christian Review* and were beginning to formulate practical plans for the establishment of a strong loyal paper.[88] William Baxter wrote Errett:

> Is it not, my dear Brother, a most mournful reflection, that we have not a paper which reflects either, the mind, or the heart of our people, and that were any one 20 years hence, to examine files of our publications, he would not be able to determine from them that a war was in progress, a war too, affecting nearly every family in the land. Look, at Lard's Review for instance, the table of contents would indicate a time of profoundest quiet. He excludes all "political articles" but political now, includes all that was formerly meant, by loyal, sympathetic, humane. Brother Shepard, Loos, Graham, and many others feel deeply, the necessity of a paper suited to the times.[89]

By 1865 the agitation for a loyalist paper had solidified and with the backing of such supporters as James A. Garfield, the wealthy Phillips brothers of New Castle, Pennsylvania, and the wealthy and ultra loyalist John P. Robison, the *Christian Standard* began publication under the editorship of Isaac Errett in April, 1866. Unquestionably the sectional motive was fundamental in the founding of the *Standard*. David Lipscomb, in a late nineteenth-century attempt to refute claims that the *Standard* was founded to support theologically liberal ideas, reported a conversation he had with Isaac Errett shortly after the founding of the paper:

> He told me that the *Standard* was started because Franklin refused to let the loyal brethren express themselves in the Review on the duty of Christians to support the government in its war upon the rebellion, its duty to punish traitors, and to express themselves on the infamy of slavery. Franklin had opposed the action of the convention, refused to let them discuss what they believed right on these subjects, and they were determined to have a paper in which they could express themselves freely in favor of sustaining the government, and on the infamy of slavery.[90]

---

[88]William Baxter to Isaac Errett, December 16, 1863; John Rogers to Isaac Errett, August 10, 1863; R. Milligan to Isaac Errett, October 29, 1863, Butler Manuscript Collection.

[89]William Baxter to Isaac Errett, December 16, 1863, Butler Manuscript Collection.

[90]"The Truth of History," *G.A.*, XXXIV (July 14, 1892), 436. Lipscomb is hardly an unbiased authority on the founding of the *Christian Standard* but there is little reason to doubt that this conversation is accurately reported. There unquestionably was another and less sectional motive for founding the paper. McGarvey's description of the motivations behind the paper is fairer, although his account was written in 1905 and is not accurate factually: "After the death of Mr. Campbell and the subsequent suspension of the *Harbinger*, there arose a

James A. Garfield wrote his friend Burke Hinsdale, who was one of the associate editors of the new paper: "I am greatly rejoiced that Bro. Errett has seen the essential wickedness of rebellion as manifested in Kentucky. We must have no soft side for it in the *Standard*."[91] Although the *Standard* in the years to come did not fulfill all the expectations of its most ardent loyalist supporters and founders, it was, in its inception, a marked expression of sectional Christianity.[92]

The move toward sectional Christianity was by no means confined to the church in the North. Thomas M. Allen wrote his old friend John Allen Gano in 1861: "I could not make you believe the bitterness of secessionists towards all those who are Union men."[93] Communications with the leaders of the church in the South had been almost completely severed during the war years and it was not until 1866 that a few letters began to trickle in to the church periodicals. In the early months of 1866, however, it became apparent that the Southerners were going to have their own sectional reaction. Nathan W. Smith of Jonesboro, Georgia, wrote Isaac Errett: "We hear that the brotherhood formed societies, and organizations, unscriptural in name, and without precedent in the word of the Lord.—And in this zeal for God . . . they passed sundry resolutions

---

strong feeling among the leading brethren in the northern States, in favor of a weekly paper of higher literary merit than the *American Christian Review* then conducted by Benjamin Franklin and exerting a powerful influence throughout the brotherhood, and one which would be more 'loyal' as the phrase went, to the Federal Government then engaged in the struggle of the civil war." *The Autobiography of J. W. McGarvey* (Lexington: The College of the Bible, 1960), p. 73.

[91]Mary L. Hinsdale, ed., *Garfield-Hinsdale Letters* (Ann Arbor: University of Michigan Press, 1949), p. 79.

[92]Errett deeply disappointed the most bitter loyalists in the years immediately after the war with his editorial policy of moderation and conciliation. Hinsdale, *Garfield-Hinsdale*, pp. 107-109. Lewis L. Pinkerton became a merciless critic of the *Standard*. In 1870 he wrote: "Seldom, in the history of life, is so great an opportunity lost for accomplishing measureless good, as was thrown away when the *Standard*—The *Christian* standard was lowered in deference to the *spirit* of a cruel and godless insurrection against liberty, right and justice. What the *Christian Standard* has done, or attempted to do, which the *Christian Review* and the *Apostolic Times* are not doing as well, I would like to learn." "Letter from Dr. Pinkerton," *Independent Monthly*, II (April, 1870), 109.

[93]T. M. Allen to J. A. Gano, September 19, 1861, John Allen Gano Papers, University of Missouri.

of a political character and import, maintaining that men may fight and kill each other." Smith drew prophetic conclusions: "I have thought and often said our brethren could never divide—but oh how our fairest and brightest prospects fade away through the operations of weak and erring humanity."[94]

The most significant sign of an emerging Southern sectional Christianity was the course of the Nashville *Gospel Advocate*, which resumed publication in January, 1866, after four years' interruption. David Lipscomb and Tolbert Fanning, the editors of the weekly, immediately denounced the course of the church in the North during the war: "Those brethren who believe that political resolutions are the Gospel can do so; and those who desire to contribute to such an object can do so; *we cannot do it*."[95] It became increasingly apparent that the *Gospel Advocate* was going to fill the place among Southern sympathizers that the *Christian Standard* was designed to fill among the staunchly loyalist elements in the church. Isaac Errett charged: "It [*Gospel Advocate*] commenced its new issue with an appeal to men of southern blood, and proposed cooperation among them only. It has constantly denounced the brethren of the North who shared in the military defense of the government."[96] By 1866, in both North and South, institutional power concentrations were being formed which would represent and appeal to the diverging sectional interpretations of the restoration plea.

By the end of 1865 it was apparent that the churches of the border states of Kentucky and Missouri, Disciples strongholds, were faced with a crucial problem in reconciling sectional factions. Although many of the churches in Missouri had weathered the storms of battle with a minimum of disturbance, others had been "well nigh wrecked."[97] John W. McGarvey with great difficulty managed to hold the church together in Lexington; in Louisville, the Disciples divided into two congregations along

---

[94]"A Letter from Georgia," *Christian Standard*, I (June 9, 1866), 76.

[95]"A Reply to the Call of W. C. Rogers, Corresponding Secretary of the A. C. M. Society for All to Disseminate the Gospel," *G.A.*, VIII (March 27, 1866).

[96]"The Gospel Advocate," *Christian Standard*, II (February 16, 1867), 52.

[97]William Gooch, "Reports from the Brethren," *C.P.*, VII (August 29, 1867), 511.

sectional lines;[98] in some places the churches completely disbanded.[99] In both Missouri and Kentucky a compromise, middle-of-the-road policy began to emerge by 1865. The large group of neutralist preachers of these states united with returning Southern sympathizers around a platform which mildly condemned the participation by brethren in the war and denounced the passage of the war resolutions while remaining markedly conciliatory in tone.[100]

In sum, by 1865 the Disciples were rapidly coalescing around three distinct sectional emphases. In the North (although the groups were never simply geographic) the preachers who had condemned slavery, supported the war, and instigated the passage of the war resolutions by the American Christian Missionary Society felt, at most, that the South ought to be reminded again and again of its wickedness and that the church members of that section who had participated in the rebellion ought either to repent or be refused fellowship. At least, they believed that their own course had been righteous and certainly were unwilling to entertain protests from their Southern brethren. In the churches of the South there was a seething deep resentment against the actions of the missionary society during the war. Many Southern church leaders emerged from the Civil War convinced that the Northern radicals had defiled the

---

[98]D. Pat Henderson to Isaac Errett, March 17, 1865, Butler Manuscript Collection.

[99]See T. P. H., "The Cause of Christ in Missouri," *C.P.*, IV (February and March, 1864), 84-85; S. B. Maywell, "Our National Troubles," *M.H.*, 5th S., IV (July, 1861), 412-413; Lamar, *Errett*, I, 276-277; "Union Troops Occupied First Christian Church During Civil War," Henderson Kentucky *Gleaner and Journal*, June 24, 1960, typed copy of article, Disciples of Christ Historical Society, Nashville, Tennessee.

[100]Lewis G. Vander Velde describes a similar struggle among border-state Presbyterians during the war years. See *Presbyterians and the Union*, pp. 183-279. Border-state Presbyterians went through the same process that Disciples in these areas did; they first tried to moderate the actions of the Northern church but finally the Synods of Kentucky and Missouri joined the Southern church. The merging of neutralist Disciples and Southern sympathizers during the last years of the war was in keeping with this common pattern. See, for further information on the Southern orientation of border-state churches, E. Merton Coulter, *The Civil War and Readjustment in Kentucky* (Chapel Hill, N. C.: University of North Carolina Press, 1926), pp. 287-339, 394-400; and the chapter entitled "Clerical Disloyalty in Loyal States," in R. L. Stanton, *The Church and the Rebellion* (New York: Derby & Miller, 1864), pp. 207-246.

kingdom and that the only pure remnant of God's people was the church in the South. In the border states a third faction was developing. It was built around the nucleus of those who had opposed the war, had especially tried to forestall the involvement of the church, and were determined to try to reconcile the discordant elements in the church by reverting to the old time-tested principles of moderation and repression of the controversial. The scars of these wounds are yet visible in the movement.

CAN WE DIVIDE?

"For it is impossible for those who were once enlightened . . . if they shall fall away, to renew them again unto repentance; seeing they crucify to themselves the Son of God afresh, and put him to an open shame." Hebrews 6:4-6.

In his classic study of the impact of social forces on American religious history, H. Richard Niebuhr states: "In few instances have schisms been so obviously due to the operation of social factors as in the case of the break which the Civil War and its antecedents affected in the churches of America."[101] Never before in American history had churchmen been so willing to renounce long-held convictions, rationalize fragile and unconvincing arguments, and spring to the defense of the socio-economic interests of their section—"the kingdom of Mars had conquered the kingdom of Christ."[102] Reeling under the pressures of public opinion, every major American Protestant denomination shattered.

In a premature attempt at self-analysis in 1866, Moses E. Lard asked and answered the pregnant question: "Can we divide?" Although Lard admitted that it was "not extremely rare" to receive an affirmative answer to the interrogation in 1866, he was decidedly optimistic. The pacifist editor believed that the Disciples had survived the slavery controversy and the war without any real schism, and hopefully added: "May we not boldly say, trusting in God to help us, *we can never divide?*"[103]

---

[101]Niebuhr, *Social Sources*, p. 187, see pp. 187-199.

[102]Niebuhr, *Kingdom of God*, p. 121. Charles C. Cole, Jr., in his study of the attitudes of Northern evangelists during the ante-bellum period, comes to similarly harsh conclusions. He writes: "After 1840 . . . the minister, by and large, followed, rather than shaped, public opinion." Cole charges that the churches generally not only did nothing to halt the disintegration of the nation but that they "contributed in no small way to the state of mind which helped bring on the Civil War." *Northern Evangelists*, p. 220.

[103]"Can We Divide?" *L.Q.*, III (April, 1866), 336, see 330-336.

But the rumor that the Civil War had been a divisive influence on the movement persisted and over thirty years later another Disciples preacher who had been an important figure in the church during the war felt compelled to reaffirm Lard's conclusions: "Recently it has been intimated that the Disciples were practically divided during the war, although no formal division actually took place. This view of the matter is entirely erroneous. . . . There was never at any time the slightest possibility of a real division among the Disciples."[104] In general, Disciples historians have accepted the optimistic conclusions of these early church leaders. While some recent historians have recognized the deep sectional animosities created by the struggle, they have generally agreed that "in a short time the sectional feeling was forgotten."[105]

---

[104]W. T. Moore, "Reformation of the Nineteenth Century, The Turbulent Period," *Christian Evangelist*, XXXVI (June 1, 1899), 680.

[105]Alonzo Willard Fortune, *The Disciples in Kentucky* (n.p.: The Convention of the Christian Churches in Kentucky, 1932), p. 367. The question of whether or not the Disciples "divided over the Civil War" could easily be oversimplified. The union of the movement was always tenuous and intangible. There were many factors involved in the ultimate severing of these nebulous ties: theological, economic, social, and personal. It is certainly true, however, that the Civil War was a major divisive influence in the history of the movement—a fact which has long been ignored by Disciples historians. Most students of the church have unquestioningly accepted the interpretation of Winfred Garrison: "Its [Civil War] ultimate effect was less divisive than might have been expected; in fact, not divisive at all." *Religion Follows the Frontier*, p. 221. Garrison contended that lack of organization precluded division within the movement: "The weakness of the Disciples in organization became their strength in maintaining unity in this crisis, for they had no court or convention empowered to put any church or individual out of the general fellowship." *Ibid.*, p. 222. And yet, Garrison recognized that "forty years later" there was a major schism in the group; no fundamental change in the organizational structure of the church had taken place during these years. The truth is that the church was in the process of dividing into antagonistic factions at least as early as the 1850's, incompatible themes had been present in the mind of the movement from the beginning, the Civil War left deep geographic imprints on the ultimate nature of the schisms, and new issues and social forces in the postwar period brought the conflict to its final fruition. See, for some examples of Disciples historians who have uncritically accepted Garrison's conclusions, A. T. DeGroot in Garrison and DeGroot, *Disciples*, pp. 336-337; Whitley, *Trumpet Call*, p. 134; Mell, "Disciples Concerning Pacifism," pp. 53-54. Mell states that the Disciples opposed the war "almost to a man." This misinterpretation has been carried over into the more general literature on American religious history. John R. Bodo writes: "The Disciples of Christ . . . began as a pacifist sect. All their early

It is both naïve and inaccurate to dismiss so lightly the massive impact of the great American sectional struggle on the Disciples of Christ. As a matter of fact, during these critical years the Disciples are a vivid example of the bending of the Christian ethos to fit the frame of social necessity.[106] The essential unity of the church had been threatened for decades. Diverging economic interests, the slavery controversy, and finally the war wrecked the hopes of the American Christian Missionary Society, or any

---

leaders, with the exception of Walter Scott, were avowed pacifists." *Clergy and Public Issues*, p. 227.

Delbert Dayton Keesee, in his study of the Disciples during the war, makes one of the most penetrating analyses of the problem of any student of the movement: "The Civil War was a turning point in the general outlook of those who constituted the restoration movement. . . . Before the war the members of the restoration movement had been inclined to look upon the mistakes of the religious groups about them. The party spirit that arose as a result of the war tended to direct their attention to their own religious group. They became more conscious of their own differences." "Churches During the War," pp. 163-164. But Keesee then makes a completely incongruous statement: "This party spirit in the Churches of Christ reached its peak during the war. . . . However, except in a few places and among a few people, it was soon gone." *Ibid.*, p. 162. This same sort of contradictory interpretation is found in the writings of William T. Moore. Usually Moore completely ignores the impact of the war on the church but on one occasion he writes that the conflict "put a heavy strain upon the fellowship of the Disciples." *Comprehensive History*, p. 150. The conservative historian Earl West recognizes serious divisive problems in the pre-Civil War history of the movement but defines them too simply in exclusively theological terms and concludes that "the churches . . . weathered the issues created by the war without any serious disruption." *Ancient Order*, I, 350. In his later work on David Lipscomb, West comes closer than any other Disciples historian to recognizing the important impact of sectional bitterness on the ultimate division of the movement. *David Lipscomb*, pp. 104-109.

It should be said, finally, that many students of Disciples history have long recognized the obvious links between the sectional fracturing of the nation and the schisms in the Disciples of Christ. The author is especially indebted to Claude Spencer, Curator of the Disciples of Christ Historical Society, who has long felt that additional study needed to be done in this area of the history of the movement.

[106]A. T. DeGroot, referring to the postwar economic undertones of the *American Christian Review* writes: "If one were hunting incidents to illustrate a thesis for a modern volume entitled 'The Social Sources of Denominationalism,' an excellent example could be presented in the reaction of the *American Christian Review.*" *Disciples*, p. 357. The *Review* does vividly illustrate Niebuhr's thesis but no more so than the *Christian Standard*, or the *Gospel Advocate*, or the *Apostolic Times*, or any of the other postwar periodicals of the movement. They all represented and appealed to specific social and sectional interests.

other organization, of gaining universal support throughout the movement. In fact, if not in theory, the Disciples of Christ were divided by the Civil War.

Although reunion of the divided church was one of the major objectives of many postwar leaders of the Disciples, by 1866 the obstacles to peace were large; if not insurmountable.[107] Each segment of the church was intent on supporting its own periodicals and institutions. No Disciples paper would ever again command the patronage of the entire brotherhood as had the *Millennial Harbinger* into the 1850's. The circulation of every major Disciples periodical of the postwar period had geographic limitations.

In addition, the interchurch antagonisms bred by the Civil War reached far deeper than the simple emotional bitterness of former enemies. The church in the North emerged from the war committed to a more denominational and socially active concept of Christianity. For the first time in its history, the church had officially (or as officially as it organizationally could) endorsed social action. An intricate complex of socio-economic forces continued to encourage the development of a liberal tradition within the movement in the postwar period but the roots of Disciples liberalism reach deeply into the slavery controversy and the Civil War.

On the other hand, the church in the South emerged from the Civil War more strongly than ever committed to the extreme sectarian emphasis in Disciples thought. Repelled by the wartime actions of the American Christian Missionary Society, the already present conservative mood in the Southern churches deepened. Although the flowering of a conservative rationale in the South was fed by the developing economic and social conditions of the post-bellum period, sectional prejudices remained a basic element in the ideological evolution of the church in the South. Benjamin Franklin, David Lipscomb, Tolbert Fanning, and other important

---

[107]This, of course, is the crucial consideration in the question of whether or not the Disciples "divided over the Civil War." Disciples union was as surely ruptured during the war as that of every Protestant denomination. After the struggle, the breaches in the Episcopal and Lutheran churches were healed while those in the Baptists, Methodists, and Presbyterians deepened. Tracing the postwar sectional tensions within the Disciples must remain the work of another volume. Suffice it to say here that, although many of the church's leaders worked diligently and courageously to erase the bitterness of the war, sectional tensions continued to be an important factor in the disintegration of the movement.

conservative leaders early and often attached sectional meaning to theological questions. Sectarian theology was a natural reaction to the sociological forces which spawned the *Gospel Advocate* and the Church of Christ.

In the final analysis, the critical weakness of Disciples of Christ in 1866 (as far as maintaining unity is concerned) was that the moderates lost control. A large group of moderates remained in the church at the close of the war—largely located in the border areas. These men represented much of the common heritage of the movement—men who were both sectarian and denominational; opposed to political fervor and yet not opposed to Christians participating in politics; unwilling to join the national struggle but willing to forgive both Northerners and Southerners. But there were not enough of them left. Fratricidal strife had fattened the fanatical fringes of the movement into sizable and obstinate factions.

Certainly not all Disciples became conservatives or liberals because of where they lived; there continued to be liberals in the South, conservatives in the North, and middle-of-the-roaders everywhere. But sectional animosities were an important and persistent force in the future course of the church.

But if the Civil War is, in the history of the Disciples as in the history of American Protestantism, one of the most obvious examples of the subservience of the church to social forces, it also is a striking example of the unbending and uncompromising spirit of militant Christianity standing against the forces of social conformity. Scattered prophets in all sections, led by the fading but courageous Alexander Campbell, fearlessly raised their voices in Christian protest against the madness of their kinsmen and brethren. As a body, the Disciples valiantly resisted involvement in the holocaust—had the struggle been shorter, they might have succeeded.

CHAPTER VI

THE CHRISTIAN AND THE WORLD

DEMON RUM

"Wine is a mocker, strong drink is raging: and whosoever is deceived thereby is not wise." Proverbs 20:1.

FROM ALL ACCOUNTS, the average American at the turn of the nineteenth century was a prodigious consumer of "spirits." It has been estimated that in 1823 the yearly consumption of liquor in the United States amounted to seven and one-half gallons per person. During the early years of the century most American churchmen offered little protest against drinking; as a matter of fact, many clergymen shared the tastes of their parishoners for stimulating beverages. While this attitude began to change quite markedly by the 1830's, many American church leaders retained a "moderate and tolerant attitude" toward temperate drinking throughout the first half of the nineteenth century.[1]

Many early Disciples defended the usefulness of a little ardent spirits on festive occasions. Thomas W. Caskey, pioneer Disciples preacher and storyteller extraordinary, was fond of relating a tale of "two prominent church members" who had been "to market to lay in supplies for the annual revival at their church." The following conversation took place as they journeyed home:

"How much 'sperits did you git?"
"Ten gallons."
"Jest sech stinginess as that will sp'ile the meetin' and kill the church. I got

---

[1]Posey, *Presbyterians*, p. 99. For some general descriptions of the early liberal attitude of church leaders on the drinking question, see Tyler, *Freedom's Ferment*, p. 311; Cole, *Northern Evangelists*, pp. 116-117; Herbert Asbury, *The Great Illusion* (Garden City, N. Y.: Doubleday & Company, Inc., 1950), pp. 13-19; Posey, *Presbyterians*, pp. 99-100.

twenty gallons, myself, an' you are jest as able to support the gospil as I am, if you wuzn't so dog stingy."[2]

While Caskey's yarn is most likely apocryphal, such an incident was not improbable.

Although church leaders who believed it proper to "indulge in the use of ardent spirits" were increasingly on the defensive by the decade of the thirties, there remained a sizable recalcitrant group in the church which insisted that Christians could imbibe " 'a little' when they are too cold or too dry, or feel unwell."[3] Through the decade of the thirties the periodicals of the movement were sprinkled with defenses of the "moderate" use of strong drink. As the press of the church swung more and more behind the plea for total abstinence, one disgruntled tippler wrote: "Now, sir, much more cogent reasons and authoritative arguments than have as yet been given must be adduced to satisfy my mind that a *temperate* use of what is provided by an indulgent Providence is sinful."[4]

After 1840 apologies for moderate drinking virtually ceased in Disciples publications but the fervent protests of temperance leaders within the church furnish vivid evidence that many Disciples, including some of the preachers, retained their earlier tastes. One Kentucky temperance advocate woefully wrote: "In our village we have the singular spectacle of a brother building a meeting-house at the top of a hill, and working a whisky still at the bottom of it."[5]

---

[2]Srygley, *Seventy Years*, p. 176. Not only were the early pioneer preachers given to occasional imbibing, they were sometimes paid a portion of their wages in homemade "spirits," a common medium of exchange on the frontier. See Russell, *Church Life in the Blue Grass*, pp. 42-43; Abner Hill, Obituary of Abner Hill, 1788, typed copy of autobiographical manuscript, Disciples of Christ Historical Society, Nashville, Tennessee, pp. 11-12, 22-23.

[3]"Queries," *W.E.*, II (December, 1851), 359. Editor Daniel Bates's comment on this statement was: "We incline to the belief that those who take a 'little' when too cold or too dry, are apt to take 'a little' when too *hot;* and they are certain to take 'a little' when they are too *wet*. Ardent spirits, with some, is like the negro's rabbit—'good for ebrything.' "

[4]"To the Editor of the Christian Index," *M.H.*, II (September, 1831), 429-430.

[5]Z. Coons, "Letters," *Evangelist*, VII (August, 1839), 207-208. An irate and overimaginative opponent of the Disciples charged that the Old Union Church in Kentucky "turned out one man for *not* drinking strong drink." J. A. Gano to Mr. French, undated letter, John Allen Gano Papers, Disciples of Christ Historical Society.

By the middle of the decade of the 1820's the hard drinking habits of the nation began to come under heavy attack from a growing group of reformers. The temperance movement became highly organized and developed techniques which became "a model for pressure groups."[6] Unlike early American temperance reformers, who simply worked to curtail the intemperate use of whisky, the temperance agitators of the post-1830 period generally demanded total abstinence. The crusade gained new momentum in the 1840's with the formation of new societies, the most notable of which were the Washingtonians and the Sons of Temperance; and increasingly the object of the reformers became the enactment of legal prohibition. Although some states experimented with local option laws in the 1830's, the first major breakthrough in temperance legislation was the passage of a state prohibition act in Maine in 1846. The passage of the Maine law was followed by similar enactments in other states. By 1855 fourteen states and territories had passed prohibition legislation, but shortly after this high tide interest in the reform began to lag until after the Civil War. During all this crusade the churches were the leading force behind the temperance movement. Charles C. Cole, Jr. writes: "The drive against intemperance was an integral part of the expanded revivalism of the 1830's."[7]

By 1830 most of the vocal leaders of the Disciples of Christ were firmly committed to total abstinence. In 1833 Walter Scott warned "professed Christians" who manufactured and used whisky: "Surely the darkness of your damnation will be increased ten-fold, if you reform not from such unholy doings."[8] In the same year John T. Johnson launched a crusade for total abstinence in the *Christian Messenger* and by 1840 every

---

[6]Tyler, *Freedom's Ferment*, p. 322.

[7]Cole, *Northern Evangelist*, p. 116. For general accounts of the temperance movement and the churches' relations to it, see John Allen Krout, *The Origins of Prohibition* (New York: Alfred A. Knopf, 1925); Asbury, *The Great Illusion*, pp. 6-67; Ernest H. Cherrington, *The Evolution of Prohibition in the United States of America* (Westerville, Ohio: The American Issue Press, 1920), pp. 39-164; Tyler, *Freedom's Ferment*, pp. 308-350; Olmstead, *Religion in the United States*, pp. 354-355; Cole, *Northern Evangelists*, pp. 116-125; Bodo, *Protestant Clergy*, pp. 183-190.

[8]"Drunkenness," *Evangelist*, II (July, 1833), 167. See, also, "Letter from A. R. to Alonzo," *Evangelist*, IX (June, 1841), 137-139.

paper in the movement was firmly committed to this position.[9]

Local churches generally considered "drunkenness" a proper cause for church discipline. Early church records abound in notices of those who were "excluded for intemperance."[10] Prior to 1840 there was some question about whether the moderate use of alcoholic beverages was just cause for excommunication[11] but after that date most of the churches, theoretically at least, made total abstinence a condition of church membership. When queried about what action to take in the case of a brother who drank and sold "spirits of brandy," Alexander Campbell caustically replied: "If, on remonstrance and admonition, he does not reform, put him away from the church."[12]

During the 1850's many Disciples leaders joined the blossoming prohibition crusade. Alexander Campbell praised the Maine law and urged his readers to support the growing agitation for prohibition in other states.[13] Prohibition sentiment was especially strong among Disciples leaders in Indiana and Ohio, where antislavery sentiment had already convinced many church leaders that social reform was not incompatible with Christianity. John Boggs's militant Cincinnati abolitionist papers, the *North-Western Christian Magazine* and the *Christian Luminary*, vigorously backed the prohibition campaign. When prohibition legislation was

---

[9]See J. T. Johnson, "Ardent Spirits," *C.M.*, VII (April, 1833), 102-103. Also consult the June and July issues of this same volume.

[10]For some examples, see Minute Book of the Christian Church of Jacksonville, Illinois, II, January 14, 1840, Disciples of Christ Historical Society, Nashville, Tennessee; Church Register and Record of the Lawrence Creek Christian Church, Mason County, Kentucky, College of the Bible, Lexington, Kentucky.

[11]Many church leaders prior to 1840 believed that total abstinence was only an "opinion" and that it should not be made a "test of fellowship." See Thomas M. Henley and J. T. Johnson, "Letter," *C.M.*, VII (June, 1833), 168-171; A.C., "Query from T. J. Matthews," *M.H.*, N.S., III (September, 1839), 431.

[12]"Queries," *M.H.*, 4th S., I (March, 1851), 172-173. The question arose as to whether it was proper for a Christian farmer to sell his products to a distiller. Alexander Hall made a nice distinction in intent which left a large loophole: "If I sell my grain to a distiller whose ostensible business is to make liquor to sell to taverns, doggeries, etc. I am guilty of sin. . . . But if the distiller's professed object in manufacturing this commodity, were only for mechanical and medicinal purposes, under such circumstances a Christian would be justifiable in furnishing grain at a fair price." "Query," *G.P.*, II (November, 1848), 179.

[13]"Temperance and the Maine Law," *M.H.*, 4th S., III (October, 1853), 582. See, also, Richardson, *Memoirs of Campbell*, II, 600.

passed in Indiana in 1855, the elated Boggs printed the entire text of the law.[14] James M. Mathes, editor of the Indianapolis *Christian Record,* hailed the enactment as the most "glorious day" in the history of the state.[15] Several years previously the Disciples of Indiana had publicly placed themselves on record in favor of prohibition by passing a resolution favoring this policy at their state convention—at at time when resolutions on social subjects were almost without precedent.[16]

In short, the Disciples of Christ were never completely united on the liquor problem in the years before 1865 but increasingly they came to support the temperance movement. While some leaders continued to claim and to exercise the right of "moderate" drinking, for the most part, after the 1830's, the doctrine of total abstinence reverberated from most pulpits. In general, Disciples leaders prior to 1865 believed that the proper method of regulating the evil was through local church discipline. By 1850, however, there was considerable backing for the prohibition movement, especially among the churches of the North.

If most Disciples favored total abstinence by 1865, there was no such agreement on the propriety of Christians joining temperance societies. The attitude of the Disciples of Christ toward the organized temperance movement was deeply affected by the group's Western antiinstitutionalism and distrust of "secret societies," as well as its left-wing Protestant aver-

---

[14] J. B., "No More Drunkards in Indiana," *N.W.C.M.,* I (March, 1855), 275.

[15] "Liquor Traffic in Indiana," *C.R.,* 2d S., VI (March, 1855), 92.

[16] "Abstract of the Minutes of the Annual State Meeting of Indiana," *C.R.,* 2d S., II (November, 1851), 150. While interest in prohibition agitation was strongest in Ohio and Indiana, individuals in all sections participated in the crusade. The militant liberal Lewis L. Pinkerton edited a temperance paper in Lexington, Kentucky. Shackleford, *Pinkerton,* p. 50. Another preacher, Warren A. Belding, opened a "Temperance Hotel" in Slankertown, Pennsylvania, after failing in efforts to persuade the local innkeeper to stop selling whisky. W. S. Belding, *Biography of Dr. W. A. Belding* (Cincinnati: John F. Rowe, Publisher, 1897), pp. 52-53. William D. Carnes, influential Disciples educator and preacher in Tennessee, lobbied for prohibition legislation in his state, M. Norvel Young, *A History of Colleges Established and Controlled by Members of the Churches of Christ* (Kansas City: The Old Paths Book Club, 1949), p. 58. Although the interest of Disciples in the prohibition crusade during the ante-bellum period was significant, it was mild compared to the fervor of postwar church leaders. See David Edwin Harrell, "A Decade of Disciples of Christ Social Thought, 1875-1885" (unpublished M.A. thesis, Vanderbilt University, August, 1958), pp. 150-192.

sion to organization. As early as 1828 Alexander Campbell attacked temperance societies as a clerical stratagem to gain control of the people and their money.[17] Barton Stone, while he did not oppose temperance societies as such, never joined a temperance organization and warned that such enterprises could easily be "prostituted to the purpose of swindling the people out of their money."[18] In 1835 Alexander Campbell vigorously summed up early Disciples opposition to the organized temperance movement:

At the same time we have borne our testimony against Temperance Associations, Missionary Societies, and every other human institution opposed to the honor, dignity, and usefulness of the Christian Institution. . . . There is not an infidel in America . . . who would not, could the Temperance Society banish one vice from the land, sound the triumph of human wisdom over the Christian Institution. They would boast that a human institution had done for the world what Christianity had not done—what the gospel could not do.[19]

Many important Disciples leaders remained unrelenting opponents of organized temperance in the years before 1865. Tolbert Fanning, conservative Southern church leader, denounced all "moral societies" as a usurpation of the authority of the church: "Where there is government in a church no frail auxiliaries of human device are necessary, and these can never be foisted into the congregations of the Lord, without throwing marked contempt upon God's authority."[20] In an annual meeting of representatives of seventeen churches in eastern Ohio, the delegates agreed "that no Bro. present, should hereafter take part in those abstract institutions, which, without controversy have a tendency to detract from the glory and honor of the Church of Christ."[21]

[17]"Suppression of Intemperance," C.B., V (January, 1828), 146. Campbell's distrust of "moral societies" is described in Lunger, Political Ethics of Alexander Campbell, pp. 44-48.
[18]"Advice to Christians," C.M., IV (October, 1830), 248-250.
[19]"Temperance Associations," M.H., VI (September, 1835), 388-389.
[20]"Temperance and Temperance Societies," C.Rev., II (March, 1845), 50.
[21]G.P., II (September, 1848), 69-70. In 1836 a Congregational minister reported that his work in the temperance cause was hindered by the opposition of some of the religious leaders of his community: "Even members of the Christian and Baptist churches, saw in the Temperance cause, danger of a Union between Church and State." Sweet, Congregationalists, p. 261. In 1833 an Arkansas Presbyterian evangelist sent a report on the "Campbellites" to his state secretary. Included was the following: "As a denomination they are opposed to creeds, to S. Schools, to Temperance Societies." Sweet, Presbyterians, p. 697.

By the last half of the decade of the thirties there was a significant tendency among the leaders of the movement to be more tolerant of the temperance movement. In an important article in 1835 Alexander Campbell outlined the changes which he thought should take place as the Disciples made the transition from a protesting element within denominationalism to an independent religious group. One of Campbell's suggestions was: "We would advise that the white horse which carries the message of peace, should not be broken down by carrying heavy loads of declamation against Temperance Societies."[22] This was a welcome change for many church leaders, who from the beginning had been more receptive to the temperance movement than had Campbell.

During the decade of the 1840's the interest of the Disciples in the organized temperance movement reached its peak. For a few years there was a bitter controversy within the church over the subject. The propriety of Christians uniting with such organizations as the Washingtonians and the Sons of Temperance was extensively discussed in Disciples periodicals; several of the papers published debates on the subject.[23] Local churches were often seriously disturbed when members joined a temperance society. Those opposed to societies sometimes favored disfellowshiping the church members who enlisted in the temperance cause.[24] On the other hand, temperance advocates within the churches often charged that those who opposed the societies were "in league with the Devil."[25]

In general, however, a more moderate mood dominated the dispute over temperance societies. Alexander Campbell remained opposed to temperance organizations but his disapproval slowly mellowed into toleration. In 1842 he reprimanded "some of our brethren" for being "too fastidious on this subject"[26] and said:

Let me then say to you that this is an extraordinary case—an effort to dethrone one of the most desolating monsters that ever usurped a throne. . . . Let those

---

[22]"The Crisis," *M.H.*, VI (December, 1835), 595.

[23]There was a debate between Rees Jones and J. R. Naylor in the *Gospel Proclamation* beginning in October, 1848, which lasted for nearly a year. A similar debate was conducted in the *Western Reformer* beginning in February, 1847.

[24]See "Teetotalism," *M.H.*, N.S., VI (August, 1842), 370-372; "Total Abstinence," *P.U.*, IV (March 1, 1848), 50.

[25]See A. R., "Temperance," *C.J.*, III (February 15, 1845), 767.

[26]"Temperance Societies," *M.H.*, N.S., VI (February, 1842), 94-95.

brethren who are for doing what they think right allow those who differ from them to do what they think right, and mutually respect each others sincerity and integrity, and all will do well.[27]

Other church leaders made similar transitions to more tolerant attitudes toward the organized temperance movement. By the 1840's Barton Stone was a staunch supporter, if not a member, of temperance societies.[28] Walter Scott joined the Washingtonians and hailed the whole temperance movement as a precursor of the millennium.[29] Jacob Creath, Jr. summed up the moderate stand on the society question: "Every christian has a right to become a member of a temperance society, if he thinks proper to do so; and he has the right not to join if he thinks it best for him to do so. Here is where the matter ought to rest; all beyond this is *intemperance.*"[30]

The debate in Disciples periodicals over temperance societies subsided in the 1850's. The moderate attitude on the question generally prevailed and church members in different localities either did or did not join temperance societies depending on the attitude of the church in that section. In some sections Disciples became important local leaders in the temperance movement[31] but by and large interest in the crusade began to dwindle as the decade wore on and was finally overwhelmed by the more pressing social issues raised by the sectional crisis.

As a body, the Disciples of Christ during the ante-bellum era was committed to total abstinence but was divided in its attitude toward the organized temperance movement. The radical sectarian wing of the church

---

[27]"Teetotalism," *M.H.*, N.S., VI (August, 1842), 372. Campbell never really approved of the organized temperance movement, however, and in 1848 he wrote a stinging series of articles on "moral societies" which prompted a rash of protests from temperance advocates among the Disciples. The series, entitled "Moral Societies," begins in April, 1848, in the *Millennial Harbinger.*

[28]See *Christian Messenger*, XII (April, 1842), 191.

[29]See "Sons of Temperance," *P.U.*, III (June 23, 1847), 114; "Total Abstinence," *P.U.*, IV (March 1, 1848), 50.

[30]"Masonry and Temperance—No. 3," *M. and A.*, V (November, 1847), 244.

[31]See Evans, *Pioneer Preachers*, p. 310; "A New Move," *C.R.*, 2d S., II (April, 1852), 314; W. F. M. Arny, "Temperance Convention," *P.U.*, I (April 9, 1845), 95; J. G. T., "Temperance," *E.R.*, V (July 1, 1852), 288-290; Harmon, *Churches in Mississippi*, p. 96; Alvin Ray Jennings, "Thomas M. Allen Pioneer Preacher of Kentucky and Missouri" (unpublished M. A. thesis, Division of Graduate Instruction, Butler University, 1951), p. 183.

opposed all organized reform—including the temperance movement. On the other hand, that element which was moving toward a more denominational concept of the church ardently supported the temperance cause. Most Disciples leaders however, remained in the moderate middle-of-the-road. Harold Lunger's explanation of Campbell's lack of enthusiasm for the temperance campaign is applicable to many Disciples leaders: "Campbell had neither the temperament nor the theological viewpoint for a crusader of the emotional type."[32] The varied reactions of Disciples to the temperance movement were the natural harvest of the divided mind of the church.[33]

THE NOXIOUS WEED

"Know ye not that ye are the temple of God, and that the spirit of God dwelleth in you? If any man defile the temple of God, him shall God destroy." I Corinthians 3:16-17.

Although the use of tobacco was never a major issue among the Disciples of Christ, it was subjected to some colorful criticism by the pioneer exhorters of the movement. Smoking, chewing, dipping, and, occasionally, tobacco growing, were indicted on charges of the waste of money involved, the encouragement such activities gave the drunkard, the uncleanliness of the tobacco habit, and the lack of scriptural authority for using "the noxious weed."[34] Most frequently, however, church leaders attacked the use of tobacco on the ground that it was injurious to one's health. Jacob Creath, Jr., the most fervent Disciples antitobacco crusader of the period, wrote: "The injurious effects of tobacco are seen in its causing vomiting, purging, universal trembling, staggering, convulsions, languor, feebleness, relaxation of the muscles, great anxiety of mind and a tendency to faint, and blindness."[35] Creath gravely recorded one of the more shock-

[32]Lunger, *Political Ethics of Alexander Campbell*, p. 152.

[33]During the postwar period the two extreme views on the temperance question again became prominent. The more denominational element in the church became deeply involved in the temperance crusade while the sectarian element continued to exhibit the same old antiorganizational bias so long present in the movement. See Harrell, "Disciples Social Thought," pp. 150-192.

[34]See, for examples, "Tobacco," *M.H.*, I (June, 1830), 281-283; "Smoking," *C.M.*, IV (December, 1830), 278; "Tobacco," *Morning Watch*, II (December, 1839), 364-367.

[35]Jacob Creath, *A Tract on the Use and Abuse of Tobacco* (n.p.: J. Sosey & Sons, 1871), p. 6.

ing cases which had come to his attention of the allegedly harmful results of the habit:

Tobacco has produced many cases of emasculation. I am informed by a gentleman,
whose name I am not at liberty to mention, that a popular writer of the present
day married a lady, and that immediately after their marriage, he proposed separate
beds, which was agreed to. But on telling her situation to her mother, the latter
had the condition of the two parties investigated and learned that the husband
was *impotent,* and that he had been an inveterate smoker. A separation and divorce
were immediately obtained, and the lady was married again, and in the ordinary
time became a mother. I could give other instances, but it is needless.[36]

The antitobacco reformers in the church were particularly stern in their
denunciations of preachers and women who used the "weed." Jacob
Creath, Jr. wrote: "The FILTHY practice of chewing tobacco and spitting on floors is bad enough for Jews and Turks, for negroes and rowdies,
but it is worse in Christian men—still worse in Christian preachers—
but worse of all, in Christian women."[37] In spite of such heated attacks
and admonitions from their brethren, however, many Disciples continued to use tobacco and the matter was never considered serious enough
to demand discipline.[38]

The practice of chewing tobacco caused some real, practical problems
for the local churches. One writer vividly described the discomforts of
nonchewers:

A single tobacco chewer in a seat may put all the rest to a serious inconvenience;
the fumes arising from his ejected saliva, offend at least one sense, and the little
pools which he forms around him, are highly detrimental to those who have any
regard for the cleanliness of their garments, in such cases it is altogether out of
the power of the worshipper to kneel, and the effluvium which his lips may leave
in the wine cup during the celebration of the Lord's Supper, may be anything but
agreeable to some of his weaker brethren or sisters.[39]

The conflict over the use of tobacco was also the source of many hu-
morous stories, one of which is recorded in the *Recollections* of William
C. Rogers:

---

[36]*Ibid.,* p. 15.
[37]"Miscellaneous," *C.E.,* IX (December, 1858), 553.
[38]J. A. Butler, "News From the Churches, &c.," *B.A.,* IV (June, 1846), 140.
[39]REFORM, "A Word to Tobacco Chewers," *P.U.,* III (February 24, 1847), 46.

Once he [John Rogers] preached at the town of G_____M against "Common Sins or Vices." . . . He spoke of money thrown away for tobacco. . . . Not only so, the habit was filthy—sustained, it is true, by one and only one passage of Scripture: "Let him that is filthy be filthy still." While enlarging upon the evil attending its use, he noticed that two or three brethren occupying front seats were very restless. At last they could stand it no longer, but concluded to offer him a direct insult, by spurting their filth on the naked floor and toward him. As they increased in spitting, he also increased in the violence of his opposition. These men were never anxious to hear another philippic against common sins, nor was he very much inclined to preach soon again in that part of the Lord's vineyard.[40]

The result of this preaching-spitting match illustrates the stalemate over the tobacco question—neither side progressed very far toward converting the other.

WORLDLY ALLUREMENTS

"Now we command you, brethren, in the name of our Lord Jesus Christ, that ye withdraw yourselves from every brother that walketh disorderly, and not after the tradition which he received of us." II Thessalonians 3:6.

During the first half of the nineteenth century the church leaders of the West fought a running battle with their rowdy parishioners in an attempt to elevate the morals of the community. They combatted the surly ungodliness of the frontier with an unwavering puritanical code of morality and an unbending rule of discipline. The more popular frontier sects made no compromise with the "sins of the flesh" but their strictness never seemed to hinder their popularity. As a matter of fact, the hard-drinking, hard-fighting Westerner liked his religion hard; "simple alternatives such as doubt or faith, sin or righteousness, hell or heaven" made religion more comprehensible to the common man.[41]

The expanse of "wordly allurements" which came under the disapproving scrutiny of Disciples leaders during these years was enormous; virtually every facet of the private life of a church member was subject to congregational investigation. The struggle to keep the saints "unspotted from the world" was nowhere more heated than in the area of enter-

---

[40]Rogers, *Recollections*, pp. 199-200.

[41]Olmstead, *Religion in the United States*, p. 251. See, for general discussions of the role of the churches as guardians of frontier morality, Cole, *Northern Evangelists*, pp. 113-116; Sweet, *Methodists*, pp. 640-679; Sweet, *Congregationalists*, pp. 141-144; Posey, *Baptists*, pp. 38-53; Posey, *Presbyterians*, pp. 93-101; Posey, *Methodists*, pp. 100-111.

tainment. Balls, masquerades, routes, grand levees, sumptuous dinners, theater-going, gambling, cards, dice, cockfights, horse races, puppet shows, checkers, backgammon, novels, fairs, parties, and other such "frivolities" all received attention from the moral guardians of the West.[42]

Most early Disciples leaders agreed that a really good Christian seldom had any desire to participate in such "pleasures of sin." Aaron Chatterton remarked that he had never seen a "faithful, devoted Christian" who enjoyed such amusements and then added: "When we see the like, we shall expect in the next instance to see a white blackbird."[43] There were also deep undertones of class prejudices in the objections of Disciples leaders to "popular entertainment." Writers in church periodicals repeatedly denounced amusement as "fashionable," "luxurious," and "sumptuous." The moral code of the movement was molded out of both puritanical moral values and Western disrespect for the social amenities of established society.

All of the sins of the flesh railed against by early Disciples leaders were by no means of equal weight. While participation in some forms of amusement was universally regarded as a cause for church discipline, other breaches of the moral code of the movement were tolerated. There were local variations in what was considered sinful and, more and more, as the economic status of the church's membership rose, local congregations often became lax in exercising discipline.[44]

The entertainment most vigorously and persistently attacked was "the giddy ball." In 1831 Barton Stone warned that of "all the fashionable amusements of the world," dancing "stands preeminent to captivate the mind, and to destroy all serious and religious impressions on the heart."[45] Twenty years later Alexander Campbell, emphasizing his economic as

---

[42]See, for examples of the extensive field of amusements which was examined by church leaders, "Aberrations of Professing Christians," *M.H.*, 3d S., I (June, 1844), 278-281; "Worldly Allurements," *W.R.*, VI (September, 1848), 697-702; "District Meeting," *E.R.*, III (November 9, 1850), 703.

[43]"Unchristian Amusements," *Evangelist*, XIII (March, 1862), 111.

[44]In the 1850's reports of the "worldliness" of church members became more and more frequent. See "District Meeting," *E.R.*, III (November 9, 1850), 703; "Declined," *C.E.*, VII (April, 1856), 187-188.

[45]"Reply to an 'Observer,' " *C.M.*, V (March, 1831), 71.

well as his scriptural objections to dancing, commented that "wealthy and honorable sinners" were the class who usually enjoyed such activities.[46]

While most Disciples preachers were unwavering in their assaults on "the popular dance" in the years before 1865, they were waging a difficult, and apparently losing, battle in many of the local churches. In 1844 Barton Stone woefully noted that dancing was "beginning to be advocated and practiced by some among us."[47] Similar protests became more and more frequent until in 1864 Moses E. Lard announced that the group was "scandalized at the prevalence" of dancing church members.[48] Most Disciples preachers continued to demand that dancing members be excluded and many congregations continued to discipline wayward members but the years, the evolving character of the church, and the national laxity of morals during the wartime years did much to narrow the gap between the church and the world.

Theater-going, which was never a practical problem of any consequence for the Western Disciples, was universally condemned by the leaders of the movement and was occasionally the cause of an excommunication.[49] More important than their objections to such an urbane amusement were the stern observations of church leaders on such Western pastimes as circuses and political barbecues. One Missouri Disciple advertised for signatures to the following petition, which he intended to send to the state

[46]"Dancing," M.H., 4th S., I (September, 1851), 504-505.

[47]"Dancing," C.M., XIII (March, 1844), 313. See, for some other examples of similar concern, "Conformity to the World," M.H., VI (September, 1835), 427-428; "Dancing," M.H., N. S., II (April, 1838), 155-157.

[48]"Instrumental Music in Churches and Dancing," L.Q., I (March, 1864), 333. In his article, Lard tried to link moral "liberalism" with the advocates of instrumental music. He was not the only antebellum preacher to make this connection. John Rogers wrote: "But my brother (would you believe it?) a popular preacher has come out in two numbers in the 'E. Reformer,' in favor of instrumental music in churches and social dancing in our families!" "Dancing," M.H., 4th S., I (August, 1851), 467. Although the conservative element in the church increasingly tried to prove that the liberals were morally suspect, there was little foundation for such suspicions in the nineteenth century. All of the factions in the movement remained committed to puritanical morals throughout these years.

[49]See Minute Book of the Christian Church of Jacksonville, Illinois, 1832-1889, Disciples of Christ Historical Society, Nashville, Tennessee; J. W. M., "The Stage," P.U., II (August 26, 1846), 149.

legislature: "Your petitioners would therefore pray your Honorable Body to prohibit all shows, circuses, magicians, menageries and other humbugs, from coming into the State."[50] In spite of such protests there was never any suggestion that the enjoyment of such hardy entertainments should be made a test of fellowship and from every indication many church members occasionally broke the monotony of back-breaking work and two-hour sermons by visiting a "humbug show."[51] A few early preachers denounced fairs, especially because of their connection with horse racing,[52] but, for the most part, both preachers and laymen looked askance on derogatory remarks about this pillar in Western social structure.[53]

Church leaders generally disapproved of all sorts of "games of chance." Alexander Campbell advised: "The truly good and great man never can be a selfish man, never can seek to rise at the expense or detriment of any man."[54] Included under the "gaming" ban were lotteries, "carnal cards," dice, checkers, backgammon, and "pitching quoits."[55] While it was not uncommon for church members to be disciplined for such activities, especially during the early years of the century, by 1865 most of the churches tended to overlook all but the worst infractions of these rules.

A more troublesome problem for church leaders was regulating the lusty language of their rugged parishoners. Jacob Creath, Jr. warned that "profane swearing" was "one of the sins for which God permits these great marts and cities to be so often scourged with fire and pes-

---

[50]"A Petition to the Missouri Legislature," *C.E.*, VIII (October, 1856), 452.

[51]See, for some typical protests about church members participating in such amusements, "Circuses," *E.R.*, III (February 2, 1850), 86; Omega, "Attending Barbecues, Dancing, &c.," *M. and A.*, V (August, 1847), 194-195.

[52]See "Public Morality—The Races," *B.A.*, VI (December, 1848), 234-235; "Cattle Shows, &c.," *C.E.*, VI (July, 1855), 325-328.

[53]Some early church leaders, such as Tolbert Fanning, John Allen Gano, and Thomas M. Allen, were prominent stock breeders and leaders in the introduction of agricultural fairs into their communities. See John Allen Gano Papers; B. Franklin, "Observation of a Day," *P. and R.*, I (October, 1850), 659-661; "Fairs and Cattle Shows," *C.E.*, VI (February, 1855), 62-65; Josephine Murphy, "The Professor and His Lady," The Nashville *Tennessean Magazine*, April 3, 1949, pp. 22-30.

[54]"Responses to Questions Propounded by Brother Hundley," *M.H.*, 5th S., III (September, 1860), 512.

[55]See "Query," *G.P.*, I (July, 1948), 548-550; J. H. Green, "The Charm of Gambling," *B.A.*, VII (September, 1849), 87-89.

tilence."[56] The records of local churches frequently note exclusions for "using profane language" and occasionally the culprit gave a colorful demonstration for the church messenger who called to confront him with his sin.[57] Not infrequently the charge of swearing was accompanied by others which showed the general surliness of the guilty party, such as "fighting," "quarrelling," and "general bad conduct."

Other, more genteel, "allurements" also claimed the attention of church leaders. Laymen were persistently warned about the evils of "poisonous literature." Most church leaders strongly discouraged reading fiction. One writer concisely summed up the major objections:

1st. *Novel-reading is a waste of time.* . . .
2d. *Novel-reading conduces to ignorance by monopolizing the time which should be given to useful study.* . . .
3d. *Novel-reading dissipates and weakens the mind, and renders it unfit to investigate truth.* . . .
4th. *Novel-reading induces a morbid ideality and sensitiveness wholly incompatible with true happiness, and it unfits the mind for the realities of life.* . . .
5th. *Novel-reading predisposes to extravagance, and induces to crime.*[58]

Most of the popular magazines of the day fell under the ban of church leaders. Mrs. Selina Campbell, the wife of Alexander Campbell, branded all the "popular periodicals," "nonsense," and urged Christian women to confine their reading to weightier matter.[59]

The women of the church were frequently cautioned about the evils of "fashionable dress." "Ribbands," "rings," "bracelets," "hooped

---

[56]"Correspondence," *C.E.*, VII (May, 1856), 234.

[57]See Minute Book of the Christian Church of Jacksonville, Illinois, 1832-1889; Russell, *Church Life in the Blue Grass*, pp. 58-59.

[58]"Popular Literature—No. VI," *M.H.*, 3d S., I (December, 1844), 599-600.

[59]"Popular Periodicals," *M.H.*, 4th S., VI (February, 1856), 90. Occasionally a writer would warn the church members about the "kind of pictures" they hung in their houses. John R. Howard wrote that he was "perfectly astonished" by some of the art displayed "in the houses of our brethren." He further elaborated: "For instance, I have seen hanging up in the houses of brethren, scenes of a gentleman and lady kissing, the gentleman with his arm around the lady's waist, &c! Now, what is the effect of these 'courting scenes,' but to arouse and cherish some of the most improper and immoral passions! I once saw in the house of a brother and sister, a *dancing* scene on the chimney [*sic*] screen! . . . What must be the effect of such pictorial examples on the minds of children, but to excite in them a love for dancing!" "Moral Influence of Pictures," *M.H.*, 4th S., III (April, 1853), 212-213.

sleeves," and any number of other articles of adornment were denounced by church leaders.[60] Barton Stone complained that the tastes of many women kept their "husbands in perfect drudgery to support them."[61] Another writer reported that the "adornment" of the contemporary ladies was such that "the passions of men should be excited, and their principles shaken."[62] The symptoms of lower-class prejudice were everywhere apparent in the remonstrances of Disciples leaders against "costly array." Barton Stone chastized the "female sisters" for their "servile imitation of the *fashionables* of Europe,"[63] while other preachers condemned wearing "gold, pearls, and costly array" simply on the grounds that "they are costly."[64] But while a good deal was said on the subject by church leaders, most church members probably dressed as they pleased, or as they could afford, the question was seldom made a matter of discipline, and most preachers simply demanded that their parishioners "dress rationally."[65]

THE LORD'S DAY

"Let no man therefore judge you in meat, or in drink, or in respect of an holy-day, or of the new moon, or of the sabbath days." Colossians 2:16.

The Puritan concept of Sabbath-keeping remained a dominant theme in American religious history throughout the ante-bellum period. Most American churchmen insisted that all secular activity should cease on the Sabbath and they generally felt that it was quite proper to enforce their view legally. In 1828 a national organization was formed to promote

[60]See "The Times," *C.M.,* IV (September, 1830), 227-228; "Modesty of Dress in Females," *C. Ex.,* II (September, 1831), 215.

[61]"To the Female Members of the Christian Churches of the United States of America," *C.M.,* VI (August, 1832), 242.

[62]"Modesty of Dress in Females," *C. Ex.,* II. (September, 1831), 215.

[63]"To the Female Members of the Christian Churches of the United States of America," *C.M.,* VI (August, 1832), 242.

[64]See C. K., "Gold, Pearls and Costly Array," *C.J.,* IV (March 22, 1845), 7-8; "Domestic Relations—No. 2," *G.P.,* I (October, 1847), 153-155; Whitley, *Trumpet Call,* p. 105.

[65]See "Address to Christian Women," *M.H.,* III (July, 1832), 325-326; A. Reynolds, "Practical Reformation, No. 7," *C.M.,* IX (November, 1835), 243-246. One preacher who was particularly offended by the "wearing of gold" was forced to explain that the "gold bands on his silver watch" were "nothing but brass." "Domestic Relations—No. 2," *G.P.,* I (October, 1847), 153-155.

such legislation—the General Union for Promoting the Observance of the Christian Sabbath. Many factors were present in American society in the first half of the nineteenth century which tended to promote a more liberal concept of Sunday-keeping: continental imigration, industrialization and urbanization, the rise of commercialized recreation and sports, improved transportation, and currents of secular and theological liberalism. For the most part, however, the Protestant clergy were successful in checkiny any real inroads into the established concept of the Sabbath prior to 1865.[66]

The dispensational theology of the Disciples of Christ markedly affected their attitude on Sunday-keeping. Since the Disciples insisted that the "old law" had been supplanted by the New Testament of Christ, they were opposed to anything which smacked of forcing Jewish standards of morality on Christians. Disciples leaders consistently insisted that the first day of the week was completely unrelated to the Jewish Sabbath.[67] Alexander Campbell pointedly attacked the claim that the Sabbath had been transformed into a Christian institution: "If it be changed, it was that august personage changed it who changed times and laws *ex-officio* —I think his name is DOCTOR ANTICHRIST."[68]

Another factor which made the Sabbath movement unacceptable to early Disciples leaders was their devotion to the principle of separation of church and state—a tenet well-rooted in the movement's left-wing Protestant and liberal Western background. Alexander Campbell repeatedly warned that national Sabbath legislation was simply the first step toward the establishment of a national church—an end which he often accused Protestant leaders of promoting.[69] Leaders of the Disciples also pointed out that such laws would be discriminatory against minority religious groups: "And what would you have Congress to do for the Jews—the

---

[66]See, for general surveys of the Sabbath movement, Stokes, *Church and State,* II, 12-13; III, 153-176; Olmstead, *Religion in the United States,* pp. 355-357; Cole, *Northern Evangelists,* pp. 105-109; Bodo, *Clergy and Public Issues,* pp. 39-43.

[67]See, for examples of the Disciples doctrinal position on the Sabbath, A. Campbell, "To Mr. Eli S. Bailey," *C.B.,* III (August, 1825), 22-24; "The First Day of the Week Is Not the Seventh Day," *M.H.,* V (September, 1834), 465-466.

[68]"Address," *C.B.,* I (February, 1824), 129-130.

[69]See "Sabbath Mail Report," *C.B.,* VII (April, 1830), 233-234; "Letter from Charles Cassedy, Esq.," *M.H.,* IV (September, 1833), 464-467.

Sabbatarians, who regard the seventh day as holy to the Lord?—pass no act of Congress for them because they are too few in number."[70]

Agitation for Sabbath legislation reached its peak in the late 1820's when Congress was overwhelmed with petitions demanding that all post offices be closed on Sundays. The protest movement was so strong that in 1828 a special congressional committee, headed by Senator Richard M. Johnson of Kentucky, was appointed to study the matter. Johnson's report (along with a similar one he made the following year as the head of a House committee to study the same question) is recognized as one of the classic state documents defining the American doctrine of separation of church and state. Johnson persuasively argued that such legislation would be dangerous, discriminatory, and unconstitutional; his reports virtually crushed the campaign to stop the Sunday mails.[71]

---

[70]"Reply to Mr. Waterman," *M.H.,* V (May, 1834), 215.

[71]See, for general information on the Sunday mail controversy and Johnson's part in it, Stokes, *Church and State,* II, 12-20; Schlesinger, *Age of Jackson,* pp. 137-143; Leland Winfred Meyer, *The Life and Times of Colonel Richard M. Johnson of Kentucky* (New York: Columbia University Press, 1932), pp. 256-263. The authorship of the Johnson reports was a matter of some dispute at the time they were presented; recent historians are still uncertain about who composed the documents. Arthur M. Schlesinger, Jr. writes: "The actual authorship of the report is a matter of some question. It was produced in the home of Reverend O. B. Brown, for some years the center of the Kentucky influence in Washington. . . . The reports are written in a loose rhetorical style, at which Johnson, Barry, Brown and Kendall were all adept. Probably Brown did most of the actual writing, in consultation with Johnson. Kendall later revised the report. Johnson took the responsibility and never refused the credit." *Age of Jackson,* p. 139, n. 18. Many Disciples believed that Alexander Campbell wrote the reports. Robert Richardson wrote: "As it was perfectly well known that Richard M. Johnson possessed neither the education nor the ability to write such a document, a great desire was manifested by the people to discover its real author; and public sentiment was not long in deciding that it could be no one else than Alexander Campbell. . . . If this was the case, it was, of course, a matter entirely confidential; and Mr. Campbell was too honorable ever to acknowledge himself the author. It is proper to say, however, also, that when the authorship was charged upon him, as it often was, by his intimate friends, he was not known in any case positively to deny it, but always evaded giving a direct reply." *Memoirs of Campbell,* I, 536-537. Richardson's guess is almost certainly incorrect. See Lunger, *Political Ethics of Alexander Campbell,* pp. 46-48. On the other hand, Campbell's views probably had an influence on Johnson's reports. There is a striking similarity between the arguments in Johnson's Sabbath reports and Campbell's often-repeated views on the subject. Johnson was unquestionably familiar with the Bethany reformer's ideas. His brother, John T.

Although the Protestant clergy generally were leaders of the Sunday mail agitation,[72] Disciples editors unanimously backed Johnson's militant expression of left-wing religious freedom and Western democracy. Alexander Campbell wrote of Johnson's report: "It is one of the ablest state papers on the question, we have ever read. It cannot be resisted by good logic or sound policy."[73] Barton Stone agreed: "I have disapproved the attempt to urge Congress to legislate on the subject, and have been disgusted at the zeal of the clergy in their bold attempts to have it effected."[74]

Although most Disciples leaders insisted that their peculiar views on the Sabbath were not meant to encourage desecration of the Lord's Day, the church was often charged with laxity on this count. A disturbed church member wrote:

The sects charge us with denying the divinity of Christ . . . *and with badly keeping the Lord's day*. In the latter charge we justly stand guilty before God. . . . Because no positive command is found in the new Testament, to "remember the Sabbath day and keep it holy," the moral obligation to keep it holy is thrown off by thousands of our brethren, with the example of many of our teachers "in high places."[75]

While some of such criticism was probably the result of outsiders misunderstanding the Disciples Sabbath-Lord's Day distinction, much of it was, no doubt, well founded.

For the most part, however, Disciples leaders were as concerned as other churchmen about the tendency to "destroy the idea of a Sabbath under any name."[76] Throughout the ante-bellum period preachers insisted that Sunday be devoted exclusively to religious activity. They argued that

---

Johnson, who was the senator's close confidant, early became the most influential Disciples preacher in Kentucky. Campbell himself visited in the Johnson home. Although Richard M. Johnson remained a Baptist, the views expressed in his reports were much nearer the doctrine of the Disciples than of the Baptists.

[72]See Stokes, *Church and State*, II, 19; Schlesinger, *Age of Jackson*, pp. 139-140.

[73]"Transportation of the Mail on the Sabbath," *C.B.*, VI (April, 1829), 213.

[74]"Sunday and Sunday Mails," *C.M.*, IV (May, 1830), 141. Another important editor, David S. Burnet, warned: "Let the prayer of the petitioners be granted and Judaism is established by law." "Sunday Mails—No. 1," *Evangelical Inquirer*, I (January, 1831), 175.

[75]S. M. McCorkle, "Lord's Day," *C.J.*, III (May 11, 1844), 120.

[76]"Sundays and Sunday Mails," *C.M.*, IV (May, 1830), 141.

such a course was both a religious requirement[77] and a physical necessity.[78] Although Disciples leaders continued to make a distinction between the Sabbath and the first day of the week, after 1840 they more and more came to support the Sabbatarian movement and by 1850 it was not unheard of for a church leader to defend the observance of Sunday on the grounds of Old Testament authority.[79] In 1849, at the first General Convention of the church, Samuel Ayers of Kentucky introduced a resolution commending "to all our brethren in the Lord the importance of sanctifying and observing the Lord's day in their conversation and behaviour."[80]

---

[77]See, for some examples, "The Lord's Day, No. 2," *C.T.*, III (March, 1844), 182-188; "Desecration of the Lord's Day in Germany," *P.U.*, I (January 1, 1845), 38.

[78]Some early Disciples defended Sabbath legislation on these practical grounds. An early Pennsylvania church member wrote: "If it be a human institution [the Sabbath], it is a good one and its observance should be enforced by every legal sanction. It gives necessary rest to men and beasts that labor, and tends to the adoption of regular habits." Bradford Clark, "The Christian Sabbath," *Primitive Christian and Investigator*, II (December, 1836), 193. Campbell made a significant switch on the question of Sunday legislation by 1854. In that year Judge Jeremiah Sullivan Black of the Pennsylvania Supreme Court, an outstanding Disciples layman and personal friend of Campbell, ruled that "driving an omnibus through the streets of the city of Pittsburgh on Sunday" was a violation of an old state blue law which prohibited any activity which was not "a work of charity or necessity" on that day. Campbell remarked: "We cannot but most cordially acquiesce in said decision, and regret that such a provision is not in all our cities, as to allow a peaceful and undisturbed attention upon the duties, privileges and honors of Christian worship, in every Christian sanctuary in the land." "The Sanctification of the Lord's Day Protected and Defended in Pennsylvania," *M.H.*, 4th S., IV (June, 1854), 351-353.

[79]In 1851 David S. Burnet defended the concept of a "Christian Sabbath:" "A distinction was drawn between the 'Sabbath of the Lord,' which Israel was commanded to *remember,* and the peculiar observances which they were to regard, connected with that day, as a nation. The latter were abrogated. The former was written by the finger of God, on the tables of stone, because it, like the other precepts, was enduring." "Popular Vices—No. VIII," *P. and R.*, II (February, 1851), 85.

[80]*Report of the Proceedings of the General Convention of the Christian Churches of the United States of America, Held in Cincinnati, Wednesday, October 23, 1849, Together With the Third Annual Report of the American Christian Bible Society, and the Second Annual Report of the Cincinnati Christian Tract Society With Appendices* (Cincinnati: American Christian Depository, 1849), p. 39. Sig-

Disciples leaders recommended a rigid code for Sunday observance. Under this code, "secular labor" was prohibited and church members were advised that "every preparation" necessary for the activities of the family on Sunday "should be made on the preceding day."[81] Readers of Disciples periodicals were encouraged to boycott businesses which operated on Sunday[82] and other activities which fell under the Sunday ban including "visiting," "feasting," "amusements," and "unnecessary travelling."[83] Alexander Campbell even frowned on "secular" conversations:

Those Christians too, who, while on the way to the Lord's institutions, or returning from the house of song and prayer on 'the day of breaking bread,' converse on the affairs of state, the times, the crops, the business of the pleasures of time and sense, show that their conversation is not in heaven.[84]

Tolbert Fanning urged that "the observance of the Lord's day, like all other great gospel truths, should be a test question"[85] but church members were seldom disciplined except for gross neglect in attending church services.

By the 1840's there had been enough relaxation of the early anti-Sabbatarian prejudices among Disciples leaders for some preachers to become active in the organized Sabbath movement. Disciples ministers attended and participated in "Lord's Day Conventions" in Kentucky, Missouri, and Indiana, as well as the National Sabbath Convention in Baltimore in 1844. Indiana Disciples were especially active in the organized movement; James M. Mathes was elected vice-president of a convention in that state in 1846 and ardently supported the crusade in his paper,

---

nificantly, the resolution was not adopted. A compromise resolution was introduced which made no mention of the "Lord's day" but simply urged all Christians to "a more faithful performance of their duties." Sentiment against the Sabbath movement was strong enough that some of the members of the convention objected to Ayer's motion.

[81]Samuel Church, "The Lord's Day," *P.U.*, I (December 18, 1844), 30.

[82]See D. S. B., "Sunday Milk," *C.A. and P.U.*, VI (June 14, 1850), 94; D. S. B., "Popular Vices—No. XI," *P. and R.*, II (March, 1851), 178-180.

[83]See "Queries," *C.R.*, V (February, 1848), 246-248; D. S. B., "Popular Vices—No. X," *P. and R.*, II (February, 1851), 121-124.

[84]"Reformation—No. XII," *M.H.*, VII (September, 1836), 420.

[85]"The Lord's Day," *C. Rev.*, II (January, 1845), 5.

the *Christian Record*.[86]

In short, the radically sectarian theme in the mind of the Disciples, inextricably interwoven with lower-class and Western prejudices, motivated militant protests against the Sabbath movement. Never less strict than other denominational leaders in their demands for rigid observance of the Lord's Day, conservative Disciples leaders bitterly denounced the agitation to legislate on a religious question. More and more, however, especially after 1840, many church leaders took a more tolerant view of the Sabbath campaign. Some preachers, especially in the North where a more denominational concept of the church was emerging, wholeheartedly backed the crusade.

MARRIAGE AND DIVORCE

"What therefore God hath joined together, let not man put asunder." Matthew 19:6.

Although divorce was uncommon, such sins as "adultery," "desertion," and common law marriage, caused frontier church leaders considerable concern.[87] Most ante-bellum Christian churches were cautious and circumspect in inspecting the marital status of their members and rigorously disciplined offenders. Some preachers, especially during the early years of the movement, believed that it was sinful for Christians to marry "infidels or unbelievers," a ban which included everyone outside the Disciples of Christ, and it was not unusual for a church member to be unchurched for such a violation.[88] James S. Lamar vividly described the policy of the congregation in Pittsburgh, Pennsylvania:

If a man married a woman who was not a member of the church, however moral and upright, and however respectful in her bearing towards Christianity and its ordinances, he was called to account for marrying contrary to the word of the Lord, and he must say—perhaps in the presence of his wife—that he was sorry

---

[86]Some of the brethren objected to Mathes's activities: "One brother beloved, writes, that he sees no use in 'Lord's day conventions,' and as we published an abstract of the Minutes of the convention held in Bloomington, 1846, and acted as an officer of said convention, he concludes to sustain us no longer as an Editor." "Conclusion," *C.R.*, IV (October, 1846), 123-126.

[87]For a general survey of the attitudes of the American churches on marriage and divorce, see Stokes, *Church and State*, III, 42-67.

[88]See T. F., "Christians Marrying With the World," *C. Rev.*, II (October 1, 1845), 237; J. R. H., "Marriage—No. 6," *M. and A.*, V (August, 1847), 209-210.

for it; and moreover—though this probably gave the poor woman some comfort—he must promise that he would not do so any more![89]

Most church leaders agreed, however, even during the 1830's, that while the brother who married an "unbeliever" was "to be pitied," he was not to be "put out."[90] Alexander Campbell wrote: "Certainly no christian can . . . exclude a person simply for marrying any person not forbidden by the laws of the land."[91]

If most Disciples leaders believed that compliance with the "laws of the land" was all that was demanded for a scriptural marriage, they were not so liberal on the question of divorce. The generally accepted standard was: "There is no release then to husband or wife from the marriage contract unless the other party has been guilty of fornication."[92] A few church leaders were liberal enough to concede that "desertion," a practice not uncommon on the frontier, was a just cause for divorce and remarriage, but they were the exceptions.[93]

In general, the churches were probably more diligent in enforcing their code of morality in this area than in any other. Cases abound in the early church records of members being excluded for "bigamy," "having two husbands living," and "marrying a man who has a living wife," as well as such sins as "adultery" and "fornication." John Dexter was arraigned before the Wellsburgh, Ohio, church for having taken a second wife after his first one had "repudiated" him. Dexter, who had not gone through the formality of getting a divorce after his first unfortunate marriage, was instructed by the church to return to his first wife. Dexter traced his first spouse down only to find that she had secured a divorce and remarried. The church then ruled that the jilted husband was free to marry so he returned home for a belated wedding ceremony with the second Mrs. Dexter. Unfortunately, "some informality in the late mar-

---

[89]Lamar, *Errett*, I, 69.

[90]Parthenos, "Marriage—No. II," *M.H.*, II (May, 1831), 203.

[91]"Remarks on Parthenos," *M.H.*, II (May, 1831), 207.

[92]"Divorce and Marriage," *C.A. and P.U.*, V (January 20, 1849), 10.

[93]See "Querist's Department," *C. Mag.*, V (January, 1852), 23-24; "Separation and Divorce," *M.H.*, 4th S., III (September, 1853), 529-533.

riage was discovered" but the determined Dexter, according to the church record, "was again married to his last wife."[94]

THE BUSINESS OF MORAL REGENERATION—
DIVERGING VIEWS

"They are not of the world, even as I am not of the world. . . . As thou hast sent me into the world, even so have I sent them into the world." John 17:16-18.

American churches were unquestionably a civilizing force on the rowdy West in the first half of the nineteenth century. Walter Posey writes: "Until civil authority was fully established on the frontier, the Presbyterian church . . . with other churches, contributed a stabilizing force that assured decency, law, and order to an ever receding frontier."[95] Committed to the sectarian principle of separation from the world, the Disciples did their share in trying to regulate the morals of the hard-living frontiersmen. Although the local church rulers never implemented all the rigorous rules advocated by church leaders, they were not hesitant to confront the most unruly sinners with their wickedness, and discipline of the recalcitrant was perhaps the most important function of their crude "business meetings."

The moral code of the Disciples of Christ was unquestionably colored by economic factors. Elmer Clark, in his study of American sectarianism, writes:

They [the sects] elevate the necessities of their class . . . into moral virtues and regard as sins the practices they are debarred from embracing. Those pinched by economic circumstances look askance on theatergoing, card playing, and "putting on gold and costly apparel," but indulge in the same when their earthly fortunes improve.[96]

While there are many individual exceptions to such a generalization, by and large the most sectarian moral protest from Disciples of Christ was voiced by the group's lower-class leaders and it was among the more urbane and sophisticated churches that left-wing discipline first began to wane.

---

[94]Record of the Origin and Proceedings of the Church of Christ at Wellsburgh, Virginia, 1823-1849.

[95]Posey, *Presbyterians*, p. 101.

[96]*Small Sects*, p. 17.

And yet, within the Disciples at any rate, there was a clearer symptom of the emerging sect-denomination pattern. In general, there was little perceptible change in the moral code of the movement prior to 1865. Although some of the churches weakened in the strictness of their discipline during the last decades of the ante-bellum period, most of the preachers remained firmly committed to puritanical morals. Even where there were noticeable changes in the church's moral code, such as on the temperance and Sabbath questions, the emerging denominational conscience within the movement was apt to be more demanding than the sectarian mind. Devotion to the doctrine of total abstinence was more characteristic of the liberal Disciples than of the conservatives—and so was outspoken agitation on the Sunday question.

The most significant symptom of the diverging emphasis within the Disciples mind was the emergence of differing attitudes on the proper method of prosecuting moral reforms. The sectarian segment of the group contended that the church ought to be the sole regulator and arbiter of Christian morality. As far as the world was concerned, it could be made moral only by first making it Christian. On the other hand, the liberal element in the movement believed that the Christian was obligated to lend his influence to the great moral crusades which recurrently swept the nation. These men were convinced that if the world could be made moral it could then be made Christian—indeed, making the world moral was a part of making it Christian. Prior to 1865, however, most Disciples did not consistently act on either of these principles. The broad, tolerant main body of the church drifted along in the ways of human inconsistency.

In sum, the three-way severing of the mind of the movement was delineated by the reaction of church leaders to the problems of moral reform. The sociological forces which were forging these divergent concepts of the Christian message affected not so much the content of the church's moral code (although sometimes the content was affected) but they deeply influenced Disciples leaders' conceptions of the proper methods of implementing Christian morality. There was no question that the Christian should be free from the sins of the world but there was no such harmony on the question of how Christians ought to go about freeing the world from sin.

CHAPTER VII

THE RESIDUE OF REFORM

CAPITAL PUNISHMENT

"Whoso sheddeth man's blood, by man shall his blood be shed: for in the image of God made he man." Genesis 9:6.

The broad currents of humanitarianism which swept across the United States and Western Europe in the early nineteenth century caused considerable agitation for reform of penal codes and institutions. By the 1840's there was significant international interest in the abolition of capital punishment. Several European states removed the death penalty from their penal codes prior to 1865 and there was strong, if unorganized, agitation for a similar reform in other nations. Although other social questions monopolized most of the energy of American social reformers, the movement for the abolition of capital punishment received persistent and vocal support from a few militant agitators.[1]

The capital punishment reform never aroused much interest among ante-bellum Disciples leaders. Occasionally an editor condemned the "inhuman practice";[2] more often, however, an irate writer attacked the humanitarian crusade as a "gull-trap, humbug or delusion."[3] The only real flurry of interest in the subject on the part of Disciples leaders came

---

[1]See, for general discussions of the movement to abolish capital punishment, Gabriel Tarde, *Penal Philosophy* (Boston: Little, Brown, and Company, 1912), pp. 530-531; Harry Elmer Barnes, *The Repression of Crime* (New York: George H. Doran, Company, 1926), pp. 156-158, 25-41.

[2]See "Notes on a Short Tour to the North West," *C.R.*, II (September, 1844), 60.

[3]B. F., "Another New Book Out," *A.C.R.*, II (January, 1857), 18.

during the years from 1846 to 1848 when the issue was rather fully discussed by several of the church's editors.[4]

In 1846 Alexander Campbell wrote a tract defending capital punishment which received wide circulation in this country and was republished
in England.[5] Campbell arrayed a massive body of pragmatic and scriptural
argument to prove that the death penalty was both necessary and compatible with Christian ethics. The editor argued that if the death penalty
were abolished, all punishment would have to be suspended: "Is not the
right to inflict upon him any penal pain whatever involved in this question: a single stripe may kill; nay, a single stripe, inflicted by an officer of
justice, and that no very violent one, has sometimes killed?"

The burden of Campbell's argument, however, was based on the scriptural examples of the death sentence found in the Old Testament. The
editor sternly cited Jehovah's injunction in Genesis 9:6: "Whoso sheddeth
man's blood, by man shall his blood be shed: for in the image of God
made he man." He repeatedly pointed out that under the Jewish the-
ocracy, a civil government directed by God, capital punishment was rigorously implemented. Although usually unwilling to accept Old Testament
authority because of his dispensational theology, Campbell contended
that the pertinent passages on this subject revealed "eternal principles"
which were applicable to civil government in every age.

Although the Bethany reformer staunchly defended capital punishment,
he was by no means opposed to the humanitarian efforts to reform the
penal code of the nation. He admitted that "our criminal code is not in
unison with the spirit of the age, nor with the presiding genius of
European and American civilization." The purpose of criminal legislation, he believed, was dual: to assure the "safety of the state" and to encourage the "reformation of the offender." He wrote:

---

[4]This reform movement reached its peak in the United States in the late 1840's.
See Barnes, *Repression of Crime*, pp. 156-158; Tarde, *Penal Philosophy*, pp. 530-
531.

[5]In February, 1847, Campbell wrote: "The essay on Capital Punishment has been
now about nine months before the public. Some six or seven thousand copies of
it have been circulated through this country. It has been republished in England;
and in that country, as well as in this, it has been presented to a number of distinguished men, constituting a portion of the government." "Capital Punishment,"
M.H., 3d S., IV (February, 1847), 61.

We have no faith either in the justice or expediency of a horizontal tariff, award-
ing one and the same punishment to each and to every one of a hundred crimes.
. . . We believe in the scriptural phrases, "worthy of stripes," "worthy of a sorer
punishment," and "worthy of death."[6]

Campbell's views on capital punishment were challenged by several
Disciples leaders.[7] Probably the most important church leader to dispute
the Bethany editor's elaborate article was Tolbert Fanning. Shortly after
Campbell's tract had been published, the influential Southern preacher
denounced the concept of *"Christian* capital punishment." Fanning insisted
that war and capital punishment were "so nearly connected that they must
stand or fall together" and ridiculed Campbell's efforts to condemn one
and defend the other. The Nashville preacher leaned heavily on the dispensational theology of the movement and while he admitted that the
death penalty had been lawful during the Jewish age, he contended that
such punishment was "utterly subversive of all the principles of the Gospel of Christ." Actually, however, Fanning's opposition to capital punishment was rooted in his extreme sectarian commitment to nonparticipation in civil government; the Christian simply had nothing to do with the
matter. If civil governments decided to punish the evildoer by putting
him to death, that was within their realm of authority—but Christians
had no business defending the practice.[8]

In sum, the Disciples were never particularly interested in this minor
reform movement. The discussion ignited by Alexander Campbell's tract

---

[6]Campbell, "Is Capital Punishment Sanctioned by Divine Authority," *Popular
Lectures*, pp. 311-341. See, also, A. C., "Capital Punishment," *M.H.*, 3d S., IV
(February, 1847), 61-70; A. C., "Capital Punishment—No. II," *M.H.*, 3d S., IV
(March, 1847), 158-160; A. C., "Capital Punishment—No. III," *M.H.*, 3d S., IV
(April, 1847), 186-189. Disciples leaders seldom commented on the efforts being
made to reform penal institutions. When the matter did come to their attention,
they generally approved of the reform measures. See A. C., "Notes on a Tour to
the North-East—No. V," *M.H.*, VII (November, 1836), 481-482; "First Annual
Report," *Monthly Christian Age*, I (April, 1852), 125-127.

[7]Campbell commented that several of his brethren seemed intent on correcting
his views on capital punishment: "We have some two or three brethren who are
so peculiarly partial to me, that they are determined to correct all my errors almost in advance." He revealed that one "brother" wrote a twenty-page tract refut-
ing his defense of the death penalty. The reference is probably to Tolbert Fanning,
although if his articles were ever published in tract form the author has failed
to find them. "Capital Punishment," *M.H.*, 3d S., IV (February, 1847), 61.

[8]"Capital Punishment," *C. Rev.*, IV (May, 1847), 148-154.

on capital punishment was short-lived and without any lasting influence on the movement. Individual Disciples disagreed about the question but their disagreement was overshadowed by a lack of concern.

THE RIGHTS OF WOMAN

"But I suffer not a woman to teach, nor to usurp authority over the man, but to be in silence." I Timothy 2:12.

Although the reform temperament of midnineteenth-century America, and especially the equalitarian philosophy of the West, was a powerful stimulant to efforts to elevate the position of women, for the most part American women remained under a political and legal protectorate of men prior to the Civil War. A number of outstanding women broke the barriers imposed on their sex and gained prestige in the professions and as leaders in reform crusades, but it was not until 1848 that women organized in their own behalf. In 1850 a national "women's rights" convention was held for the first time. These early feminine crusaders were zealous and courageous but, by and large, they made little progress, except in the area of education.[9]

Most American religious groups had little sympathy for the expanding aspirations of women reformers. While there were exceptions, notably among the Quakers and Shakers, most of the nations's religious leaders insisted that the proper sphere of women was in the home. Very few women were admitted into the ministry prior to 1865 and most churchmen agreed that while it was proper for the ladies to address female assemblies, prayer meetings, and private gatherings, it was improper for them to speak in mixed meetings, and especially in the church.[10]

The "sphere" of the Christian woman, according to Alexander Campbell, was the "domestic circle," where she was the "power, the light, the

---

[9]See, for general discussions of the women's rights movement, Tyler, *Freedom's Ferment*, pp. 424-462; Curti, *Growth of American Thought*, pp. 382-388; Arthur Meier Schlesinger, *New Viewpoints in American History* (New York: The Macmillan Company, 1934), pp. 126-148; T. V. Smith, *The American Philosophy of Equality* (Chicago: The University of Chicago Press, 1927), pp. 85-129.

[10]See, for the churches' attitudes toward women, Olmstead, *Religion in the United States*, p. 360; Cross, *Burned-Over District*, pp. 37-38, 237; Arthur W. Calhoun, *A Social History of the American Family* (3 vols.; Cleveland: The Arthur H. Clark Company, 1918), II, 79-101; Lillian O'Connor, *Pioneer Women Orators* (New York: Columbia University Press, 1954), pp. 21-31.

life, the glory."[11] Winthrop H. Hopson, influential Missouri preacher, summed up the typical Disciples view on "woman's realm:"

> Educated, protected, honored, loved, what more could she ask. Would she yield the genteel voice of supplication and persuasion for the boisterousness of command? Would she give up her fireside and its pleasures for the council hall and its cares? . . . Would she at one fell stroke destroy the sacred altar, at which man has ever knelt with an adoration that stops but little short of idolatry. . . . No, no! if she be wise.[12]

Most ante-bellum Disciples leaders insisted that the "women keep silence in the church" in accordance with the injunction of the Apostle Paul, as well as the "modesty" and "delicacy of their sex."[13] Although many congregations appointed women as "deaconesses" to direct the charitable activities of the church, they were universally excluded from the "eldership," the ruling office in the local congregation, and were usually not allowed to vote in the congregational "business meetings."[14] There were Disciples leaders as early as 1840, however, who insisted that "the sisters" had the right to "pray and prophesy" in the public assembly. These early liberals believed that the Bible sanctioned such activities and argued that a strict application of Paul's injunction of silence would prohibit even congregational singing. Most early preachers who contended that it was right for women "to pray in the Church, or speak a word of exhortation for the edification and encouragement of the brethren" still insisted, however, that "*it is* unlawful for women to be set up as public Teachers, or Preachers, or to preside over the congregation as officers."[15] It was extremely rare before 1865 for a Disciples minister to defend the

---

[11]"An Address on the Amelioration of the Social State," *M.H.*, N. S., IV (July, 1840), 322.

[12]"An Address on Female Education," *Evangelist*, X (November, 1859), 484.

[13]See "Reply," *Primitive Christian and Investigator*, II (March, 1837), 282-285. Even women Disciples disapproved of ladies entering the ministry: "When a lady ascends the pulpit, or seeks to become an expounder of Coke and Blackstone, she parts with almost everything which, as a woman, should constitute her chief attraction." M. Helen Lucy, "Woman's Rights," *Ladies' Christian Annual*, III (April, 1855), 314. See Elizabeth Ann Hartsfield, "Shall the Sisters Speak?'" *College of the Bible Quarterly*, XXXI (January, 1954), 5-22.

[14]See J. R. H., "Practical Religion—No. 15," *M. and A.*, V (March, 1847), 51-52; "Queries," *C.E.*, VI (October, 1855), 465-467.

[15]"Queries," *C.E.*, VI (October, 1855), 466.

right of women to become "evangelists" or "missionaries."[16]

No Disciples leader prior to 1865 showed much sympathy for the "women's rights" movement. Although Alexander Campbell believed that the zeal of the reformers was "commendable," he was convinced that they were trying to accomplish something contrary to nature.[17] The fact that women reformers were often linked with radical religious and social experiments often prejudiced church spokesmen against the whole movement for women's rights.[18] Even the most advanced women writers in the church, while they approved of moderate efforts at reform, denounced the agitation of "women's rights" reformers.[19]

In one area of women's reform, however, Disciples were well advanced by 1865. Most early leaders were staunch advocates of "female education." In 1837 Alexander Campbell wrote: "If the question rested on my vote, *whether, as a general rule, the female sex, or the male sex, ought to be better educated* . . . I would say, the ladies should have it."[20]

The Disciples contributed fully their share to the prolific national growth of "female seminaries" after 1830. In 1840 Alexander Campbell listed five such schools operated by Disciples in Kentucky, Ohio, and Tennessee.[21] Claude Spencer, Curator of the Disciples of Christ Historical Society, has compiled a list of over forty women's educational institutions operated by Disciples prior to 1865.[22]

---

[16]See John Flick, "Answer to R. Faurott's Query," *G.P.*, II (January, 1849), 314-317; "Education of Female Missionaries," *P. and R.*, II (August, 1851), 524-526.

[17]Campbell was gentle with the movement. He wrote: "If failings they be, they lean on virtue's side." "Women's Rights," *M.H.*, 4th S., IV (April, 1854), 203-206. President P. H. Murphy of Abingdon College, an ardent advocate of coeducation, took a similar moderate view on the women's rights movement. See "Baccalaureate Address," *Christian Sentinel*, IV (September, 1857), 257-267.

[18]See "Editors' Table," *C.E.*, IX (September, 1858), 432.

[19]See Eliza, "To My Own Sex," *Ladies Christian Annual*, III (January, 1855), 224; Mrs. Sigourney, "The Rights of Woman," *E.R.*, IV (October 15, 1851), 560-561; "The Woman's Sphere," *C.Mon.*, II (February, 1864), 61-62.

[20]"Education," *M.H.*, N. S., I (June, 1837), 257.

[21]"Female Seminaries," *M.H.*, N. S., IV (August, 1840), 384.

[22]Claude E. Spencer, Educational Institutions of the Disciples of Christ (unpublished typed manuscript, Disciples of Christ Historical Society, Nashville, Tennessee, 1955).

Even more significant were the early efforts of Disciples in coeducation. Especially were Disciples educational leaders in Illinois pioneers in promoting coeducation.[23] Eureka College, begun in Eureka, Illinois, in 1850 (it was the successor of Walnut Grove Academy which was established in 1848), was chartered on a coeducational basis. Abingdon College, begun in Abingdon, Illinois, in 1853, and Berean College, founded in Jacksonville, Illinois, in 1854, also admitted both sexes from their beginnings. Oberlin College graduated women nine years before the founding of Eureka and was chartered as a coeducational college in 1833 but the Disciples schools were certainly the first such ventures in Illinois and were quite possibly the first institutions after Oberlin to test the experiment.[24]

Although some Disciples leaders reserved judgment about the educational experiment,[25] most of the church's educational leaders were active promoters of the reform. Western Reserve Eclectic Institute (later Hiram College) was established in Hiram, Ohio, in 1850 on a coeducational basis, although, as a rule, women took a "shorter course of study" which

---

[23]H. O. Pritchard writes: "In this [coeducation] the Disciples were not forelopers, but they were pioneers. They followed closely in the path of those who blazed the trail." "The Contributions of Disciples to Higher Education," *Culver-Stockton Quarterly,* IV (January, 1928), 5.

[24]See Haynes, *Disciples in Illinois,* p. 33; Dickinson, *Eureka College,* pp. 326-327; A. C., "Our Literary Institutions and Colleges," *M.H.,* 4th S., V (June, 1855), 356-357; Wm. Maxwell, "Abingdon College," *C.E.,* VI (August, 1855), 373-374. Alfred T. DeGroot states that these Disciples schools were the first coeducational ventures in Illinois, *Disciples,* p. 304. Most historians of American education list Horace Mann's Antioch College in Yellow Springs, Ohio, as the second coeducational institution in the country. It was established in 1853. See Thomas Woody, *A History of Women's Education in the United States* (2 vols.; New York: The Science Press, 1929), II, 224-303; Schlesinger, *New Viewpoints,* p. 140; Calhoun, *American Family,* II, 13-14; Stuart G. Noble, *A History of American Education* (rev. ed.; New York: Rinehart and Company, Inc., 1954), p. 281. Several Disciples schools admitted women at about this time. Woody points out that there were three different plans in early coeducational institutions: "education of the sexes together in the same college (but not necessarily the same education for both), identical education of the sexes together, and education in coordinate colleges." *Women's Education,* II, 224. By the mid-1850's there were Disciples colleges operating on each of these plans.

[25]See A. C., "Our Literary Institutions and Colleges," *M.H.,* 4th S., V (June, 1855), 356-357; A. C., "Berean College," *M.H.,* 4th S., VII (August, 1857), 465-466.

was provided especially for them.[26] North-Western Christian University, in Indianapolis, also provided for the equal education of the sexes in its 1850 charter. This abolitionist-oriented school, which did not open until 1855, had a woman in its first graduating class and was "one of the early educational institutions to have women on its faculty."[27] Christian University, chartered in 1853 in Canton, Missouri, also began as a coeducational institution, according to its founders, "the only one known to us" in the "great valley of the Mississippi."[28] W. D. Carnes, preacher and President of Burritt College in Spencer, Tennessee, in spite of "quite a bit of opposition," opened the doors of that institution to women in 1851.[29]

In short, while the Disciples were not the first to introduce the practice of "educating the sexes together," they proved apt students of this reform movement. After 1850 virtually every instiution of higher education established by Disciples was coeducational. Perhaps in no other area did they so clearly mark themselves as the children of the equalitarian West. And yet, the Disciples heritage from the frontier was not the only motivation for the liberalism of Disciples on this question. Probably more important than anything else, the Disciples were simply devoted to education—for both men and women—the spread of knowledge would surely hasten the coming of the millennium.

INDIANS

"Go ye therefore, and teach all nations, baptizing them in the name of the Father, and of the Son, and of the Holy Ghost." Matthew 28:19.

Americans were never completely without a sense of responsibility for Christianizing the Indians but, generally, they were more concerned with dispossessing them of their lands. While most American Protestant

---

[26]F. M. Green, *Hiram College* (Cleveland, Ohio: The O. S. Hubbell Printing Co., 1901), pp. 179-180.

[27]Commodore Wesley Cauble, *Disciples of Christ in Indiana* (Indianapolis: Meigs Publishing Company, 1930), pp. 224-225. See, also, Thomas W. Grafton, *Men of Yesterday* (St. Louis: Christian Publishing Company, 1899), pp. 272-273; N. Banshee, "Western Reserve Eclectic Institute," *N.W.C.M.*, IV (August, 1857), 61-62.

[28]"Christian University," *C.E.*, VII (November, 1856), 494.

[29]Young, *History of Colleges*, p. 56.

churches supported missionary activities among the Indians during the ante-bellum period, they did little to protest effectively against the recurrent encroachments on Indian rights and lands. During the critical decade of the 1830's, when the brutal policy of Indian removal was vigorously enforced by the Federal government, some churchmen, especially the missionaries who worked among them, tried to defend the treaty rights of the tribes, but, generally, their protests were uncoordinated and ineffectual.[30]

The constant encroachment of the white man on the lands of the Indians passed by with little comment from pre-Civil War Disciples leaders. There were occasional protests, such as this fervent plea for the Cherokee written in 1830 by Alexander Campbell:

> I humbly trust that there is yet so much justice, so much pure republicanism, so much regard to truth and national faith, in the bosoms of the American people and of their representatives in congress, as will not permit them to give up an innocent and harmless nation to the cupidity of a few capitalists in Georgia or any where else.[31]

Campbell's interest in the Indians, however, was not deep-seated enough to sustain an extended protest, nor was that of any other Disciples editor.

Neither did the Disciples make much effort to support mission work among the Indians during these years. A few of the early Christian preachers did some teaching among the Southern tribes shortly after the turn of the century, especially among the Cherokee in North Georgia and Alabama.[32] According to tradition, both Alexander Campbell and Barton Stone preached at a Christian church in Athens, Alabama, which

---

[30]See, for general accounts of Indian removal and the churches' relations with the Indians, Bodo, *Clergy and Public Issues*, pp. 85-111; Olmstead, *Religion in the United States*, pp. 274-277; Posey, *Baptists*, pp. 80-88; Posey, *Presbyterians*, pp. 61-72; Posey, *Methodists*, pp. 81-90; R. S. Cotterill, *The Southern Indians* (Norman, Oklahoma: University of Oklahoma Press, 1954); Ruth Murray Underhill, *Red Man's America* (Chicago: The University of Chicago Press, 1953).

[31]"The Cherokee Indians," *M.H.*, I (January, 1830), 46.

[32]John Thomas, Rice Haggard, and Rueben Dooley were early Christian preachers who worked among the Indians. See Thomas, *Life of the Pilgrim*, p. 115. In 1805 Barton Stone wrote to Richard M'Nemar: "Brother Dooley is among the Cherokees again—His last rout there was successful—some poor Indians received the gospel—He was solicited to return—He is truly an Apostle of the Gentiles." M'Nemar, *Kentucky Revival*, p. 78. Such independent work among the Indians apparently stopped in the 1830's.

included both white and Indian members.[33] By and large, however, Disciples were never able, or willing, to expend the funds and effort necessary to make major inroads among the Indians. They were too busy converting white men to bother with the more costly job of going to the heathen. John T. Johnson, an Indian fighter in the War of 1812, wrote: "It is safe to calculate, that, at least fifty of our citizens can be converted to christianity by an amount of time, labor, &c. not excluding what would be requisite for the conversion of *one* savage Indian."[34]

As early as 1850 the corresponding secretary of the American Christian Missionary Society suggested that the Disciples needed to begin a mission among the Indians. In the secretary's report in both 1853 and 1854 it was stated that everything was in readiness to begin a mission among the Cherokee, but nothing ever came of the project.[35]

The only significant Disciples missionary among the Indians during the ante-bellum period was James J. Trott. Trott began working among the Cherokee of Georgia as a Methodist missionary in the mid-1820's. He denounced the efforts of the state of Georgia to strip the Cherokee of their land (as did most of the missionaries working among them), refused to leave the Indian Territory when ordered to by state officials, and as a result was "arrested, chained, imprisoned, condemned, reprieved, and

---

[33]Barton Stone apparently spoke the Cherokee language. Several of his sermons written in Cherokee are extant. Harrell C. Biard (typed memorandum concerning Barton Stone and the Cherokee Indian, Disciples of Christ Historical Society, Nashville, Tennessee).

[34]"Indian Missions—A Hoax," *B.A.*, II (July, 1844), 182.

[35]The missionary who was to undertake the project was never named. In 1853 the report stated: "Owing to the state of his private affairs the missionary elect to the Cherokee has not been enabled yet to depart to the Indian territory. We hope to communicate some favorable intelligence next spring." *Proceedings* of the Convention of Churches of Christ, 1853, p. 42. The following year the secretary reported: "It was expected to open this mission among the Cherochees [*sic*] as early as last May, but in consequences of difficulties in the disposition of the property of our missionary elect, and disturbances among the Indians, by which blood was spilled and some relations of the missionary family slain, the whole enterprize was necessarily postponed. If possible it will be commenced early this winter, or at all events, at as early a day as practicable, the effort will be made." *Ibid.*, 1854, p. 49. See, also, *Report of the Proceedings of the American Christian Bible, Missionary and Tract Societies, For the Year 1850, Together With Other Documents, and an Address to the Christian Churches* (Cincinnati: American Christian Depository, 1850), p. 30.

banished [from] the territory of the state."[36] While in prison in 1831 Trott read the works of Alexander Campbell and later that year became a Disciple. Shortly after his banishment from Georgia, the missionary, who had married a Cherokee woman, wrote Campbell that he was determined to continue work among the Indians:

> The Cherokees are an interesting people; and with them (God willing), whatever their destiny may be, I expect to live and die. My heart's desire and prayer to God is, that the *primitive* gospel may be introduced, prevail, and triumph among this oppressed people. The days of inspiration have passed away; nevertheless, I believe I am divinely called to proclaim the word of salvation to the Cherokees.[37]

Trott returned to work among the Indians until the spring of 1837, when the nation was removed to the West, and then began doing evangelistic work among the churches of the South.[38]

The missionary retained his determination to preach to the Indians, however, and nearly twenty years later, in 1856, he departed for the Indian Territory. Tolbert Fanning announced in the *Gospel Advocate* that Trott was about to commence work among the Cherokee and urged his readers to provide the "necessary pecuniary support."[39] Support for the project was difficult to raise. Trott reported: "The richest Christian brother, whose heart and purse were appealed to, said he had 'no sympathy for the Indian!' "[40] Not until 1858 did Trott receive sufficient funds to buy a tract of land in the Indian Territory, which he promptly christened, "Christian Mission."[41] Trott's mission was never regularly supported, although from 1859 through 1861 the congregation in Franklin,

---

[36]"To the Editor of the Millennial Harbinger," *M.H.*, III (February, 1832), 85. See, also, "Letter from James J. Trott," *M.H.*, III (August, 1832), 389-390. J. Edward Moseley's sketch of Trott is especially good for the early years of the missionary's life. *Georgia*, pp. 123-131. See, also, Emmet Star, *History of the Cherokee Indians and Their Legend and Folklore* (Oklahoma City: The Warden Company, 1921), p. 605. See, for general accounts of the Cherokee before and after their removal, Grant Foreman, *Advancing the Frontier* (Norman, Oklahoma: University of Oklahoma Press, 1933); Grant Foreman, *Indian Removal* (Norman, Oklahoma: University of Oklahoma Press, 1932).

[37]"To the Editor of the Millennial Harbinger," *M.H.*, III (February, 1832), 85.

[38]See T. F., "James J. Trott," *G.A.*, XI (March 25, 1869), 271-274.

[39]"Mission to the Cherokees," *G.A.*, II (February, 1856), 63-64.

[40]"The Indian Mission," *G.A.*, II (April, 1856), 110.

[41]"Mission to the Cherokees," *N.W.C.M.*, IV (April, 1858), 317-318.

Tennessee, where he had lived for many years, served as a clearinghouse for contributions intended for him.[42] By the end of 1860 the missionary reported seventy-five converts among the Indians and revealed that several Southern preachers had visited him in the Territory to aid in the work.[43] The Civil War again interrupted Trott's mission work; in 1862 he was forced to leave the reservation and did not return until the conflict was over.[44]

To sum up, Disciples interest in the Indians was spasmodic and ill-organized at best. What was done, was accomplished almost totally as the result of the dedicated determination of one man—James J. Trott. Deeply committed to the conversion of the Indians to the "ancient gospel," Trott also worked untiringly for their social, political, and educational elevation.[45] But, by and large, the movement had neither the organization, the funds, nor the interest necessary for serious work among the Indians.

SECRET SOCIETIES

"Unto him be glory in the church by Christ Jesus throughout all ages, world without end." Ephesians 3:21.

---

[42]Tolbert Fanning often pointed to this project to demonstrate that mission work could be done without a missionary society. See *Report of the Proceedings of the Anniversary Meeting of the American Christian Missionary Society, Held in Cincinnati, October 19, 20, 21, 1859* (Cincinnati: G. B. Bentley and Co., Printers, 1859), pp. 24-25; T. F., "James J. Trott," *G.A.,* XI (March 25, 1869), 271-274. Apparently Trott never received any financial support from the society.

[43]With reference to the converts, Trott wrote: "Some of these are the result of our humble efforts in the old nation more than twenty years ago. Some are the fruits of the able efforts of Bro. Graham, and the pious labors of Br. Robertson; and some 50 were converted by the zealous efforts of brethren Goodnight and Phillips." *Proceedings* of the General Christian Missionary Convention, 1860, p. 16. See, also, J. J. Trott, "The Indian Mission," *M.H.,* 5th S., III (September, 1860), 505-507.

[44]See T. F., "James J. Trott," *G.A.,* XI (March 25, 1869), 271-274; Moseley, *Georgia,* pp. 123-131.

[45]Trott wrote: "The very best thing the tribes of this Territory could do, would be to hold a convention, form a constitution, and petition Congress for adoption into the United States as a free and independent State; and the very best thing the United States could do for them would be to admit them at once as a State. The intelligent Indians would then feel that they were *somebody* and somewhere." "The Indian Mission," *M.H.,* 5th S., III (September, 1860), 506. He not only preached among the Indians but also tried to start schools wherever possible. See *Proceedings* of the General Christian Missionary Convention, 1860, p. 16.

Masonry gained considerable prestige during the period of the American Revolution because many of the leading American patriots had been members of the society but by the mid-1820's anti-Masonic agitation had become widespread. The organized anti-Masonic movement began in 1826 in the "burned-over district" in western New York as the result of the kidnapping of a stonemason who was reportedly about to publish an exposé of Masonic secrets. The movement reached its zenith in the early 1830's, when it assumed national political importance and caused large depletions in lodge memberships, and then rapidly lost its vigor in the 1840's. Most American churches strongly supported the anti-Masonic movement; during the 1830's many congregations made lodge membership a test of fellowship.[46]

Masonry and other fraternal organizations were frequently attacked by Disciples leaders, along with all "moral societies." Prior to the 1850's some churches were seriously disturbed by anti-Masonic agitation. In 1832 Barton Stone wrote that several "conferences have resolved that Masonry is incompatible with the christian religion—therefore every Mason must be excluded from fellowship."[47] Some Christian churches divided over the question and in many areas lodge membership was a controversial issue.[48]

The most persistent objection to Masonry and other fraternal organizations was that such institutions, if Christians participated in them, de-

---

[46]See, for general accounts of the anti-Masonic movement, Stokes, *Church and State*, II, 20-25; Tyler, *Freedom's Ferment*, pp. 351-358; Cross, *Burned-Over District*, pp. 113-125. Anti-Masonry among the early Baptists is described in Posey, *Baptist*, pp. 41-42.

[47]"Extract of a letter from Bro. L. Bruen, of Dayton, Ohio, to one of the Editors, B. W. Stone, dated Dec. 3, 1831," *C.M.*, VI (February, 1832), 59.

[48]See Peter Vogel, *Tale of a Pioneer Church* (Cincinnati: Standard Publishing Co., 1887), pp. 248-256; A. C., "Elder D. S. Burnet and Elder Clark," *M.H.*, 3d S., V (November, 1848), 645-646; Russell, *Church Life in the Blue Grass*, p. 112. As late as 1846 Walter Scott reported the following proceedings at the Mayslick, Kentucky, Church: "Took up the subject of Oddfellowship & the brethren and sisters sending their children to dancing school. & discussing it lengthly [*sic*], both being disaprotiated [*sic*] by the brethren, no action taken only requested that the Elders and brethren would see those brethren and Sisters and persuade and influence them if possible from the error of their way." Walter Scott Notebook, College of the Bible, Lexington, Kentucky.

stroyed the doctrine of the all-sufficiency of the church. "Shall Masonry, Odd Fellowship, Sons of Temperance, or any such association," asked W. W. Eaton, "have our money, time, influence, and energies; or shall we consecrate all that we have and are to the 'congregation of the Lord?' "[49] Most Disciples anti-Masonic agitation was aimed not at the organization as such; church leaders were simply opposed to Christians being lodge members. Alexander Campbell wrote: "I have no controversy with any man out of the precincts of Christianity, be he called Free Mason, Abolitionist, or Odd Fellow. . . . But we have to do with those who have vowed eternal allegiance to the great and good king."[50]

As a matter of fact, a number of preachers, including Alexander Graham of Alabama, Thomas W. Caskey of Mississippi, and Winthrop Hopson and John Allen Gano of Kentucky, were lodge members throughout the ante-bellum period.[51] Most of the leaders of the movement were moderate on the question. Even Alexander Campbell, who was the most significant if not the most ardent assailant of "societies," advised that Masons ought not to be "excluded."[52] When he was earnestly "solicited" by some of his readers to join the national crusade against "secret societies," Barton Stone curtly replied that he had no intention of making the *Christian Messenger* an "anti-masonic organ."[53] Even some of the church's most conservative leaders, such as Jacob Creath, Jr., consistently

---

[49]"Letter from Brother Eaton," *G.P.*, II (October, 1848), 115.

[50]"Free Masonry, Odd Fellowship, Abolition, &c. &c.—No. I," *M.H.*, 3d S., II (March, 1845), 135. Fraternal orders were also attacked because of their "secrecy" and because of the "religious rites" connected with their meetings. See A. C., " 'Odd Fellows' and 'Free Masons,' " *M.H.*, N. S., VI (December, 1842), 557-558.

[51]See M. A. Feris and William Craig to J. A. Gano, undated letter, John Allen Gano Papers, Disciples of Christ Historical Society; Harmon, *Churches in Mississippi*, p. 96; Hopson, *Hopson*, p. 29; Pickney B. Lawson, *The Life and Character, to Which, Are Added Some of the Addresses and Sermons of Alexander Graham, Teacher of the Christian Church in Marion, Alabama* (New York: John F. Trow, Printer, 1853), p. 16. John R. Howard wrote that "many professed Christians" were extremely "sensitive" on the subject of Masonry. "An Apology—Masonry and Temperance," *M. and A.*, V (December, 1847), 283.

[52]"Moral Societies, No. IV," *M.H.*, 3d S., V (July, 1848), 402.

[53]"Extract of a letter from Bro. L. Bruen, of Dayton, Ohio, to one of the Editors, B. W. Stone, dated December 3, 1831," *C.M.*, VI (February, 1832), 59-60.

denounced the anti-Masonic crusade.[54] In short, while some Christian churches were seriously disturbed by "antisociety" agitation, especially prior to 1850, the issue was never of national importance in the movement and after 1850 Disciples periodicals increasingly ignored the question.[55]

"THE MOTHER OF HARLOTS"

"And upon her forehead was a name written, MYSTERY, BABYLON THE GREAT, THE MOTHER OF HARLOTS AND ABOMINATIONS OF THE EARTH. . . . And the woman which thou sawest is that great city, which reigneth over the kings of the earth." Revelation 17:5, 18.

The roots of nineteenth-century American anti-Catholicism reached deep into the history of the nation and its European heritage. Seventeenth- and eighteenth-century Protestant immigrants to colonial America brought with them their religious prejudices against Rome and, when they arrived, they discovered that their natural enemies in the new world were Catholic France and Spain. By the turn of the nineteenth century, however, religious toleration was well established as one of the fundamental tenets of the new American faith, in spite of these latent prejudices. The Catholics were an insignificant group numerically in the American nation at the turn of the century and until the 1820's Protestant-Catholic relations were relatively tranquil. As Catholic immigrants from northern Europe increasingly poured into the country after 1820, however, the phenomenal growth of the Roman church almost inevitably led to conflict. American Protestants more and more viewed Catholicism as a threat to their new national, evangelistic faith and after 1820 there were recurrent outbursts of militant anti-Catholicism in the nation.[56]

---

[54]Creath wrote: "Why not break our sticks over the heads of all the other societies in the land: the agricultural, the stock societies, the mechanical, the mercantile association, the literary, the military, the naval, the Bible and missionary societies, abolition societies. Why single out masonry and temperance?" "Masonry and Temperance," M. and A., V (August, 1847), 188.

[55]Henry Shaw writes: "The lodge membership issue, which split many denominations about this time, had no serious effect on the Disciples in Ohio. Lodge membership was considered in the realm of opinion, and not a matter of faith." Buckeye Disciples, p. 146.

[56]See, for general information on American anti-Catholicism before 1865, Ray Allen Billington, The Protestant Crusade 1800-1860 (New York: The Macmillan Company, 1938); Olmstead, Religion in the United States, pp. 323-328; Tyler, Freedom's Ferment, pp. 358-395; Bodo, Clergy and Public Issues, pp. 61-84.

Throughout the ante-bellum period the Roman Catholic Church was one of the favorite targets of Disciples writers. Church papers were never very long without doctrinal and historical investigations of "Romanism." Most Disciples leaders believed that the Catholic church was the prophetic "mother of harlots" and repeatedly predicted the doom of "popery"— in fact, they regarded it a historical necessity before the millennium could begin.[57]

More important were Disciples' attacks on the political and social motives of American Catholics. Throughout the period there was an ever-present fear among the church's leaders that the ultimate design of the Catholic church was to "subjugate anew to her despotic rule those whom she would fain style her revolted subjects."[58] Charles Louis Loos, a very able German immigrant preacher, who by the 1850's was the leading Disciples authority on Catholicism, summed up the widely held views of Disciples leaders: "Rome and free institutions are irreconcilable. This is the clear conviction of every one who has studied Rome in its deeds and in its doctrines."[59]

By the mid-1830's many leaders of the Disciples were seriously concerned about the threat of Catholicism to American institutions. In 1835 Alexander Campbell warned his readers that next to slavery the "most inauspicious and portentous cloud in our political horizon" was the "rapid growth of a *popish empire* in the bosom of the Republic."[60] The following year Campbell attended the annual meeting of the Western Literary Institute and College of Professional Teachers in Cincinnati, Ohio, to deliver an address and during one of the sessions of the meeting he became involved in a public dispute with the Catholic Bishop of Cincinnati, John P. Purcell, over the contributions of Catholicism and Protestantism

[57]See, for example, John Thomas, "The Mother of Harlots," *Apostolic Advocate*, I (December, 1834), 169-176; "The Coming Doom of Popery," *M.H.*, 4th S., III (August, 1833), 455-456.

[58]F., "Poperty—Our Position," *P.U.*, I (November 27, 1844), 18. James M. Mathes, militant editor of the *Christian Record*, wrote: "Let Roman Catholics in these United States prate as much as they please about *liberty, toleration*, and the *rights of conscience:* it is all a hoax. It is all a cry of *'Peace, Peace,'* when there is no peace!" "The Inquisition in America," *C.R.*, I (December, 1843), 139.

[59]"Jesuitism Against Free Political Institutions," *M.H.*, 4th S., VI (January, 1856), p. 31.

[60]"The Jesuit's Oath," *M.H.*, VI (March, 1835), p. 114.

to the advancement of civilization. The final upshot of the tiff was that the Bethany reformer challenged the Bishop to a debate on the merits of the Roman Catholic religion; Purcell promptly accepted and arrangements were made to hold the discussion in Cincinnati in January, 1837.

Although the Campbell-Purcell debate dealt mainly with doctrinal issues, the last proposition affirmed by Campbell concerned the political aims of Catholicism:

7. The Roman Catholic religion, if infallible and unsusceptible of reformation, as alleged, is essentially anti-American, being opposed to the genius of all free institutions, and positively subversive of them, opposing the general reading of the scriptures, and the diffusion of useful knowledge among the whole community, so essential to liberty and the permanency of good government.[61]

When the disputants finally reached the last proposition, Campbell concisely stated his case on the "anti-American" nature of Catholicism:

This I have so far proved, as reference has already been made to those doctrines, which make the Roman Catholic population abject slaves to their priests, bishops, and popes—to that hierarchy, which has always opposed freedom of thought, of speech, and of action, whether in literature, politics, or religion. . . . The benumbing and paralyzing influence is such, as to disqualify a person for the relish and enjoyment of political liberty. For in all history, civil liberty follows in the wake of religious liberty; insomuch, that it is almost an oracle of philosophy, that religious liberty is the cause, and political liberty an effect of the cause, without which it never has been found.[62]

Purcell retorted that Catholics had been in the forefront of the fight for religious liberty in this nation and that Protestants, rather than Catholics, had historically been the persecutors in the new world. The two men never really came to grips with one another on the proposition; Campbell argued from theory that no Catholic could be a good citizen since

---

[61]Alexander Campbell and Rt. Rev. John B. Purcell, *A Debate on the Roman Catholic Religion*. . . . (Cincinnati: J. A. James & Co., 1837), p. viii. Winfred Garrison points out that the Campbell-Purcell debate was a unique incident in American religious history: "This is, so far as is known, the only occasion on which a Roman prelate of such high rank has consented to meet a Protestant in open debate on the validity of his church's claims." *Disciples*, p. 228. Alice Felt Tyler calls the debate the "climax" of the anti-Catholic controversy in the West and Ray Allen Billington interprets it as the most significant of the many Protestant-Catholic discussions of the 1830's. Tyler, *Freedom's Ferment*, p. 369; Billington, *Protestant Crusade*, p. 65.

[62]*Debate on the Catholic Religion*, p. 311.

his loyalty was divided, while Purcell persistently labored to prove from history that Catholics had been good Americans.[63] Whatever may be the merits of the debate, at its conclusion Alexander Campbell was probably the most widely known anti-Catholic spokesman in the West.

Numerous local and national issues and incidents recurrently stirred anti-Catholic feeling among Disciples leaders. Protestant-Catholic riots,[64] the internal strife in the American Catholic church over ownership of property,[65] the alleged immorality of the new Catholic immigrants in the mushrooming Western cities,[66] repeated rumors of Catholic political coalitions,[67] and similar issues constantly stirred simmering prejudices. Throughout the antebellum period, however, the two most persistent causes of anti-Catholic agitation, both in the nation and among Disciples, were the startling growth of Catholicism in the West and the church's attacks on the public school system.

National anti-Catholic agitation was closely linked throughout this period with a surging nativist movement. After 1830 many American Protestants believed that European Catholics were encouraging, and even financing, the emigration of their fellow religionists in a concerted effort to gain control of the American West. Other motives besides anti-Catholicism were important in the pre-Civil War nativist movement—race prejudice, fear of economic competition on the part of the American laborer, and the poverty and illiteracy of many of the immigrants were all important factors—but as often as not, whatever the motive might have been, the immigrant was attacked on the grounds of his religion.[68]

During the 1830's and 1840's some Disciples leaders showed serious concern over the growth of Catholicism in this country. In 1841 Walter Scott warned that the "great number of Jesuits who are flocking into our country and commencing operations in every part of it" might well be the

[63]*Ibid.,* pp. 310-334.

[64]See A. C., "Philadelphia Riots," *M.H.,* 3d S., I (September, 1844), 410.

[65]See "Editor's Table," *C.E.,* VI (June, 1855), 289-291.

[66]See B. Franklin, "Romanism," *P. and R.,* I (November, 1850), 730-734.

[67]See A. C., "Romanism," *M.H.,* 4th S., I (October, 1851), 541-546.

[68]See, for accounts of the relation of nativism to anti-Catholicism, Billington, *Protestant Crusade,* pp. 118-135; Tyler, *Freedom's Ferment,* pp. 374-377; Curti, *Growth of American Thought,* pp. 315-317.

first step in a "Romish plot" to overthrow the government.[69] Several
years earlier Scott had urged legislation banning Catholic immigration:

If they [Catholics] have not, if they cannot be at once a subject of the Pope, and
a citizen of the United States, then let our courts of law, cease to extend to them
that citizenship for which Protestants eminently bled and died under the great
fathers of the Revolution, and if any law of prohibition be framed, let it run
thus: "That no Catholic, or subject of the Pope of Rome, shall emigrate to the
United States." We are no alarmists; but we pledge ourself to prove, that every
true Catholic is a subject of the Pope of Rome, and as such, is not entitled to
the citizenship of these States.[70]

A similar article in the *Christian Messenger* proposed that all Catholic
immigrants be placed on probation for ten years before they were granted
citizenship.[71]

Other Disciples leaders took a calmer view of the Catholic menace.
Alexander Campbell strenuously objected to the "violent [anti-Catholic]
publications in our religious papers" even though he agreed that the ever-
increasing influx of Catholics gave "much reason for alarm." The usually
moderate Bethany editor scoffed at the talk of immigration restrictions:

Yes, says one, let our government prevent their migration hitherward any more—
then down goes our temple of equal rights and our boasted indifference to all
political concern in religion. We cannot place Catholics under disabilities.

Campbell believed that the only solution to the problem of growing Catholic strength was "universal education." He wrote: "An enlightened
community cannot be enslaved—an ignorant and uneducated society cannot be free."[72]

Disciples concern over the rapid growth of American Catholicism continued through the decade of the fifties but it was markedly less frantic
than in the preceeding two decades. In 1855 Jacob Creath, Jr., warned
that the "Papists" were making "strenuous efforts" to "subjugate this
country [Kentucky] to that most Loyal Son of the Devil, the Pope of
Rome."[73] Other church leaders wrote with similar concern but, by and

---

[69]"The Romish Church Since the Reformation," *Evangelist*, IX (May, 1841),
101.

[70]"Catholicism," *Evangelist*, IV (December, 1835), 280.

[71]"Roman Catholicism," *C.M.*, X (October, 1835), 147-151.

[72]"Education—No. 2," *M.H.*, VI (February, 1835), 63-67.

[73]"Correspondence," *C.E.*, VI (January, 1855), 37.

large, they recommended moderate solutions such as unwavering support of public education and more united concern on the part of all Protestants.[74]

An even-more-important source of Protestant-Catholic friction was their differences on the subject of education. The American Catholic church was totally unprepared to meet the educational needs of the swarms of lower-class immigrants who flooded into the nation in the decades after 1820. Most of the immigrants could not afford to send their children to private schools and, generally, Catholic parishes were too poor to provide free parochial schools. The young public school systems which had arisen in many localities by 1830 were almost always Protestant-dominated; the King James version of the Bible was read and often studied in the classrooms and many of the texts used gave a decidedly anti-Catholic version of religious history. Beginning in the 1830's American Catholic leaders loosed a two-pronged attack on the American school system. Their major aim, based on the contention that the public schools were in fact Protestant schools, was to gain a share of public funds for parochial schools. Never very successful in this campaign (although they gained minor victories in several cities), Catholic leaders agitated for the banning of the use of the Bible in public schools.[75]

Most Disciples were fanatical supporters of education, both sectarian and public. Alexander Campbell often equated "Protestantism," "universal education," and "free republican institutions"—he believed that they must all stand and fall together. The Campbell-Purcell debate was triggered by a discussion in the Teacher's Institute of Cincinnati on whether the Bible ought to be banned from use in the public schools.[76] In 1853 Campbell warned that both "light and Liberty" would soon be "extinct" if Catholics ever gained the "power" necessary to carry through their plans on education.[77] According to the editor of the *Harbinger*,

[74]See "The Aspects of Romanism—No. I," *M.H.*, 4th S., II (February, 1852), 66-72; I. E., "Scylla and Charybdis," *M.H.*, XXXVI (May, 1865), 193-200.

[75]See, for general accounts of the dispute over education, Billington, *Protestant Crusade*, pp. 142-165; Tyler, *Freedom's Ferment*, pp. 377-382; Curti, *Growth of American Thought*, p. 317.

[76]See "Catholics and Free Schools," *M.H.*, N. S., II (February, 1838), 71-74; Richardson, *Memoirs of Campbell*, II, 422-437; Garrison, *Religion Follows the Frontier*, pp. 170-172.

[77]"Romanism versus Common Schools," *M.H.*, 4th S., III (March, 1853), 150.

the question involved "more of our good or evil destiny, as a people, than any politico-ecclestiastic . . . question now before the public mind."[78]

Several Disciples editors applauded the formation of the American Protestant Association in 1842, an organization designed to coordinate the activities of anti-Catholic agitators.[79] Alexander Campbell wrote: "Such an association I have long thought the peculiar signs of the times loudly call for." In commenting on the organization, Campbell revealed that several years previously he had proposed the establishment of such a society to Lyman Beecher, prominent Cincinnati minister:

Deeply penetrated with the conviction that the plan was profoundly concocted and the measures already adopted at Rome, in Austria, in the very bosom of the Papal See, to subjugate all America to the Catholic faith and the tyranny of its ambitious and tyrannical Pontiff, I proposed to Dr. Beecher, of Cincinnati, and some others about the time of my debate with Bishop Purcell, to have an association got up in the valley of the Mississippi, and to hold state annual meetings for the very purposes displayed in the address following the Constitution . . . but the Doctor thought that in the openings of Providence the time was not yet come; or that it would make too great a draft on ministerial time and services to attend such great annual meetings as I proposed.[80]

Other leaders of the Disciples also supported the Association. Especially outspoken was Walter Scott in his ardently anti-Catholic weekly, the *Protestant Unionist*.[81]

In general, however, Disciples leaders never supported the most violent variety of anti-Catholic agitation. Alexander Campbell tenaciously disclaimed any personal antipathy toward Catholics[82] and repeatedly censured Protestant "alarmists, agitators, and panic-makers."[83] He deeply resented it when the Catholic press classed him with "Maria Monk" and "Rebecca Reed"[84] and persistently insisted that he was "no friend to

[78]"Common Schools," *M.H.*, 4th S., III (August, 1853), 439-440.

[79]See, for information on the American Protestant Association, Tyler, *Freedom's Ferment*, pp. 382-385.

[80]"Protestant Association," *M.H.*, N. S., VII (April, 1843), 182-183.

[81]See "Anniversary of the American Protestant Society," *P.U.*, I (June 25, 1845), 114; "Roman Catholicism—No. I," *O.P.*, I (March, 1843), 61.

[82]See *Debate on the Catholic Religion*, p. 304; "The Jesuit's Oath," *M.H.*, VI (March, 1835), 114.

[83]"Popery in America," *M.H.*, VI (September, 1835), 411.

[84]"Debate on Roman Catholicism," *M.H.*, N. S., I (March, 1837), 111. See, also, "Brethren Creath and Eaton," *C.E.*, VI (January, 1855), 30-35.

Protestant Popery any more than to Papal Popery."[85] Jesse B. Ferguson, popular Nashville preacher, summed up the moderate approach to the Catholic question which probably represented the views of most Disciples leaders:

> I repeat it, Catholics are men; let us never forget it. Protestants also are men, subject to like infirmities with other men, and were they placed where Catholics have been, we have every reason to believe, and a little experience to assure us that they will do as Catholics have done. Then let us rail no longer against Catholics; but in the spirit of enlightened investigation, direct our efforts against a system, and not against the men. And when we shall do this, we will find in many instances as much Roman Catholicism in Protestant sects as in the Old Roman church herself.[86]

In short, Disciples and Roman Catholics ideologies clashed at many points. Not only were the two groups bitter theological enemies, but Catholicism loomed as the archenemy in the battle of Disciples to establish the millennial kingdom of Anglo-Saxon, Protestant America. But if Disciples often, and sometimes violently, objected to Catholic encroachments on their concept of Christian America, they were seldom completely carried away by emotional prejudices. As the expanding young American nation matured, Disciples and Catholics clashed in many troublesome areas but, for the most part, their battles were fought on a fairly rational plane.[87]

---

[85]"Protestant Association Address," *M.H.*, N. S., VII (August, 1843), 352. Other early leaders shared Campbell's fear of "Protestant Popery." See Iota Tau Kappa, "An Analytic Sketch," *Apostolic Advocate*, I (August, 1834), 73-81; "Murder Will Out!" *C.M.*, II (September, 1828), pp. 241-244.

[86]"Roman Catholicism," *C. Rev.*, II (March, 1845), 76.

[87]Whitney Cross comments that in western New York "'the Protestant Crusade' against Catholicism . . . was more largely urban." *Burned-Over District*, p. 231. Perhaps part of the explanation for the moderate reaction of Disciples to the Catholic question is that they were not extremely numerous in the cities, where most of the Catholic immigrants were going. Once again, however, it should be noted that the Disciples had a strong rational and moderate background.

CHAPTER VIII

THE QUEST

The vision of a regenerated nation was a pervasive one in nineteenth-century Disciples thought. Disciples were most deeply concerned about the spiritual salvation of mankind, but they also believed that the Christian message had a deep meaning for this world. If every backwoods evangelist had a well-used sermon of the "gospel plan of salvation," he also was prepared to speak on "practical Christianity."

Disciples' views on the mold in which a Christian America was to be cast were by no means homogeneous. The varied battery of spokesmen for the "restoration of the ancient order" applied the Christian doctrines of love, mercy, and justice to the social problems which they knew and in doing so they expressed the hopes and aspirations of much of the society in which they lived. It may be true that these nineteenth-century preachers often did not understand the problems of their society, but they were never uninterested in or unsympathetic about social injustice. Whatever their status in society, they agreed that before their job was done sinfulness in every form would give way to a rule of justice. To overlook them in a search for prophets of a better America would be a serious mistake.

Of course, the story of the Disciples' quest is not greatly different from that of other religious groups that shared their heritage and environment. Which poses an interesting question: If it is clear that the social philosophy of the Disciples was substantially that of all major Protestant groups, and if the social pressures on the church were the same ones which divided other American religious streams, is it not fair to surmise that the same diversity of class expressions and the same vision of a Christian America was common to them all? Studies in depth of the thought of other religious movements will reveal, I believe, a class of "people's preachers" who, long ignored, played an important role in American religious life and whose message was deeply influenced by the social views of their parishioners.

It is interesting that the conflicting views of the regenerate nation were not, within themselves, the major source of trouble within the church. Disciples displayed a catholic ability to tolerate differences of opinion on social issues.

The irrepressible problem which placed an unbearable strain on the unity of the movement was the question of methodology. As long as there was little intrachurch organization within the stream, disagreement on social subjects caused little disturbance. Even after the emergence of weak state and national organizations, Disciples long respected an un-official ban on institutional statements on social issues. Many of the church's leaders clearly understood that this proscription was the price of peace.

From the beginning there had been little agreement among the leaders of the church about the means of Christianizing America. Some, prob-ably most during the early years, insisted that the only religious duty of the Christian was to convert sinners—social improvement would follow. A middle group believed that the Christian was obligated to actively par-ticipate in organized social reform, but only in his capacity as a compas-sionate Christian individual. By the 1850's, however, a growing group within the movement became committed to a philosophy of active church participation in social regeneration. The social salvation of society was a Christian end in itself—spiritual benefits would follow.

Diverse social views could remain nondivisive only as long as intra-church organizations did not become involved. As the social conscience of the Christian activists pressed them into action in the years before the Civil War, the unity of the movement collapsed.

As it happened, the circumstances of history gave a sectional flavor to the schism. The first burning issue which made social activists of a sig-nificant group of Disciples was the crusade for the abolition of slavery. The offensiveness of slavery convinced many Northerners that it was sinful for the church to remain silent. The same issue convinced South-erners that the only possible position that the church could take was one of toleration of philosophical differences. They insisted that the solution to problems of social evil would have to come by individual conversion. Social circumstances made denominational activists of Northern Disciples; the same conditions caused Southern churchmen to emphasize the le-galistic concept of a church limited to spiritual functions.

The Civil War drove the wedge deeper. Although most Disciples in both North and South became political activists during the war, when it was over both sections found reinforcement for their prewar philosophies of the role of the church in social reform. Northerners were convinced that righteousness had been served by their Christian commitment to po-litical action. On the other hand, the doctrine of the separation of the church from the entanglements of the world seemed more true than ever to sympathizers with the lost cause.

Events after the war hardened the fissures which had clearly appeared by the end of the struggle. Diverging economic interests added to the sectarian tendencies of the religion of the South and to the rise of middle-class denominationalism in the North. There were many individual ex-ceptions—but a clear pattern had emerged.

BIBLIOGRAPHY

PRIMARY MATERIAL

GENERAL BOOKS

Baxter, William. *Pea Ridge and Prairie Grove; or Scenes and Incidents of the War in Arkansas.* Cincinnati: Poe and Hitchcock, 1864.

Campbell, Alexander. *The Christian System.* . . . 4th ed.; Bethany, Virginia: A. Campbell, 1857.

Campbell, Alexander, and Right Reverend John B. Purcell. *A Debate on the Roman Catholic Religion.* . . . Cincinnati: J. A. James & Co., 1837.

Campbell, Alexander, and Robert Owen. *The Evidences of Christianity; A Debate Between Robert Owen . . . and Alexander Campbell.* . . . 5th stereotyped ed.; Cincinnati: American Christian Publication Society, 1854.

Challen, James. *Christian Morals.* Philadelphia: James Challen & Son, 1859.

Goodwin, Elijah. *The Family Companion.* . . . Cincinnati: Moore, Wilstach, Keys & Overend, 1856.

Lamar, James S. *The Organon of Scripture.* Cincinnati: H. S. Bosworth, Publisher, 1860.

Lipscomb, David. *Civil Government.* Reprint; Nashville: Gospel Advocate Company, 1957.

M'Nemar, Richard. *The Kentucky Revival.* . . . Reprint; Albany: E. and E. Hosford, 1808.

Richardson, Robert. *The Principles and Objects of the Religious Reformation.* . . . Bethany, Virginia: A. Campbell, 1853.

Scott, Walter. *The Gospel Restored.* . . . Cincinnati: O. H. Donogh, 1836.

——. *The Messiahship or Great Demonstration.* . . . Cincinnati: H. S. Bosworth, 1859.

AUTOBIOGRAPHIES, MEMOIRS, AND REMINISCENCES

Caskey, Thomas W. *Caskey's Book.* St. Louis: John Burns Publishing Co., 1884.

Clark, Randolph. *Reminiscences Biographical and Historical.* Wichita Falls, Texas: Lee Clark, Publisher, 1919.

Crutcher, Samuel W. *My Experience with the Liquor Traffic.* St. Louis: Christian Publishing Co., 1891.

Davies, Eliza. *The Story of an Earnest Life.* Cincinnati: Central Book Concern, 1881.

Emmons, Francis Whitefield. *The Voice of One Crying in the Wilderness.* . . . Noblesville: L. H. Emmons—Printer, 1837.

Fee, John G. *Autobiography of John G. Fee.* Chicago: National Christian Association, 1891.

Garrison, James Harvey. *Memories and Experiences.* St. Louis: Christian Board of Publication, 1926.

Graham, Robert, ed. *Autobiography of Frank G. Allen.* Cincinnati: Guide Printing & Publishing Co., 1887.

Harrison, Ida Withers. *Forty Years of Service.* 2d ed.; Indianapolis: Christian Women's Board of Missions, n.d.

Hoshour, Samuel K. *Autobiography of Samuel K. Hoshour.* St. Louis: John Burns Publishing Co., 1884.

McGarvey, John W. *The Autobiography of J. W. McGarvey.* Lexington: The College of the Bible, 1960.

Manire, Benjamin F., ed. *Caskey's Last Book.* Nashville: The Messenger Publishing Co., 1896.

——. *Reminiscences of Preachers and Churches in Mississippi.* Jackson, Mississippi: Messenger Publishing Company, 1892.

Mullins, George G. *My Life Is an Open Book.* St. Louis: John Burns, Publisher, 1883.

Rogers, John I., ed. *Autobiography of Elder Samuel Rogers.* Cincinnati: Standard Publishing Company, 1880.

——. *The Biography of Eld. Barton Warren Stone.* . . . Cincinnati: J. A. & U. P. Jones, 1847.

Srygley, Fletcher D. *Seventy Years in Dixie.* Nashville: Gospel Advocate Publishing Co., 1891.

Summerbell, Nicholas, ed. *The Autobiography of Elder Matthew Gardner.* Dayton, Ohio: Christian Publishing Association, 1874.

Thomas, Joseph. *The Life of the Pilgrim, Joseph Thomas.* . . . Winchester, Virginia: J. Foster, Printer, 1817.

Vogel, Peter. *Tale of a Pioneer Church.* Cincinnati: Standard Publishing Company, 1887.

PUBLISHED SERMONS, ADDRESSES, AND LETTERS

Campbell, Alexander. *Familiar Lectures on the Pentateuch.* St. Louis: Christian Publishing Company, 1901.

——. *Popular Lectures and Addresses.* Philadelphia: James Challen & Son, 1863.

Crihfield, Arthur. *Orations on the Origin and Destiny of Man, on the Evidences of the Christian Religion, and on the Reformation of Society.* Cincinnati: published by the author, 1845.

Errett, Isaac, ed. *Life and Writings of George Edward Flower.* Cincinnati: Standard Publishing Company, 1885.

——. *Lindsey-Woolsey and Other Addresses.* Cincinnati: Standard Publishing Company, 1893.

Hawkins, J. W., ed. *Speeches and Lectures of Dr. M. C. Hawkins.* Canton, Missouri: Canton Press Job Print, 1874.

Hinsdale, Mary L., ed. *Garfield-Hinsdale Letters.* Ann Arbor: University of Michigan Press, 1949.

Hopson, Ella L. *Sermons of Dr. W. H. Hopson.* Cincinnati: Standard Publishing Company, 1889.

Mathes, James M. *The Western Preacher.* Bedford, Indiana: published for the author, 1865.

Moore, William T., ed. *The Living Pulpit of the Christian Church.* Cincinnati: R. W. Carroll & Co., Publishers, 1868.

TRACTS AND PAMPHLETS

A Southern Clergyman [Iverson L. Brooks]. *A Defence of Southern Slavery Against the Attacks of Henry Clay and Alex'r Campbell.* Hamburg, South Carolina: Printed by Robinson and Carlisle, 1851.

Butler, Pardee. *Reply of Elder Pardee Butler, to Attacks Made by Elders Isaac Errett and Benj. Franklin, in Recent Numbers of the American Christian Review.* Cincinnati: published by the author, 1859. Photostatic copy in the Disciples of Christ Historical Society Library, Nashville, Tennessee.

Campbell, Alexander. *The Rank and Dignity of Man.* Bethany, Virginia: A. Campbell, 1838.

Creath, Jacob. *Biographical Sketches of Elder Wm. Creath.* . . . St. Louis: T. W. Ustick, Printer, 1866.

——. *Some Essays on Marriage and Divorce.* St. Louis: T. W. Ustick, Printer, 1845.

——. *A Tract on the Use and Abuse of Tobacco.* n.p.: J. Sosey & Son, 1871.

Davis, E. C. *Female Education.* Columbia, Missouri: Davis & Millan— "Sentinel" Office, 1852.

Lawson, Pinckney B. *The Life and Character to Which Are Added Some of the Addresses and Sermons of Alexander Graham.* . . . New York: John F. Trow, Printer, 1853.

Pinkerton, Lewis L. *To the "Union Men" of the Church of Christ (Called "Reformers") in Kentucky, Especially to Those in Lexington.* No publication information. 4 page pamphlet.

Rogers, John. *Discourse on the Subject of Civil and Religious Liberty Delivered on the 4th of July, 1828 in Carlisle, Ky. Rewritten by the Author, in 1856, with Alterations and Additions.* Cincinnati: Moore, Wilstach, Keys & Co., Printers, 1857. Microfilm copy, Disciples of Christ Historical Society, Nashville, Tennessee.

Shannon, James. *An Address Delivered Before the Pro-Slavery Convention of the State of Missouri, Held in Lexington, July 13, 1855, on Domestic Slavery.* St. Louis: Republican Book and Job Office, 1855.

——. *Inaugural Address, Delivered Before the Curators of the University of the State of Missouri, at His Installation as President of that Institution.* n.p.: printed by D. S. Burnet, 1850.

——. *Inaugural Address Delivered by James Shannon Before the Trustees of Bacon College, at His Installation as President of that Institution.* . . . Bethany, Virginia: A. Campbell, 1841.

——. *The Philosophy of Slavery, as Identified with the Philosophy of Human Happiness.* 2d ed.; Frankfort, Kentucky: A. G. Hodges & Co., 1849. Photostatic copy, Disciples of Christ Historical Society, Nashville, Tennessee.

Smith, Benjamin H. *Discourse, Delivered on the Occasion of the Dedication of the Christian Church, Corner of Seventeenth and Olive Streets, St. Louis, Mo.* . . . St. Louis: [n. pub.], 1863.

Stone, Barton W. *An Address to the Christian Churches in Kentucky, Tennessee & Ohio.* 2d ed., rev. and enl.; Lexington: Printed by I. T. Cavins & Co., 1821.

PERIODICALS

The American Christian Preacher and Disciples' Miscellany. (Kinston, North Carolina.) 1855-1856.

The American Christian Quarterly Review. (Cincinnati.) 1862-1863.

The American Christian Review. (Cincinnati.) 1856-1887.

The Apostolic Advocate. (Philadelphia, Richmond, and Amelia, Virginia.) 1834-1839.

The Bible Advocate. (Paris, Tennessee and St. Louis.) 1842-1850.

Challen's Illustrated Monthly. (Philadelphia.) 1851-1859.

The Christian Baptist. (Buffalo, Brooke County, Virginia.) 1823-1830.

The Christian Examiner. (Lexington and Louisville.) 1829-1831.

The Christian Herald. (Wappala and Eureka, Illinois.) 1864-1869.

The Christian Intelligencer. (Georgetown, Kentucky, Scottsville, Virginia, and Richmond.) 1840-1864.

The Christian Journal. (Harrodsburg, Kentucky.) 1842-1845.

The Christian Journal and Union. (Covington, Kentucky.) 1847.

The Christian Luminary. (Cincinnati.) 1858-1863.

The Christian Magazine. (Nashville.) 1848-1853.

The Christian Messenger. (Georgetown, Kentucky and Jacksonville, Illinois.) 1826-1837; 1839-1845.

The Christian Messenger and Bible Advocate. (St. Louis.) 1847.

The Christian Monitor. (Cincinnati.) 1863-1869.

The Christian Pioneer. (Lindley, Trenton, and Chillicothe, Missouri.) 1861-1870.

The Christian Preacher. (Cincinnati and Georgetown, Kentucky.) 1836-1840.

The Christian Publisher. (Richmond.) 1839.

The Christian Publisher. (Charlottesville, Virginia.) 1836-1842.

The Christian Record. (Bloomington, Indianapolis, and Bedford, Indiana.) 1843-1866.

The Christian Reformer. (Paris, Tennessee.) 1836.

The Christian Review. (Nashville.) 1844-1847.

The Christian Sentinel. (Springfield and Peoria, Illinois.) 1853-1857.

The Christian Teacher. (Lexington and Paris, Kentucky.) 1843-1847.

The Christian Teacher. (Little Rock, Arkansas.) 1852.

The Christian Teacher. (Woodland, California.) 1858-1866.

The Christian Union. (Augusta, Georgia.) 1856.

The Christian Union. (Baltimore and New London, Pennsylvania.) 1851-1855.

The Disciple. (Somerset, Pennsylvania.) 1851-1853.

The Ecclesiastic Reformer. (Frankfort and Lexington.) 1848-1852.

The Evangelical Inquirer. (Dayton, Ohio.) 1827-1831.

The Evangelist. (Cincinnati and Carthage, Ohio.) 1832-1844.

The Evangelist. (Mt. Pleasant, Ft. Madison, and Davenport, Iowa.) 1850-1864.

The Gospel Advocate. (Georgetown, Kentucky.) 1835-1836.

The Gospel Advocate. (Nashville.) 1855-1861; 1866-.

The Gospel Proclamation. (St. Clairsville, Ohio.) 1847-1849.

The Herald of Truth. (Buffalo, New York.) 1861-1864.

The Heretic Detector. (Middleburgh, Ohio.) 1837-1841.

The Ladies' Christian Annual. (Philadelphia.) 1852-1857.

Lard's Quarterly. (Georgetown and Frankfort, Kentucky.) 1863-1868.

The Millennial Harbinger. (Bethany, Virginia.) 1830-1870.

The Monthly Christian Age. (Cincinnati.) 1845-1857.

The Morning Watch. (Evergreen, South Carolina.) 1837-1840.

North-Western Christian Magazine. (Cincinnati.) 1854-1858.

North-Western Christian Proclamation. (Waupun, Wisconsin and Buchanan, Michigan.) 1865-1869.

The Orthodox Preacher. (Cincinnati and Covington, Kentucky.) 1843-1846.

The Primitive Christian and Investigator. (Auburn, New York.) 1835-1838.

The Proclamation and Reformer. (Milton, Indiana and Hygenia, Ohio.) 1850-1851.

The Protestant Unionist. (Pittsburgh and Cincinnati.) 1844-1848.

The Reviser. (New York.) 1855.

The Weekly Christian Record. (Indianapolis.) 1862-1865.

The Weekly Gospel Echo. (Carrollton, Illinois.) 1865.

The Western Reformer. (New Paris, Ohio, Centerville, Indiana, and Milton, Indiana.) 1843-1851.

OFFICIAL PUBLICATIONS

Address to the People of the United States, Together with the Proceedings and Resolutions of the Pro-Slavery Convention of Missouri, Held at Lexington, July, 1855. St. Louis: Republican Office, 1855.

Annual Report of the American and Foreign Anti-Slavery Society. New York: William Harned, Office Agent, 1851.

Proceedings and Debates of the Virginia State Convention of 1829-30. Richmond: Samuel Shepard & Co., 1830.

Proceedings of the General Christian Missionary Convention. 1849-65. Title, publisher, and place of publication varies.

Report of the Trustees of the Indiana Asylum for the Education of the Deaf and Dumb to the General Assembly, December, 1846. Indianapolis: J. P. Chapman, State Printer, 1846.

MANUSCRIPTS

Butler Manuscript Collection. Microfilm copy, Disciples of Christ Historical Society, Nashville, Tennessee.

Creath, Jacob, Collection. Disciples of Christ Historical Society, Nashville, Tennessee.

Darsie, James L., Journals. 7 vols. Disciples of Christ Historical Society, Nashville, Tennessee.

Fall, Philip, Papers. Microfilm copy, Disciples of Christ Historical Society, Nashville, Tennessee.

Fanning, Margaret T. Letter to B. Henry, August 27, 1850. Typed copy, Disciples of Christ Historical Society, Nashville, Tennessee.

Gano, John Allen. Biographical Notebook. College of the Bible, Lexington, Kentucky.

Gano, John Allen, Papers. Disciples of Christ Historical Society, Nashville, Tennessee.

Gano, John Allen, Papers. University of Missouri, microfilm copy, Disciples of Christ Historical Society, Nashville, Tennessee.

Garrison, James H., Collection. Disciples of Christ Historical Society, Nashville, Tennessee.

Henderson, David Patterson. Letter to J. S. Lamar, November 26, 1860. Typed copy, Disciples of Christ Historical Society, Nashville, Tennessee.

Irvin, Joshua R. Notebook. College of the Bible, Lexington, Kentucky.

Loos, Charles L., Collection. Disciples of Christ Historical Society, Nashville, Tennessee.

Moore, William Thomas. Notebook. College of the Bible, Lexington, Kentucky.

Raines, Aylette, Collection. College of the Bible, Lexington, Kentucky.

Reneau, Isaac Tipton, Collection. College of the Bible, Lexington, Kentucky.

Scott, Walter. Notebooks. College of the Bible, Lexington, Kentucky.

Shannon, James, Collection. Disciples of Christ Historical Society, Nashville, Tennessee.

CHURCH RECORDS

Canton (and Sully, Missouri), Minute Book, 1850-1866. Disciples of Christ Historical Society, Nashville, Tennessee.

Jacksonville, Illinois, Minute Book, Christian Church, 1832-1889. 3 vols. Disciples of Christ Historical Society, Nashville, Tennessee.

Lawrence Creek Christian Church, Mason County, Kentucky, Church Register and Record, 1807-1859. College of the Bible, Lexington, Kentucky.

Monticello, Lewis County, Missouri, Church Minutes, 1839-1871. Disciples of Christ Historical Society, Nashville, Tennessee.

Mount Zion, Illinois, Minute Book, 1855-1876. Disciples of Christ Historical Society, Nashville, Tennessee.

Old Union Church, Fayette County, Kentucky, Church Register and Record, 1823-1893. College of the Bible, Lexington, Kentucky.

Owingsville, Kentucky, Church Register, Church of Christ, 1828-1858. College of the Bible, Lexington, Kentucky.

Providence Christian Church, Jessamine County, Kentucky, Church Register and Record, 1817-1875. College of the Bible, Lexington, Kentucky.

South Elkhorn Church, Church Register and Record, 1817-1897. College of the Bible, Lexington, Kentucky.

Sulphur Creek Church of Christ, Cumberland County, Kentucky, Minute Book, 1802-1849. College of the Bible, Lexington, Kentucky.

Washington Christian Church, Mason County, Kentucky, Church Register and Record, 1853-1890. College of the Bible, Lexington, Kentucky.

Wellsburgh, Virginia, Record of the Origin and Proceedings of the Church of Christ, 1823-1849. Disciples of Christ Historical Society, Nashville, Tennessee.

Western Reserve Christian Association, Minutes, 1863-1898. Disciples of Christ Historical Society, Nashville, Tennessee.

MANUSCRIPT AUTOBIOGRAPHIES

Allen, Basil Louis. Autobiography of Basil Louis Allen. Typed manuscript, Christian Theological Seminary, Indianapolis, Indiana.

Hill, Abner. Obituary of Abner Hill, 1788-. Typed manuscript, Disciples of Christ Historical Society, Nashville, Tennessee.

Ogden, George Washington. Autobiography of George Washington Ogden. Typed manuscript, Disciples of Christ Historical Society, Nashville, Tennessee.

SECONDARY MATERIAL

There is a massive body of literature dealing with American religion and society. The works which have been most helpful in this study have been cited in the footnotes.

BOOKS ON DISCIPLES HISTORY

Bower, William Clayton, and Roy G. Ross, eds. *The Disciples and Religious Education*. St. Louis: Christian Board of Publication, 1936.

Braden, Gayle Anderson, and Coralie Jones Runyon. *A History of the Christian Church, Maysville, Kentucky*. Lexington: The Official Board of the Maysville Christian Church, 1948.

Brown, John T. *Churches of Christ*. Louisville: John P. Morgan and Company, 1904.

Butler, Lorine Letcher. *History of First Christian Church, Paris, Kentucky*. Lexington: The Keystone Printers, Inc., 1960.

Cauble, Commodore Wesley. *Disciples of Christ in Indiana*. Indianapolis: Meigs Publishing Company, 1930.

Centennial Convention Report. Cincinnati: The Standard Publishing Company, 1909.

Chalmers, Thomas. *Alexander Campbell's Tour in Scotland*. Louisville: Guide Printing & Publishing Co., 1892.

Chenault, John Cabell, ed. *First Christian Church, Frankfort, Kentucky.* No place or publisher, 1957.

Cole, Clifford A. *The Christian Churches of Southern California.* St. Louis: Christian Board of Publication, 1959.

Darst, H. Jackson. *Ante-Bellum Virginia Disciples.* Richmond: Virginia Christian Missionary Society, 1959.

DeGroot, Alfred T., ed. *Central of Des Moines.* Des Moines: Wallace-Homestead Company, 1945.

Dickinson, Elmire J., ed. *A History of Eureka College.* St. Louis: Christian Publishing Company, 1894.

Disciples in Illinois. Jacksonville: Centennial Convention of the Disciples of Christ in Illinois, 1950.

Forster, Ada L. *A History of the Christian Church and Church of Christ in Minnesota.* St. Louis: Christian Board of Publication, 1953.

Fortune, Alonzo Willard. *Adventuring With Disciple Pioneers.* St. Louis: The Bethany Press, 1942.

———. *The Disciples in Kentucky.* N.p.: The Convention of the Christian Churches in Kentucky, 1932.

Garrison, James Harvey. *The Reformation of the Nineteenth Century.* St. Louis: Christian Publishing Company, 1901.

Garrison, Winfred E. *An American Religious Movement.* St. Louis: Christian Board of Publication, 1945.

Garrison, Winfred E., and Alfred T. DeGroot. *The Disciples of Christ.* St. Louis: Christian Board of Publication, 1948.

Garrison, Winfred E. *Religion Follows the Frontier.* New York: Harper & Brothers, 1931.

———. *Whence and Whither Disciples of Christ.* 3d printing; St. Louis: Christian Board of Publication, 1950.

Gates, Errett. *The Early Relation and Separation of Baptists and Disciples.* Chicago: The Christian Century Company, 1904.

Giovannoli, Harry. *Kentucky Female Orphan School.* Midway, Kentucky: [n. pub.], 1930.

Green, Francis M. *Hiram College.* Cleveland: The O. S. Hubbell Printing Co., 1901.

Hailey, Homer. *Attitudes and Consequences in the Restoration Movement.* 2d ed.; Rosemead, California: The Old Paths Book Club, 1952.

Hall, Colby D. *History of Texas Christian University*. Ft. Worth: Texas Christian University Press, 1947.

——. *Texas Disciples*. Ft. Worth: Texas Christian University Press, 1953.

Harmon, Marion F. *A History of the Christian Churches in Mississippi*. Aberdeen, Mississippi: [n. pub.], 1929.

Haynes, Nathaniel S. *History of the Disciples of Christ in Illinois*. Cincinnati: The Standard Publishing Company, 1915.

Hodge, Frederick Arthur. *The Plea and the Pioneers in Virginia*. Richmond: Everett Waddey Company, 1905.

Jennings, Walter Wilson. *Origin and Early History of the Disciples of Christ*. Cincinnati: The Standard Publishing Company, 1919.

Lewis, Grant K. *The American Christian Missionary Society and the Disciples of Christ*. St. Louis: Christian Board of Publication, 1937.

Lowry, J. E., ed. *A History of the Christian Church of Mexico, Missouri*. No place or publisher, 1953.

McPherson, Chalmers. *Disciples of Christ in Texas*. Cincinnati: The Standard Publishing Company, 1920.

Moore, William Thomas. *A Comprehensive History of the Disciples of Christ*. New York: Fleming H. Revell Co., 1909.

Moseley, J. Edward. *Disciples of Christ in Georgia*. St. Louis: The Bethany Press, 1954.

Murch, James DeForest. *Christians Only*. Cincinnati: Standard Publishing, 1962.

Nance, Ellwood C. *Florida Christians*. Winter Park: The College Press, 1941.

Peters, George L. *Dreams Come True, A History of Culver-Stockton College*. Canton, Missouri: Culver-Stockton College, 1941.

Peterson, Orval D. *Washington-Northern Idaho Disciples*. St. Louis: Christian Board of Publication, 1945.

Philputt, James M. *That They May All Be One*. St. Louis: Christian Board of Publication, 1933.

Rogers, James R. *The Cane-Ridge Meeting-House*. Cincinnati: The Standard Publishing Company, 1910.

Russell, Ward. *Church Life in the Blue Grass 1783-1933*. A special limited edition, serially numbered and autographed. Lexington: published by the author, 1933.

Scobey, James E., ed. *Franklin College and Its Influence.* Reprint; Nashville: Gospel Advocate Company, 1954.

Shaw, Henry K. *Buckeye Disciples.* St. Louis: Christian Board of Publication, 1952.

Spencer, Claude E. *An Author Catalog of Disciples of Christ and Related Religious Groups.* Canton, Missouri: Disciples of Christ Historical Society, 1946.

——. *Periodicals of the Disciples of Christ and Related Religious Groups.* Canton, Missouri: Disciples of Christ Historical Society, 1943.

Stevens, J. Edward, and Vernon J. Rose. *Historical Sketches of the Christian Churches of Kansas and of Representative Workers.* Newton, Kansas: Journal Print, 1902.

Swander, Clarence F. *Making Disciples in Oregon.* Portland: published by the author, 1928.

Ware, Charles Crossfield. *North Carolina Disciples of Christ.* St. Louis: Christian Board of Publication, 1927.

Ware, Elias B. *History of the Disciples of Christ in California.* Heraldsburg, California: F. W. Cooke, Publisher, 1916.

West, Earl Irvin. *The Search for the Ancient Order.* 2 vols.; Nashville: Gospel Advocate Company, 1953.

Whitley, Oliver Read. *Trumpet Call of Reformation.* St. Louis: The Bethany Press, 1959.

Wilcox, Alanson. *A History of the Disciples of Christ in Ohio.* Cincinnati: The Standard Publishing Company, 1918.

Woolery, William K. *Bethany Years.* Huntington, West Virginia: Standard Printing & Publishing Company, 1941.

Young, Charles Alexander. *Historical Documents Advocating Christian Union.* Chicago: The Christian Century Company, 1904.

Young, M. Norvel. *A History of Colleges Established and Controlled by Members of the Churches of Christ.* Kansas City: The Old Paths Book Club, 1949.

BIOGRAPHICAL WORKS

Abbott, Byrdine A. *Life of Chapman S. Lucas.* Baltimore: Christian Tribune, 1897.

Ainslie, Peter. *Life and Writings of George W. Abell.* Richmond: Clemmitt & Jones, Publishers and Printers, 1875.

Barrow, Frank. *R. C. Barrow.* Lincoln, Nebraska: State Journal Company, Printers, 1892.

Baxter, William. *Life of Elder Walter Scott with Sketches of His Fellow-Laborers.* . . . Reprint; Nashville: Gospel Advocate Company, n.d.

Belding, Warren S. *Biography of Dr. W. A. Belding.* Cincinnati: John F. Rowe, Publisher, 1897.

Brigance, William Norwood. *Jeremiah Sullivan Black.* Philadelphia: University of Pennsylvania Press, 1934.

Campbell, Selina Huntington. *Home Life and Reminiscences of Alexander Campbell.* St. Louis: John Burns, Publisher, 1882.

Clayton, Mary Black. *Reminiscences of Jeremiah Sullivan Black.* St. Louis: Christian Publishing Company, 1887.

Egbert, James. *Alexander Campbell and Christian Liberty.* St. Louis: Christian Publishing Company, 1909.

Elam, Edwin A. *Twenty-Five Years of Trust: A Life Sketch of J. M. Kidwell.* Nashville: Gospel Advocate Pub. Co., 1893.

Evans, Madison. *Biographical Sketches of the Pioneer Preachers of Indiana.* Philadelphia: J. Challen & Sons, 1862.

Garrison, Winfred E. *The Sources of Alexander Campbell's Theology.* St. Louis: Christian Publishing Company, 1900.

Grafton, Thomas W. *Men of Yesterday.* St. Louis: Christian Publishing Company, 1899.

Green, Francis M. *The Life and Times of John Franklin Rowe.* Cincinnati: F. L. Rowe, Publisher, 1899.

Hale, Allean Lemmon. *Petticoat Pioneer.* Columbia, Missouri: [n. pub.], 1956.

Haley, Jesse J. *Makers and Molders of the Reformation Movement.* St. Louis: Christian Board of Publication, 1914.

Haley, Thomas P. *Historical and Biographical Sketches of the Early Churches and Pioneer Preachers of the Christian Church in Missouri.* St. Louis: Christian Publishing Company, 1888.

Hamlin, Griffith Askew. *The Life and Influence of Dr. John Tomline Walsh.* Wilson, North Carolina: published by the author, 1942.

Hanna, William Herbert. *Thomas Campbell.* Cincinnati: The Standard Publishing Company, 1935.

Harding, Samuel Bannister. *Life of George R. Smith.* Sedalia, Missouri: privately printed, 1904.

Hastings, Rosetta B. *Personal Recollections of Pardee Butler*. Cincinnati: Standard Publishing Company, 1889.

Hay, Kenneth McKinley. *The Life and Influence of Charles Carlton 1821-1902*. Fort Worth: published by the author, 1940.

Henry, Frederick A. *Captain Henry of Geauga*. Cleveland: The Gates Press, 1942.

Hinsdale, Burke Aaron. *President Garfield and Education*. Boston: James R. Osgood and Company, 1882.

———. *The Republican Textbook for the Campaign of 1880*. New York: D. Appleton & Co., 1880.

Hopson, Ella Lord. *Memoirs of Dr. Winthrop Hartly Hopson*. Cincinnati: Standard Publishing Company, 1887.

Keith, Noel L. *The Story of D. S. Burnet: Undeserved Obscurity*. St. Louis: The Bethany Press, 1954.

Lamar, Clarinda Pendleton. *The Life of Joseph Rucker Lamar 1857-1916*. New York: G. P. Putnam's Sons, 1926.

Lamar, James S. *Memoirs of Isaac Errett*. 2 vols.; Cincinnati: The Standard Publishing Co., 1893.

The Life and Times of John Tomline Walsh. Cincinnati: Standard Publishing Company, 1885.

Lindley, D. Ray. *Apostle of Freedom*. St. Louis. The Bethany Press, 1957.

Lipscomb, David. *Life and Sermons of Jesse L. Sewell*. Nashville: Gospel Advocate Publishing Co., 1891.

Lunger, Harold L. *The Political Ethics of Alexander Campbell*. St. Louis: The Bethany Press, 1954.

Mathes, James M. *Life of Elijah Goodwin*. St. Louis: John Burns, Publisher, 1880.

Morro, William C. *Brother McGarvey*. St. Louis: The Bethany Press, 1940.

Moses, Jasper T. *Helen E. Moses*. New York: Fleming H. Revell Company, 1909.

Osborn, Ronald E. *Ely Vaughn Zollars*. St. Louis: Christian Board of Publication, 1947.

Page, Emma, ed. *The Life Work of Mrs. Charlotte Fanning*. Nashville: McQuiddy Printing Company, 1907.

Patterson, Henry C., ed. *Our Living Evangelists of the Church of Christ*. St. Louis: Christian Publishing Company, 1894.

Powell, Anna D. *Edward Lindsay Powell.* Louisville: The Herald Press, 1949.

Power, Frederick D. *Life of William Kimbrough Pendleton, LL.D.* St. Louis: Christian Publishing Company, 1902.

Purviance, Levi. *The Biography of Elder David Purviance.* . . . Dayton, Ohio: B. F. & G. W. Ells, 1848.

Rains, Paul Boyd. *Francis Marion Rains.* St. Louis: Christian Board of Publication, 1922.

Reid, Elizabeth Jameson. *Judge Richard Reid.* Cincinnati: Standard Publishing Company, 1886.

Rice, Perry J. *The Life and Labors of Henry Cornelius Kendrick.* Los Angeles: [n. pub.], 1944.

Richardson, Robert. *Memoirs of Alexander Campbell.* 2 vols.; Philadelphia: J. B. Lippincott & Co., 1868.

Rogers, John. *The Biography of Elder J. T. Johnson.* Cincinnati: published for the author, 1861.

Rogers, William C. *Recollections of Men of Faith.* St. Louis: Christian Publishing Company, 1889.

Shackleford, John, Jr. *Life, Letters and Addresses of Dr. L. L. Pinkerton.* Cincinnati: Chase & Hall, Publishers, 1876.

Smith, Benjamin Lyon. *Alexander Campbell.* St. Louis: The Bethany Press, 1930.

Smith, Clayton C. *The Life and Work of Jacob Kenoly.* Cincinnati: Methodist Book Concern, 1912.

Stanford, Belle. *Elder Elijah Martindale.* Indianapolis: Carlon & Hollenbeck, Printers, 1892.

Stevenson, Dwight E. *Home to Bethpage.* St. Louis: Christian Board of Publication, 1949.

———. *Walter Scott.* St. Louis: Christian Board of Publication, 1946.

Tiers, M. C., ed. *The Christian Portrait Gallery.* Cincinnati: Stereotyped at the Franklin Type Foundry, 1864.

Ware, Charles Crossfield. *Barton Warren Stone.* St. Louis: The Bethany Press, 1932.

Warren, William Robinson. *The Life and Labors of Archibald McLean.* St. Louis: The Bethany Press, 1923.

Wasson, Woodrow Wilson. *James A. Garfield: His Religion and Education.* Nashville: Tennessee Book Company, 1952.

West, Earl Irvin. *The Life and Times of David Lipscomb*. Henderson, Tennessee: Religious Book Service, 1954.

West, Robert Frederick. *Alexander Campbell and Natural Religion*. New Haven: Yale University Press, 1948.

West, William Garrett. *Barton Warren Stone: Early American Advocate of Christian Unity*. Nashville: The Disciples of Christ Historical Society, 1954.

Williams, John Augustus. *Life of Elder John Smith*. Cincinnati: The Standard Publishing Company, 1904.

Woolery, Lewis C. *Life and Address of W. H. Woolery, LL.D.* Cincinnati: The Standard Publishing Company, 1893.

ARTICLES ON DISCIPLES HISTORY

Ames, Edward Scribner. "The Disciples and Higher Education," *The Scroll*, XXXVI (November, 1938), 65-77.

———. "Surveying the Disciples III," *The Scroll*, XXXVI (December, 1938), 123-124.

Bower, William C. "The Frontier Mind," *The Scroll*, XL (June, 1943), 300-309.

Brown, Sterling W. "The Disciples and the New Frontier," *The Scroll*, XXXII (May, 1936), 153-165.

———. "Heritage of Disciples Colleges," *The Scroll*, XXXVI (May, 1939), 279-283.

Butler, Charles P. "Pardee Butler: Pioneer Minister and Statesman," *Shane Quarterly*, III (January, 1942), 78-83.

Gardner, Frank N. "That Heretic—L. L. Pinkerton," *The Scroll*, XL (April, 1943), 235-243.

Garrison, Winfred E. "1896-1946," *The Scroll*, XLIII (September, 1945), 1-3.

Hamlin, C. H. "Alexander Campbell on War," *The Scroll*, XXXIX (March, 1942), 220-222.

———. "The Disciples of Christ and the War Between the States," *The Scroll*, XLI (December, 1943), 99-119.

———. "James Shannon," *The Scroll*, XLI (March, 1944), 220-223.

Harrell, Jr., David Edwin. "Disciples of Christ Pacifism in Nineteenth-Century Tennessee," *Tennessee Historical Quarterly*, XXI (September, 1962), 263-274.

——. "The Sectional Origins of the Churches of Christ," *Journal of Southern History*, XXX (August, 1964), 261-277.

Hartsfield, Elizabeth Ann. " 'Shall the Sisters Speak?' " *College of the Bible Quarterly*, XXXI (January, 1954), 5-22.

Humbert, Royal. "Convention Resolutions: A Case History," *The Scroll*, XLIII (October, 1950), 54-59.

——. "Convention Resolutions: A Case History," *The Scroll*, XLIII (December, 1950), 121-129.

——. "Convention Resolutions: Alcohol," *The Scroll*, XLIII (November, 1950), 79-82.

Kershner, Frederick D. "The Development of Ministerial Training Among the Disciples of Christ," *Shane Quarterly*, IV (July, 1943), 137-145.

——. "Robert Owen—Communist," *Shane Quarterly*, V (January, 1944), 27-42.

Lobingier, Charles S. "The Disciples in the Civil War," *The Scroll*, XLII (October, 1944), 51-59.

McQuary, Rodney L. "The Social Background of the Disciples of Christ," *College of the Bible Quarterly*, XIII (March, 1924), 3-16.

Murphey, Josephine. "The Professor and His Lady," The Nashville *Tennessean Magazine*, April 3, 1949, 22-30.

Pritchard, H. O. "The Contributions of Disciples to Higher Education," *The Culver-Stockton Quarterly*, IV (January, 1928), 1-17.

Quenzel, Carrol H. "Intimate Glimpses of Archibald W. Campbell," *The West Virginia Review*, XI (June, 1934), 258-259.

Stevenson, Dwight E. "Campbell's Attitude on Social Issues," *Christian Evangelist*, LXXVI (September 8, 1938), 977-979.

Wrather, Eva Jean. "Alexander Campbell—Portrait of a Soul: A Quest for Freedom," *Christian Evangelist*, LXXVI (September 8, 1938), 962-968.

——. "Alexander Campbell and Social Righteousness," *Christian Standard*, LXXIII (September 17, 1938), 907-908, 912, 923.

THESES

Albert, Frank J. A History of the First Christian Church of Canton, Ohio. Unpublished B.D. thesis, School of Religion, Butler University, 1944.

Ashton, Donald George. History of the Pulaski County Christian Churches. Unpublished B.D. thesis, School of Religion, Butler University, 1947.

Baim, Frank M. The Contribution of John R. Howard to the Reformation of the Nineteenth Century. Unpublished B.D. thesis, School of Religion, Butler University, 1948.

———. A History of the Churches of Christ (Disciples) in Bradford, Centre, Clinton, Lycoming, and Tioga Counties, Pennsylvania. Unpublished B.D. thesis, School of Religion, Butler University, 1956.

Barnes, Robert E. An Analytical Study of the Northwestern Christian Magazine. Unpublished B.D. thesis, School of Religion, Butler University, 1951.

Bennett, Joseph Richard. A Study of the Life and Contributions of Emily H. Tubman. Unpublished B.D. thesis, School of Religion, Butler University, 1958.

Bray, John Lester. John Smith: Pioneer Kentucky Disciple. Unpublished B.D. thesis, College of the Bible, 1955.

Cox, James Arthur. Incidents in the Life of Philip Slater Fall. Unpublished B.D. thesis, College of the Bible, 1951.

Dawson, Charles Richard. Elder Isaac Errett: Christian Standard Bearer. Unpublished B.D. thesis, College of the Bible, 1948.

Day, Charles Alvis. Moses E. Lard—A Master Builder in the Reformation of the Nineteenth Century. Unpublished B.D. thesis, College of the Bible, 1951.

Dorman, James Edward. A Study in the History of the Living Benevolent Institutions of Disciples of Christ; with Particular Reference to Their Current Status. Unpublished B.D. thesis, School of Religion, Butler University, 1946.

Dorman, Minnie Friester. A History of the First Christian Church at Selma, Alabama. Unpublished M.A. thesis, Division of Graduate Instruction, Butler University, 1945.

Dowling, Enos E. James Madison Mathes. 2 vols. Unpublished B.D. thesis, School of Religion, Butler University, 1937.

Edwards, Arthur B. Educational Problems of the Churches of Christ to 1909. Unpublished B.D. thesis, School of Religion, Butler University, 1949.

Fife, Robert O. Alexander Campbell and the Christian Church in the Slavery Controversy. Unpublished Ph.D. dissertation, University of Indiana, 1960.

Foster, W. C. The Progress of the Disciples Through Controversy. Unpublished B.D. thesis, College of the Bible, 1918.

Griggs, Roy Lee. The Life and Thought of Robert Graham. Unpublished B.D. thesis, College of the Bible, 1959.

Harrell, David Edwin. A Decade of Disciples of Christ Social Thought. Unpublished M.A. thesis, Vanderbilt University, 1958.

Hogan, Donald Thomas. A Survey of the Kentucky Christian Education Society. Unpublished B.D. thesis, College of the Bible, 1954.

Jennings, Alvin Ray. Thomas M. Allen—Pioneer Preacher of Kentucky and Missouri. Unpublished M.A. thesis, Division of Graduate Instruction, Butler University, 1951.

Keesee, Delbert Dayton. The Churches of Christ During the War Between the States. Unpublished M.A. thesis, Division of Graduate Instruction, Butler University, 1954.

LaRue, Mary Ellen. Women in the Ministry of the Church: A Disciple History. Unpublished B.D. thesis, College of the Bible, 1960.

Lillie, Harold. Alexander Campbell's Psychology of Religion. Unpublished B.D. thesis, School of Religion, Butler University, 1947.

Logan, C. LeRoy. The Disciples of Christ and Slavery. Unpublished B.D. thesis, School of Religion, Butler University, 1935.

Mell, Glen W. A Study of the Opinions of Some Leading Disciples Concerning Pacifism. Unpublished B.D. thesis, School of Religion, Butler University, 1936.

Murphy, Frederick I. North Western Christian University and the Education of the Ministry. Unpublished M.A. thesis, Division of Graduate Instruction, Butler University, 1960.

Norton, Herman A. The Organization and Function of the Confederate Military Chaplaincy, 1861-1865. Unpublished Ph.D. dissertation, Vanderbilt University, 1956.

Nunnelly, Donald Alfred. The Disciples of Christ in Alabama, 1860-1910. Unpublished B.D. thesis, College of the Bible, 1954.

Smith, Frank E. The Editorial Contributions of Charles Louis Loos to the Movement of the Disciples of Christ. Unpublished B.D. thesis, School of Religion, Butler University, 1954.

Smith, William Martin. A History of Ministerial Support, Relief and Pensions Among the Disciples of Christ. Unpublished M.Th. thesis, School of Religion, Butler University, 1956.

Thompson, James Maurice. The Stewardship Principles of A. Campbell. Unpublished B.D. thesis, School of Religion, Butler University, 1940.

Tucker, William Edward. James Harvey Garrison (1842-1931) and the Disciples of Christ: An Irenic Editor in an Age of Controversy. Unpublished Ph.D. dissertation, Yale University, 1960.

Tyler, John Willis. Preaching on Stewardship Among Disciples of Christ. Unpublished B.D. thesis, College of the Bible, 1955.

Vandergrift, Eileen Gordon. The Christian Missionary Society: A Study in the Influence of Slavery on the Disciples of Christ. Unpublished M.A. thesis, Division of Graduate Instruction, Butler University, 1945.

Walker, Claude. Negro Disciples in Kentucky, 1840-1925. Unpublished B.D. thesis, College of the Bible, 1959.

Whitson, Samuel Montgomery, Jr. Campbell's Concept of the Millennium. Unpublished M.A. thesis, Division of Graduate Instruction, Butler University, 1951.

OTHER UNPUBLISHED MATERIAL

Biard, Harrell C. Typed memorandum concerning Barton Stone and the Cherokee Indians. Disciples of Christ Historical Society, Nashville, Tennessee.

Dodd, S. T. The Church of Christ in Kansas. Typed manuscript, Disciples of Christ Historical Society, Nashville, Tennessee. Originally published by John Burns in St. Louis in 1883.

Hinsdale, Wilbert B. The Church I Was Brought Up In. Typed manuscript, Disciples of Christ Historical Society, Nashville, Tennessee.

Morro, William C. John Allen Gano. Typed manuscript, College of the Bible, Lexington, Kentucky.

Platt, Robert M. Robert Milligan Disciple. Bound typed manuscript, Disciples of Christ Historical Society, Nashville, Tennessee.

Spencer, Claude E. Educational Institutions of the Disciples of Christ. Typed manuscript dated 1955, Disciples of Christ Historical Society, Nashville, Tennessee.

INDEX

Roman numeral vii refers to new page number xiii

245

248

INDEX

Cole, Charles C., Jr., 44 (n. 68), 90 (n. 109), 177

College of Louisiana, 122

Columbia, Missouri, 122, 123

Columbus, Ohio, 84

"Common Sense" philosophy: influence on Disciples, 28

Communism, attitudes of Disciples toward, 79-84

Compromise of 1850, 92, 110, 123

Confederate States of America, 154 (n. 48), 155

Congregational church, 3, 68 (n. 19)

Congress of the United States, 86, 191, 192

Constitution of United States, 124, 220

Contracts, sanctity of, 70

Copperheads, 60, 152

Cornelius, 143

Covington, Kentucky, 79

Cox, Josiah W., 151

Creath, Jacob, Jr., 10, 34 (n. 28), 35, 48, 70, 78, 86, 122, 151, 183, 184, 188, 213, 214 (n. 54), 218

Crihfield, Arthur, 43, 45, 64

Cross, Alexander, 95, 96

Cross, Whitney R., 31 (n. 16)

Cumberland Presbyterian church, 2

Curti, Merle, 144 (n. 18)

D

Dale, Mr., 82

Dancing, attitudes of Disciples toward, 186-87

Davenport, Iowa, 75, 126

Debt, attitudes of Disciples toward, 70

Declaration and Address, 6, 7, 27

Democratic party, 106, 123

Denominational attitude: definition of, 12-14; and division of the Disciples, 222-24; economic basis in Disciples, 68-69, 88-90; encouraged by Civil War, 173-74; in Disciples thought, 10-11, 22-25, 58-61; in modern Disciples thought, vii; influence of on moral standards, 198-99, temperance, 182-83, Sabbath question, 193-96

Devil, 181

Dexter, John, 197

Disciples of Christ (*see also* Christian church, Christian movement, Church of Christ, Division and specific headings for Disciples' attitudes on various social issues): development of, 1800-1865, 4-11; social thought, 1800-1865, 18-25

Disciples of Christ Historical Society, 205

Dispensationalism: in Disciples thought, 29; influence on attitudes of Disciples toward capital punishment, 201-2, pacifism, 141, the Sabbath question, 191

Divine Standard (*see also* Bible, Biblical literalism), 27

Division, in Disciples of Christ: influence of Biblical literalism on, 33-34; influence of Civil War on, 164-74; influence on economics on, 88-90; influence of slavery on, 105-7, 129-38; influence of war resolutions on, 164-65; nature of, 9 (n. 12), 10-11, 58-61, 134, 171 (n. 105), 222-24; shown in moral code, 198-99

Divorce, attitude of Disciples toward, 196-98

Dooley, Rueben, 208 (n. 32)

Dred Scott Decision, 92

Dress, attitude of Disciples toward, 189-90

Drinking: among Disciples, 175-76; in the United States, 175

Dunlavy, John, 80

E

East (*see also* Sectionalism), 2, 3, 16, 21, 24, 39, 92, 103, 104, 127

Eaton, Clement, 103 (n. 43)

Eaton, W. W., 213

Ecclesiastic Reformer, 68

Eclectic Institute, 118

Economic interest: agrarian sentiment, 64-65, 84-89; antiaristocratic prejudice, 65-66, 88-90; influence in Disciples, ix, 23-25, 60, 64, 67-68, 173, 222-24; influence in United States, 1, 62; influence in United States religion, 2-4, 15-17; influence on Disciples' attitudes on dancing, 186-87, entertainment, 186, moral standards, 198-99, stewardship, 72-73, upper class prejudice, 38, women's dress, 189-90

Economic problems (*see also* specific topics), 62-90

Education: career of James Shannon, 123; clash with Catholics over, 219-21; Disciples' attitudes toward coeducation, 206-7; Disciples' attitudes toward education for women, 205; establishment of North-Western Christian University, 111-14

Edwards, Jonathan, 54

Eighteenth Mississippi Regiment of Volunteers, 156

Eleventh Annual Report of the American and Foreign Anti-Slavery Society, The, 93

Ellsworth, Clayton Sumner, 140

West—cont'd
  Disciples thought, 23, 28-29, 35-36, 63, 100
West, Earl, 172 (n. 105)
West, William Garrett, 29 (n. 12), 32
West Virginia, 63, 151
Western Literary Institute and College of Professional Teachers, 215
Western Reformer, 142
Western Reserve, 36, 82, 107, 154, 158 (n. 57)
Western Reserve Eclectic Institute, 206
Wheeling, Virginia, 84
Whig party, 106, 123
White, H., 94

Whitley, Oliver Read, 18 (n. 37), 19, 20, 77 (n. 69)
Wilcox, Alanson, 114
Wittke, Carl, 49
Women: and the ministry, 203-5; rights of, 203-7; standards of dress, 189-90
Woodson, Carter G., 94 (n. 8)
Wrather, Eva Jean, 36, 126
Wright, David T., 150, 151, 161

Y

Yearbook of American Churches, vii
Yinger, J. Milton, 34, 35
Youngs, Benjamin Seth, 36